THE LOWEST RUNG

Voices of Australian Poverty

The Lowest Rung is a fascinating and profoundly moving portrait of the people who are suffering the consequences of a more divided and less egalitarian Australian society. Based largely on the author's conversations with hundreds of people living and working in three areas commonly described as 'disadvantaged'—Inala in Queensland, Mount Druitt in New South Wales and Broadmeadows in Victoria—this is a book in which impoverished Australians, who are too often absent from debates about poverty, tell their own stories. Some are funny, others are sad. There are stories they can hardly bear to tell about loss, despair and an uncertain future. But there are also stories about hope, and the capacity of poorer people to imagine and create a fairer world. Rather than focusing on abstractions such as 'the underclass', this book provides an intimate account of real people's fears, hopes and dilemmas in the face of growing inequality, entrenched unemployment, and fading opportunities for the young.

This important book is essential reading for anyone concerned about the impact of social and economic change in contemporary Australia. It urges us to learn from rather than lecture those who experience first-hand the more unequal future we are now making, and it will change the way we think about poverty and its solutions.

Mark Peel is the author of *Good Times, Hard Times* and *A Little History of Australia*. He teaches history at Monash University.

THE LOWEST RUNG

Voices of Australian Poverty

MARK PEEL

CAMBRIDGE
UNIVERSITY PRESS

PUBLISHED BY THE PRESS SYNDICATE OF THE UNIVERSITY OF CAMBRIDGE
The Pitt Building, Trumpington Street, Cambridge, United Kingdom

CAMBRIDGE UNIVERSITY PRESS
The Edinburgh Building, Cambridge CB2 2RU, UK
40 West 20th Street, New York, NY 10011–4211, USA
477 Williamstown Road, Port Melbourne, VIC 3207, Australia
Ruiz de Alarcón 13, 28014 Madrid, Spain
Dock House, The Waterfront, Cape Town 8001, South Africa

http://www.cambridge.org

First published 2003

Printed in Australia by Ligare

Typeface Minion 10.5/14 pt. System QuarkXPress® [PC]

A catalogue record for this book is available from the British Library

National Library of Australia Cataloguing in Publication data
Peel, Mark, 1959– .
The lowest rung: voices of Australian poverty.
Bibliography.
Includes index.
ISBN 0 521 83062 1.
ISBN 0 521 53759 2 (pbk.).
1. Poverty – Australia. 2. Poverty – Social aspects – Australia. 3. Poor – Australia. 4. Australia – Social conditions. 5. Australia – Economic conditions. I. Title.

305.5690994

ISBN 0 521 53759 2 paperback
ISBN 0 521 83062 1 hardback

To Patrick Troy, for the inspiration,
and to Scott, for showing me
the way forward

CONTENTS

ACKNOWLEDGEMENTS

Any book – and this book more than most – is a product of people's generosity. A book that takes a long time to write further stretches that generosity. To the hundreds of people in Broadmeadows, Mount Druitt and Inala who spoke to me, I am grateful beyond measure. This book relied upon your willingness to share your stories with me, knowing that that meant they would be shared with others, and your trust that I could tell them properly. I hope I have.

I am very grateful to the people who led me through their communities or provided me with particular contacts: Jeff Fiedler, Graham Francis, Carmel McMennemin, Maria Robles, Vivien Routley and Barbara Steen in Broadmeadows; Kylie Battams, Jenny Chaves, Connie and Ray Dailey, Jon Eastgate, Iris Moir and Bet Peters in Inala; and Mark Aggar, Val Franzen, Paul Hanna, Trish Martin, Coral McLean, Joe and Wendy Munoz and Yvonne Shipp in Mount Druitt.

The librarians and archivists at the State Records Authority of New South Wales, the LaTrobe Library, the Queensland Department of Housing, Local Government and Planning Library, the Victorian Department of Housing Library, the Broadmeadows Local History Collection, the Blacktown City Library, the Inala Public Library and the New South Wales Department of Housing Library were always helpful.

I also wish to thank those who organised opportunities for me to share some of my original findings, especially Monica Wolf at National Shelter, Arnold Bailey of the Housing Communities Assistance Program, Patrick

Mullins at the University of Queensland and Rod Plant at Shelter NSW, and to the following organisations for permission to use revised parts of articles first published elsewhere: the University of New South Wales Press ('The Ends of the Earth: Mount Druitt and Inala', in Tim Bonyhady and Tom Griffiths (eds), *Words for Country: Landscape and Language in Australia*), the editorial board of *Urban Policy and Research* ('Entitlement and Justice', vol. 18, 2000) and the Australian Academy of the Humanities ('Decency and Justice: Voices from Australian Margins', in Janet McCalman (ed.), *Humane Societies*). Parts of Chapter 4 are based on 'Trusting Disadvantaged Citizens' by Mark Peel, in *Trust and Governance*, edited by Valerie Braithwaite and Margaret Levi © 1998 Russell Sage Foundation, 112 East 64th Street, New York, NY 10021. Reprinted with permission.

I devised and wrote this book within two remarkable scholarly communities. The first was the Urban Research Program at the Australian National University. Tim Bonyhady, Nicholas Brown, Steve Bourassa, Alastair Greig and Max Neutze pushed me to see the possibilities of a project that always seemed a little too large, while Heather Grant, Coralie Cullen, Rita Coles and Penny Hanley handled what they often thought were little things. For calculations and compilations of census material, I am grateful to Glenys Harding, and Virginia Rapson at Monash University. Further afield, Margaret Levi shared the fruits of her progressive wisdom. Through it all, Patrick Troy strove to smooth my path. A pioneer in tackling and solving many of the issues raised in this book, he will probably huff and gruff and say he didn't do all that much. All I can say is that if this book manages to make an argument for justice, it is largely due to his example.

From Canberra I moved to Monash University, where teaching, student welfare and administration duties probably delayed this book by several years. But it is better for the waiting, and for the ways in which my new colleagues helped me improve it. I enjoy working in a fine department; I need to acknowledge in particular Barbara Caine, David Garrioch and Andrew Markus for occasionally tugging at the reins, Graeme Davison for reading anything at a moment's notice, Bain Attwood and Esther Faye for the inspiration of their scholarship, and Jane Drakard and Peter Howard, who coincided with me and still help me keep my feet. To my other colleagues, too, my thanks for all the shared endeavours. My graduate students, too, have inspired and educated me, and special thanks go to Jeremy Sammut and Nick Fischer for their research assistance. I am grateful to other Monash colleagues for their suggestions, especially Andrew Singleton, who read two of the chapters and provided invigorating criticisms, to Ian Britain and Mary Cunnane for their advice on publishing proposals, and to Gary Swinton for drawing the map.

A range of friends listened along the way: in Sydney, Penny Russell and James Campbell in Canberra, Sheila Hughes, Monica Wolf and Rosemary Webb; and in Melbourne, Louise Persse, Erica Mehrtens, Gary Bass, John Stapleton, my brother Philip Peel, Madeleine Pitcher, Cathy Emery, Susan Keogh, Val Campbell, Pam Williams and John Murphy. At Cambridge University Press, Kim Armitage was my first contact. Her enthusiasm, support and energy were crucial to this book's completion and were matched by the people responsible for each stage of the publishing journey: Karen Hildebrandt, Amanda Pinches, Margaret Trudgeon and Sarah Cannon. I thank them all, and am grateful as well to the readers of the manuscript for their detailed comments.

Three people generously read an entire first draft. I benefited from Al Knight's publishing eye, and Janet McCalman's unstinting passion for good writing. From the time of our first ever meeting, some fifteen years ago, I have drawn frequently on Janet's kindness and intellectual rigour. The third reader was my mother, Jean Peel, who read hundreds of pages and then sent back almost as many covered in notes and thoughts. I think my father Roger Peel had a hand in it all, too. I hope they see their work and their values reflected in what they now read.

To Orlando and Doris, my thanks for reminding me about the important things, like dinner time. Finally, to my partner, Scott Evans: you brought this book to life because you made sure I knew there was something to say and that I would be able to say it.

A NOTE ON NAMES AND WORDS

Writing a book based on conversations creates a difficult decision about whether to use people's real names. To each person with whom I spoke, I promised a transcript for their amendment. I also guaranteed to let them see their words woven into mine before I used their names. I managed to keep the first promise but the second proved more difficult than I anticipated. As some people have not had the opportunity to approve my use of their words, all names in this book are pseudonyms, and, if necessary, small details of people's lives have been generalised so that they cannot be recognised. The real names of every person who participated are listed below.

When your conversations are with people living in poverty there is the added difficulty of finding the correct descriptive term. If those to whom I spoke were best characterised as disadvantaged, they mostly called themselves 'ordinary'. Some people preferred the word 'battlers', though they were growing suspicious of a term that had been twisted by conservatives to mean people with much more than they had. A few – normally those with strong union or Labor Party backgrounds – used terms such as 'working class'. In general, though, explicit class language was reserved for others: if they were called 'working people' or 'ordinary people' those outside their suburbs were called 'middle class' or 'the rich'. Their position was also indicated by where they lived: 'Inala people', 'Westies' and 'Broady folks', as opposed to 'Toorak types' in Melbourne and 'North Shore people' in Sydney. In Inala, the location of the rich seemed a bit less definite, or perhaps I never understood it as well, but there was usually a gesture in the direction of the Brisbane River and suburbs like Indooroopilly, Jindalee and Toowong.

There is, as yet, no agreed term for Australia's poorest citizens. There are good and bad names but nothing like the relative consensus over respectful identification we now have for groups such as Aboriginal and Torres Strait Islander people or people from non-English speaking backgrounds. The diversity among those to whom I spoke also made it difficult to decide upon a particular word, and I did not want to invent something that some might endorse but others would find inaccurate or offensive. Accordingly, I have used various terms, including impoverished, poor and disadvantaged, in the hope that a factual description of their situation best represents them.

Overall, this book is based upon the words of nearly 300 people who were living and working in Inala, Broadmeadows and Mount Druitt in 1994 and 1995. The full names of 249 people are listed below; the others were either momentary participants whose family names I did not know, or people who were involved in larger group discussions at neighbourhood houses, job centres or welfare agencies. While this is a larger group of people than appears in most Australian, British or American studies, a smaller group of around 150 people provided the bulk of the insights, ideas and interpretations. As I began the study with the intention of including a survey of housing, economic and social development policies, as well as local political representation, I spoke to numerous councillors, policy workers, strategic planners and housing department managers. While those conversations were very valuable, they played a much smaller role in the book that emerged.

There are 164 women and eighty-five men listed below. There are fewer men because they were less likely to be involved in community work or neighbourhood networks, and because most of the local social, community and welfare workers were female. Women do the talking in these suburbs. In terms of their relationships with Mount Druitt, Inala and Broadmeadows, these men and women can be divided into four groups. About one-third (eighty-one) were residents, and a further fifty-two were 'worker–residents' who both lived in the suburb and worked part-time or full-time in local agencies, neighbourhood houses and community centres. Of the rest, eighty-eight were social workers, youth workers and other welfare workers who did not live in or grow up in the area, and twenty-eight were people working in local councils, regional bodies or government departments outside these suburbs.

The residents were more likely to be over the age of 30 than under it; accordingly, I have been circumspect in regard to the views of younger residents, from whom I heard relatively less. Of the 133 residents and worker–residents, seventeen were Aboriginal. Twelve were born in countries other than Australia, Britain and New Zealand, and I also interviewed fourteen community workers who were first- or second-generation migrants from Turkey, El Salvador, Vietnam, Iraq, Iran, Greece and the Philippines.

This was not a study in which I collected precise details of income or expenditure, used surveys or questionnaires, or carried out quantitative analysis of people's budgets and financial strategies. However, all of the residents and a majority of the worker–residents were, by my estimation and observations, doing it hard. Eighty-six were renting from the state housing departments, ten were living in housing cooperatives, and thirty-seven had bought or were buying low-cost homes built by the Housing Commissions in the 1960s, 1970s or 1980s. Of the eighty-one residents, fifty-nine were living on a pension – either aged, disability or supporting parent – or on unemployment benefits. More than half the worker–residents also received some welfare payment alongside their wages. The twenty-two residents who were in paid employment, apart from two clerks and one saleswoman, worked for public (or at that point public) authorities such as Telecom (now Telstra) and the railways, in public works departments, as factory hands, storemen, process workers or labourers, or as part-time shop assistants, cleaners, deliverers or couriers.

CAST OF CHARACTERS

Broadmeadows

Daya Adelan
Fouad Alali
Alan Aylward
Melek Bagdas
Robbie Barry
Geoff Blair
Norma Brooks
Joy Burness
Nick Button
Ella Carruthers
Joanna Casey
Reverend Peter Clark
Connie Dew
Graham Eagles
Barry Edwards
Mary Elvey
Jeff Fiedler
Kate Fogale
Graham Francis
Pat Frawley
Frank Gallagher
Cass Gryzorowicz
Wendy Hancock
Mari Hardstaff
Sue Herbst
Jenny Holloway
Paul Hopkins
Reverend Jim Houston
Marjorie Houston
Laurie Jackson
Barbara Jones
Kym Jones
John Karageorge
Sharon Keppel
Sue Lagreca
Stephanie Langridge
Jacqui Lavis
Suzanne Lechte
Joan Legg
Sharyn Mains
Nicky Marshall
Carmel McMennemin
Antoinette Mertins
Nick Michael
Janey Muir-Smith
Nancy Nankervis
Joe Narbaluk
Lyn Nicholls
Pam O'Reilly
Michael Olijnyk
Margaret Pateman
Suzy Pinchen
Father Pat Purcell
Pam Quinton-Randall
Carmen Raspor
Maria Robles
Derek Robson
Jack Roper
Vivien Routley
Gaye Rowe
John Rutherford
Sonja Rutherford

Father Joe Ruys
Cheryl Sampson
Philip Shanahan
Irene Sharp
Jennifer Shore
Monica Sidhu
Barbara Steen
Reverend Frank Tate
Yvonne Thompson
Tony Triado
Keith Van Dome
Pam Vorbach
Jane Williamson
Ralph Willoughby
Christina Wright

Inala

Mirtha Barboza
Ellie Barney
Kylie Battams
Kevin Bell
Rosemary Bell
Jean Brett
Vanessa Brett
Ken Butler
Lynda Cawley
Shirley Cawley
Kerry Charlton
Jenny Chaves
Tony Churchill
Katherine Collins
Julie Conway
Audrey Cooper
Nettie Corbett
Penny Corbett
Connie Dailey
Ray Dailey
Dave Davidson
Lisa Dejong
Sister Vivienne Desailly
Jon Eastgate
Aureole Edwards
Matthew Evans
Lil Fellows
Di Glynn
Sister Rosemary Grundy
Paul Hauff
Jill Haug
Eric Jansink
Margaret Joughin
Karen Krarup
Lyn Lindberg
Chris Lucas
Jim Lucey
Ashok Madan
Elena Madan
Diane Marr
Iris Moir
Father Frank Moynihan
Chuong Nguyen
Chris O'Keefe
Warren Oxman
Penny Penrose
Bet Peters
Olwen Redshaw
Marianne Reid
Peta Robinson
Luisa Romano
Sue Schmidt
Shirley Schneider
Margaret Shepherd
Beth Smith
Kay Smith
Michelle Smith
Monty Smith
Sue Smith
Shirley Stark
Connie Sully
Joie Sumby
Nola Townsend
Anh Tran
Lorna Tyson
Linda Velli
Judy Walker
Donna Warrie
Margaret Warrington
John Westwood
Jule Wilkie
Chris Williams
Julie Wright
Fay Zarge

Mount Druitt

Kyla Aggar
Mark Aggar
Richard Amery, MP
Arnold Bailey
Cesar Bigornia
Julie Bosley
Tony Bowen
Caron Brown
Lesley Brown
Sue Butler
Brenda Chadwick
Lay-Yin Chiew
Jean Cinis
Maxine Conaty
Patricia Crane
Margaret Curtis
Paul Dengate
Carol Donovan
Stephen Driscoll
Pat Eastman
Brenda English
Vicky Eyles
Robyn Fallick
Mick Fell
Glenn Finnie
Simon Fox
Val Franzen
Paul Gibson, MP
Alex Gooding
Sylvia Gray
David Hall
Father Paul Hanna
Rhonda Hills
Sonia Hinkley
Jim Hook
Nancy Horner
Narelle Hosking
Naomi Houston
Claire Hutton
Matthew Johnson
Christine Kal
Lynette Knight
Konstanty Kudzielko
Terry Lett
Mark Letta
Brett Louat
Charlie Lowles
Bob Lundie-Jenkins
Sharyn Magennis
Sundar Mahtani
Trish Martin
Alison McIntyre
Coral McLean
Janet Milligan
Chris Mortimer
Lin Mountstephen
Joseph Munoz
Wendy Munoz
Lachlan Murdoch
Graham Murray
George Nicolaidis
Marlene Palmai
John Paszek
Wilma Pearce
Michelle Peisley
Laraine Presgrave
Annette Rennie
June Richards
Mel Roebuck
Aaron Romero
Coral Rosevear
Barry Ryan
Dianne Ryan
Wayne Ryan
Karen Salisbury
Greg Shaw
Lily Shearer
Kooryn Sheaves
Dick Sheppard
Yvonne Shipp
Patricia Simms
June Sinclair-Lawler
Pam Slade
Lois Smith
Matthew Smyth
Lynn Tarrant
Penny Thomas
Ric Thomas
Marie Turner
Bev Vincent
Dave Vincent
Harvey Volke
Maria Votano
Pat Wain
Helen Wilson
Tiane Wilson
Debbie Wong
Brother Bill Wright

INTRODUCTION

Journeys

Blue plastic bags stuck to wire fences by an unrelenting wind. Streaked fibrocement and grey-green besser block. Spindly trees dying in the leaded dust. At the welfare centre women pick over the used clothes, pots and pans. On the community workers' pinboard directives about best practice crowd out and almost seem to mock fading notices for social justice workshops. Closed shops, old service stations selling ten-dollar stretch jeans and cigarettes 'at Queensland prices'. Wounded cars on blocks, dead ones in front yards. Broken beer bottles crunch underfoot outside the TAB. At least the newsagent promises to 'Tatts you out of here'.

Many accounts of places such as Inala, Broadmeadows and Mount Druitt begin and end with the same sense of desolation. Granted, there are tragedies and despair. You can't just wish away entrenched unemployment. You can't ignore the men who know they will never work again, the teenage boys who tell you they'll be overdosed or dead in a car crash before they're 20, the mothers, nervous, ashamed or simply resigned, collecting their emergency food parcels at the church hall. But nor can you ignore the sparks and flashes of invention and resilience: the young jobless fathers I saw in Mount Druitt who tenderly minded their babies outside Coles while their girlfriends finished their shifts, the Broadmeadows children's playgroup that Joan, Barbara and Geraldine helped turn into a language class for their Turkish and Iraqi neighbours, or the community meeting where Val and Lorraine laughingly made a new Inala out of plasticine and crêpe paper.

You can't turn the caricatures on their heads and argue that Inala, Broadmeadows and Mount Druitt are not impoverished, for some of their neighbourhoods and some of their people most definitely are. But you can choose to see and hear something different: stories about what is happening to many ordinary Australians and what they are making happen, stories they relish sharing and others they can hardly bear to tell. You can listen to Father Patrick Nolan, who came to Mount Druitt in 1980:

> You know, you dare to read the signs of the times that are occurring here. Because they are signs that disturb the equilibrium, greatly so, and it takes a lot of guts.
>
> This is a place of great prophecy. That's what I can see, a place of great prophecy. It's a disturbing place.

Prophecy is not a skill that most outsiders would ascribe to impoverished people. Yet it is the best description because they are living in a future others will not acknowledge is already here.

The mistake of many venturers – and the mistake that I made – is to think that you already know the story when what you must do is listen. I first began listening to people in Broadmeadows, Inala and Mount Druitt in 1993. I was then working on another book, *Good Times, Hard Times*, about the town of Elizabeth in South Australia. Established in the 1950s, Elizabeth became disadvantaged during the 1970s and 1980s as the relative prosperity of its first two decades of existence gave way to increasing unemployment and as its founder, the South Australian Housing Trust, was proving itself unable to resist the forces that were turning public housing into welfare housing.

Listening to people in Elizabeth, I was able to blend in my own memories of the town in which I had grown up and gone to school, but which I had also left as soon as I could. I was a member of a fortunate group, a working-class generation born in the 1950s and early 1960s who benefited from all of the opportunities our parents could afford and were able to find a security unknown in our families' histories. We heeded our parents' warnings about the need for qualifications and safe jobs and we worked hard. For many of us it came at the cost of disconnection, though I don't think we realised that as we left Elizabeth or places like it in the 1970s.

Writing a book about Elizabeth was a way of telling an important story about the policies and promises that had given my generation our chances. I broached, if I could not resolve, my ambivalence about the emphasis on sacrifice, struggle and hard work, and about the ways of life that could and could not be imagined. I wanted to give a clearer picture of how and why a place like Elizabeth, which outsiders so often see as drably plebeian, could be so valued by the people who lived there. And in writing about the decisions that helped make Elizabeth poor I realised that there was much more to be said about places like it, and the other people who were living at the sharp end of Australia's reshaping.

I wanted to continue writing about people living in hard times, and to describe the world from their perspective. This took me beyond Elizabeth to those suburbs perceived as the most disadvantaged places in the larger eastern cities: Melbourne's Broadmeadows, on the flat lands of what used to be the city's north-western edge; Inala, one of the suburbs strung along the Cunningham Highway between Brisbane and Ipswich; and Mount Druitt, a Housing Commission suburb in Sydney's west.

For three years I asked people to tell me their stories. I started by talking with activists in neighbourhood houses or community centres, or with social workers in welfare agencies, and relied on them to suggest other people to whom I might talk. As they became convinced that I would listen carefully to what they had to say, they laced me into their networks and organised meetings with local residents. Other conversations were opportunistic, as neighbours and friends dropped by or people who were using the welfare centre decided that talking to me was an interesting enough diversion. Some thought of other people I might approach, and offered to go and get them. Because I wanted to listen to every possible point of view, I always asked people to nominate someone who might take a different perspective and maybe disagree with what they had said. In all, I talked with about 300 people.

I was interested in how people described their lives and their work, but I also wanted to know what they thought about the future and how they would change the world if they could. This wasn't a study of budgets and incomes or labour market policies. I didn't use questionnaires and surveys. Scholars more expert than I were already doing that. This was a study of people's stories, of what they wanted to say, what they could see happening, and what they hoped might yet happen.

At the time I did these interviews the recession of the early 1990s had not yet lifted: unemployment in these suburbs hovered at around 15–20 per cent, and local services were struggling to cope with dramatic increases in need. In some estates, fewer than one in ten families contained anyone earning a wage. Many people felt left behind, and that those who lived outside the area had stopped caring. Those who had managed to keep their jobs had unemployed sons and grandsons, daughters bringing up children on their own, friends and kin who were scared and didn't know what the future held.

I often heard about a world being destroyed, the world they had created in the 1960s and 1970s. I heard about the return of insecurity and poverty that many people thought had gone forever. Many people felt betrayed by the political party for which they had voted all their lives. They were tired of the stigma and unsure if the struggle was really leading anywhere. Among young people I heard of the pain of adulthood delayed by unemployment and parenting distorted by poverty. Among older people I heard fading hopes for a better world, for which they often blamed themselves. One woman from Inala insisted on telling me about her greatest failure: she hadn't taught her daughter how to be poor. She hadn't thought it would ever be needed. But, she said, Australia was changing. She shouldn't have trusted the good times, and she should have known the hard times would come back.

I heard the tragedies of youth suicide, and 40-year-old unemployed men who spoke quietly of how they had failed their families. A woman living on twenty spare dollars a week and eating every other day so her children could have milk; a woman heating the house every second night because she couldn't afford the bill and the newly privatised electricity company wouldn't cut her any more slack; the worker in an emergency relief service that had lost half its funding, who had to choose which person would wait two weeks for their emergency food parcel and who was so desperate they had to get food on the spot. It is what some people want to call 'relative poverty'. It is what some people would like to say doesn't exist in Australia. It shouldn't, but it does.

Three places

At first I was just angry for the people who shared their stories with me. I was going to write an exposé about 'hidden people' and 'Australia's shame'. I would bear witness to the inadequacies of the welfare system and to what abstractions such as 'downsizing' actually meant in people's lives. However, this wasn't the tale they wanted told. Nor did it do justice to the complicated, careful stories they shared with me. I had to learn what had to be said, about hope as well as pain.

A more immediate problem was whether I could convey the great diversity of each of these suburbs. One of the facts that is sometimes ignored in accounts of disadvantaged places is the jumble of different paths and experiences they contain. Seemingly detached from the real city – although both Inala and Broadmeadows are within 15 kilometres of the central business district, and only Mount Druitt, located 35 kilometres from central Sydney, could really be called distant – their differences are submerged in an expectation of drab sameness. Those differences, within each street and estate, trace the intricate histories of individuals and families, as well as the impact of decisions taken by powerful people who don't live there: how many public housing units are kept or sold, who moves in and who is relocated out, which factory is saved or closed.

In one street there might be several households dependent on old age or single parent pensions, others on unemployment relief, still others living on one or two low wages. Some are doing well enough, perhaps saving to buy a cheap house or a block of land, while others are redundant or retrenched. There are older couples who have purchased their homes and have a caravan, widows and widowers who live alone in public housing or are providing a home for unemployed grandchildren, families with eight children living next-door to lonely transients who close their blinds tightly against the street.

Each of these places also registers the mobility of twentieth-century people. When I was there in the middle of the 1990s almost everyone I saw had moved or been moved from somewhere else. Most of the Australian-born were displaced from inner suburbs, moved out to the city's edge in search of cheaper housing, or moved in from country towns and lost farms. Inala and Mount Druitt had large and well-organised Aboriginal and Torres Strait Islander communities, often tied through migration to

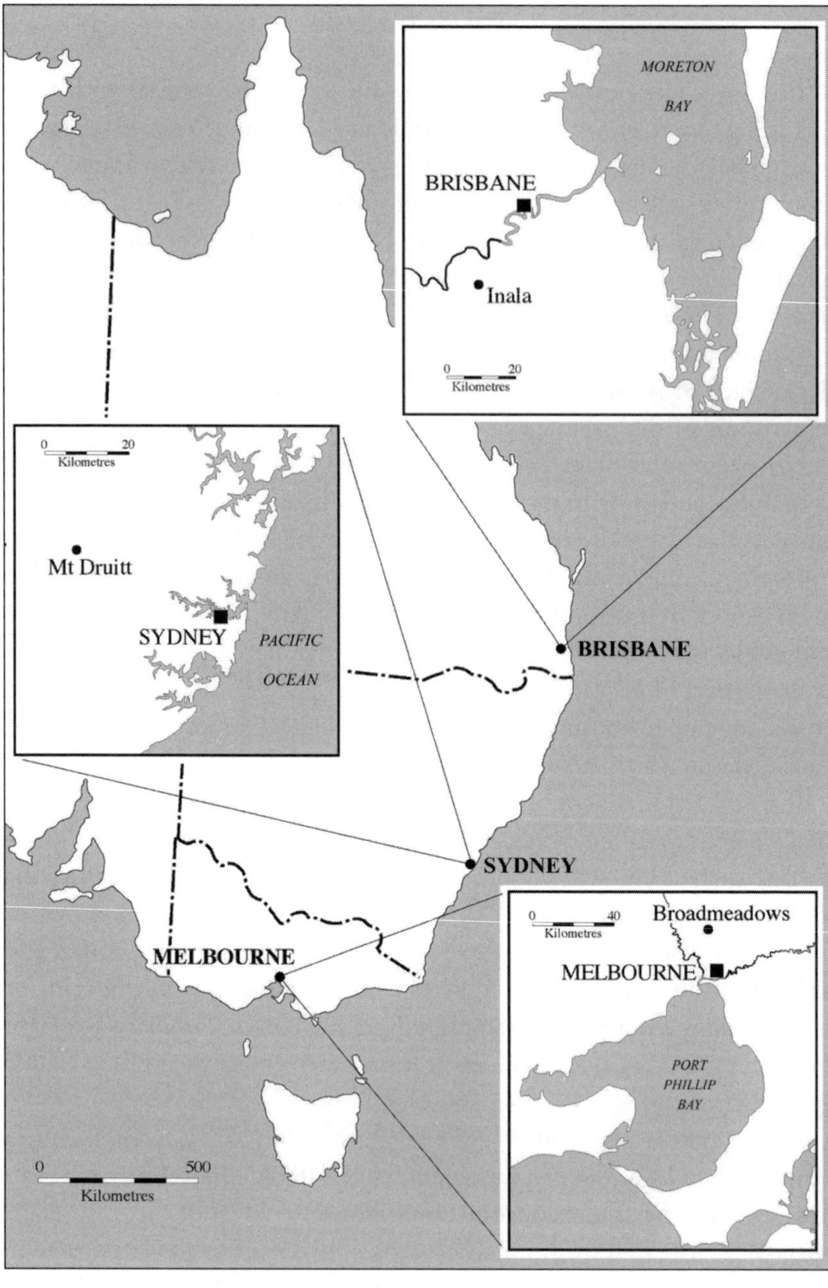

Figure 1: Inala, Mount Druitt and Broadmeadows

former missions or inner suburbs, such as Sydney's Redfern. In all three, around one-third of the adults were born outside Australia, and most spoke a language other than English. Inala, Broadmeadows and Mount Druitt had all become increasingly diverse after 1980, as longer-established groups such as Italians, Greeks and Maltese were joined by Samoans, Tongans, Filipinos, Guatemalans, El Salvadoreans, Hmong, Turks, Vietnamese, Iraquis, Kurds and Eritreans.

It is important to stress variations within places that many outsiders see as drably similar. However, I still had to make decisions about emphasis and concentration. As I spent more time in each suburb I found myself drawn to the local residents who, in their own words, were doing it hard, and to the social workers, activists, priests, nuns and volunteers who ran the hardest pressed agencies. My focus became the experiences, the ideas, the fears and the hopes of people brought together not by a particular cultural identity but by their entrenched hardship. Some were migrants, some were Aboriginal, and some were Australian-born; some were living on very low incomes, some were working in public and private welfare agencies and some were doing both. But all said that what really mattered was poverty. If it didn't dissolve boundaries of culture, language, age and gender, hardship nonetheless provided people with a common register of complaint and of vision. Anne Neilsen, a Mount Druitt community worker, talked about focusing on the people who were 'easily put down' and 'easily swept aside'. I needed to incorporate her wisdom and to see that the people most likely to be discarded and ignored had not only endured the worst injustices but knew the most about justice.

Rather than writing about these three suburbs – an immensely difficult task given their diversity – I decided to write about the people living in those parts identified as particularly poor and those who worked in the nearby agencies. In Broadmeadows this meant the public housing estates of 'old' Broadmeadows and Dallas, as well as the newer estate at Meadow Heights. In Mount Druitt it was Bidwill and Shalvey, along with the cluster of welfare centres in Emerton. Inala is a smaller, more contained place, and while I began to grasp some of its internal divisions, these seemed less significant than in the other two suburbs.

I tried as best I could to speak to a wide range of people. About two-thirds of those to whom I spoke were women, because female residents and female workers do most of the talking. While the majority were Anglo-Australian, about 10 per cent spoke another language as well as English and another 10 per cent were Aboriginal or Torres Strait Islander people. Most of the residents lived in public housing and more than two-thirds were living on pensions or unemployment benefits. The employed formed the smallest group, and they were largely labourers, factory workers, cleaners or shop assistants.

Their paths into hardship were depressingly familiar. From their perspective the best definition of poverty was its persistent insecurity. Theirs was the poverty of always being behind, always being unable to afford things everyone else takes for granted, and always putting up with run-down housing and poor health. Their hardship had a history that could not be captured in snapshots. Other people's mishaps – too many bills coming at once, getting ill, losing a part-time job, having a child with asthma, a broken appliance – were their catastrophes. Pushed into poverty by accumulating misfortune, they did not have the resources to protect themselves from its consequences. If they envied rich people anything, it was their safe distance from disaster.

Most of the people with whom I spoke came from backgrounds of rural or inner-urban hardship. Their homes had too many children and not enough money. Some had lost a father or a mother or both, or one parent was a drinker, a gambler or a drifter. Their schooling had been poor. They didn't read and write very well and when they were at school the classes were too large and the teachers too busy to help them. Out in the world at the age of 14 or 15, with no qualifications, their work histories were punctuated by unemployment. They had always received low pay and those with families generally relied on one wage while their children were small. Those who were younger had entered the labour market in the 1970s and 1980s, when it was harder to find and keep decent jobs. As recession bit in the 1980s the middle-aged men and women were in the most vulnerable jobs, in the most insecure industries. Some had worked in one factory for two or three decades, but longevity and loyalty counted for little. Others worked as mailroom clerks, railway workers, labourers, train conductors, hospital porters or school cleaners, or for the power stations and water boards. As public organisations slashed their workforces in the 1990s they were the first to go.

Some had expensive or chronic illnesses. Other people had to use their meagre savings to care for a sick mother or husband or wife. They had car accidents and were injured at work. Geraldine, Val and Michael had married gamblers; Joan had married a man who died young, leaving her with six children, no skills or experience with which to get a job and no money for childcare. Kylie, Alison and Sophie had unplanned pregnancies but decided to keep their babies. Vincent and Karen, looking back, said they had had one too many children, while Linda had triplets who quickly exhausted her husband's storeman income. Grace hadn't bargained on her fourth child, and it was a difficult pregnancy, but she was a Catholic so the few thousand dollars she'd saved for a deposit on a house were eaten up in hospital bills. Lorraine, Bill, Darren and Graeme had not done well in school: they'd had to stay home to look after a sick parent or younger children, or been dyslexic or deaf or disinterested. Jean, Jeff, Elena, Martin and Matt had lost their jobs because the company they worked for had gone broke, they'd been expendable, or they'd turned 18 and the boss didn't want to pay them an adult wage.

This is not intended to be a complete history of Mount Druitt, Inala or Broadmeadows, nor a painstaking reconstruction of a few people's lives. Instead, my aim is to present a polyphonic portrait of the most impoverished people and those who worked with them and knew them, based on the stories they wanted to tell about the world as it was in the 1990s and as it might be in the future. It is my contribution to a tradition of writing about people who are on the lowest rung. It shares the commitment that produced such powerful works as *Struggletown*, *The Hidden Injuries of Class* and *All Our Kin*, and the other compassionate accounts of hard times in Australia and elsewhere.[1] I acknowledge the concern of Lois Bryson and Ian Winter about a light of inquiry that is always shined on the powerless rather than the powerful.[2] But I knew that done well it could move hearts and change minds.

Some will not want to be moved or to change their minds. They will insist that people don't have to be poor and that they have brought it upon themselves. People will say the poor refuse to better themselves, that they are lazy and won't pull themselves up by their boot-straps; that they don't really want a job; that they always have cigarettes and beer and a colour television, perhaps these days even a mobile phone. They get themselves pregnant so they can get the single parent pension. They aren't stupid, they're clever and fraudulent and they tell lies.

If it is unearned, unfair and unlucky, poverty seems very cruel. So we reassure ourselves that poor people are to blame. Everyone seems to know someone who knows someone else who says that he knows a person who is rorting the system. The evidence can be flimsy – third- or fourth-hand, even fabricated – but it will still be held up as truthful. Invariably, people create a middle ground – 'for some, it's through no fault of their own' – and then sweep it away: 'but you can't do anything for some people'. These beliefs must be true because the alternative is unpalatable. Perhaps poverty – and wealth – stem from a fundamentally unfair structure. Perhaps those who are privileged in terms of inheritance, opportunity and ability do very well and are protected against the consequences of their failures, while those who are not must struggle harder to succeed and suffer dire consequences should they fail. In other words, the distance between a rich person and a poor person measures the weight of a whole range of advantages, earned or unearned. If you wish to be wealthy or even just comfortable it is still good advice to choose your parents carefully.

In order to do justice we must reject the fantasy that poverty is deserved. Further, we must have regard for our common humanity. We must insist that if we were in the same situation we would be just as unsure about how to solve our problems. We might make the same mistakes or worse ones. Yet somehow poor people have never quite become part of a common humanity. Other people always want to push them out. There must be something wrong with poor people after all. They don't deserve any sympathy, let alone compassion. Thankfully, no one dares use the term 'nigger' any more. But loser? bludger? people who don't count? Some of our most respectable citizens seem happy enough to use those words. To treat poor people so harshly you have to see them as unlike you in a very fundamental way. But they are not unknowably distant. In them we should see ourselves if things had been different.

The debate about social division and poverty in Australia pays too little attention to the experiences and ideas of people like Geraldine, Val, Darren, Lorraine, Elena and Matt. Discussions of welfare reform or ways of tackling unemployment too often fail to address a broader problem: a problem in the way that people who are not poor think about those who are. I don't think most people lack compassion or regard for the sufferings of strangers.

Public responses to disasters and tragedies reveal a desire to help and a desire to know about suffering that is more empathetic than voyeuristic. This is why it is so important to listen to those who suffer poverty, and to make sure that they are involved in the discussion of its remedies. Thinking about justice begins by listening to those who know about injustice.

Listening

Listening to so many people is difficult, and retelling their stories is more demanding than it might appear. By asking someone to tell you their history you are asking them, as anthropologist Elizabeth Tonkin pointed out, 'to crystallise themselves at this chance moment in time'.[3] Our stories about the past are always told with an eye on the present and on our audience: asked to describe our experiences and our lives, we do not rewind some figurative tape to a point in the past and provide a blow-by-blow account of what happened. We create personal histories that are also stories, because remembering always involves shaping events into tales that can be told to the person who has asked for them. Memory is not the past as it exactly was, but the past as it seems now.[4]

When asked to remember, the people with whom I spoke shaped their lives into paths, highlighting decisions and moments of choice and selecting what seemed to them significant. They moved back and forth between past and present to interpret why they did some things and how they must have felt. And because they wanted me to understand, they, like everyone else, used the conventions of storytelling: rise and fall, love won or lost, heroism, success, tragedy, surprises, hopes realised or deferred.[5] Sometimes they remembered themselves saying the things they wished they'd said. They slightly adjusted the timing of events to make clearer the story's ultimate conclusion and generalised impossibly detailed days and weeks into good years and hard times. This does not mean that their stories weren't true; oral testimony is not a 'repository of facts and errors' but our best attempt, at a specific moment, to describe the themes, lessons and meaning of our lives.[6]

Nor do we tell stories in isolation. We tell them in dialogue with others, as our contribution to a conversation about the ways of the world, the truth about the past and the possibilities of the future. People in Broadmeadows,

Inala and Mount Druitt talked about their place in a wider world, blending their stories together, sometimes disputing details but more often than not coming up with an agreed version. Perhaps even more than other people, however, they also told stories they were used to telling. Those who rely upon others for help must become very skilled at producing an account of themselves, and not in the relative safety of the crafted memoir or diary: their autobiographies must be produced on demand and on the run, to the social worker or the police officer or at the emergency relief counter. They must keep their story consistent, and most of all they must tell it in the right way, speaking of sufferings they don't deserve, and of their fortitude and strength of character. Their autobiographies are a way of asking for help without confirming suspicions of helplessness.[7] Again, the fact that their stories are strategic doesn't make them false, but it does make it all the more important to listen, to ask questions and to ask for more.

The most important point, perhaps, is that I helped to create these stories. People began with what they thought I might want to hear or need to know, and relied on my verbal agreement, nods, smiles and frowns. If oral historians must always be attentive to their own role in the scripting, editing and transformation of stories, for me the relationship between the listener and the teller was perhaps especially complicated. For a start, I was asking people questions different to those they often encountered, which focused on what they had done wrong or why they needed help. I was asking them to share their imaginativeness and their hope, and seeking to use oral history in its best possible way: to endorse the importance of what people said, and acknowledge them as speakers with a right to be heard.[8]

Also, I think most people saw me as being not quite an outsider to their experiences. Often poked and prodded by social surveyors with clipboards, they first of all wanted to know who I was and why I wanted to know about them. They wanted my story. So I told them that I was born and grew up in Elizabeth, a place that shared many features with their own suburbs. I made it clear that I had left Elizabeth a long time ago. Yet while I was not an insider neither was I completely an outsider. People old and young could understand my story: a man born at a particular time, in a place they could imagine, and whose life – moving away to get a university education and a good job – followed a recognisable path. I was expected to understand the truth in what they said, make the right connections and fill in the gaps. Of course, I always tried to ask questions about every story, the statements and points with which I agreed, as well as those I found unpalatable. I would ask people to explain more fully their point of view and share with me the evidence that led them to their conclusions. But I was still expected to comprehend their past and present in a way that another researcher might not.

In particular, I was expected to know two specific stories. The first portrayed the people of Inala, Broadmeadows or Mount Druitt as heroes who had built viable communities despite all the neglect and stigma they had experienced. This was their story of heroes and villains, a humorous tale of fooling the powers that be. The second story was a mournful accounting for the victims of undeserved suffering. I knew these stories well. I knew they were often inaccurate and that parts of them were manifestly untrue. People put themselves into situations they could not have witnessed and invented words they could not possibly have said. They weren't really there. It didn't really happen that way and they didn't really win. At times you knew people wished it had happened like that and the wish had become the memory. Still, their inaccuracies mattered less than the meaning they managed to convey and the truths they told about dignity, effort and sacrifice.

But there was more to hear, not really stories so much as fragments, things that people could hardly bear to say. People told me stories, cracked jokes and shared their anecdotes. But because they thought I might understand, they also shouted and cried and said things I didn't want to hear. They shared intimacies I had not expected, sad, stumbling accounts of pain and despair and loss. Some wanted reassurance that what they feared would not come to pass; somehow I would know that things were going to get better, that all the talk of 'the million unemployed' in the newspapers and on the television was just talk. Others wanted to share difficult feelings: about being helpless, about people they knew – I think sometimes it was themselves – who were tired of struggling and just wanted someone to solve their problems. There were impossible hopes. Stories broke and lost their thread; loose ends of dreams and what might have been. There was anger, flashes of scorching rage about what had been done and said to them because people like them didn't matter.

It took a long time for me to know what to do with their anger and desperation. There were words I didn't hear properly; worse, there were words I tried to silence. Listening to the tapes, I hear my discomfort stop people in their tracks. I say stupid things, reassuring and empty things. I know what that is about: the past I shared with them was both an advantage and an obstruction. I could understand the stories of heroes and villains and undeserved suffering; I knew those and I could place myself in them. But not the stories about hopelessness and pain, or shouting, angry despair; those stories I had to learn how to hear. When I was growing up I never knew real poverty. There was hardship, but only until my father got a decent job and my mother started working again. However, poverty was near enough to see and especially to smell. It was in the houses I didn't like to visit. It was the mother who didn't get out of bed, the father who didn't go to work, the friends who didn't ever seem to have anything for lunch and who drank all the free school milk, even when it had been curdled by the summer sun. I knew we weren't meant to be like them. We didn't look down on them, we looked across at them, because theirs was the hopelessness that might have been ours if we didn't keep trying and if we weren't careful.

In backing away from the despairing, angry stories, I was making clear my own investment. I wanted all the people with whom I spoke to know what had to be done, to show their courage and their capacity. They did, but some of them also wanted to show me something else. When you ask people to tell you their stories there is a responsibility to hear everything: the half-spoken conclusions, the despair, the longings, the hopes; what you want to hear and what you don't. It's not that the stories about heroes and suffering were false and the stories about anger and loss were true. It's that there were expected and unexpected ways of telling true stories. Some were less sculpted and less often rehearsed. Some told truth through allegory, others through tragedy, others more directly. Some I shared, but others I had to learn to understand because they conveyed difficult feelings in a fragmentary way, sometimes through silence and words that could not be said.[9] In the end I had to learn how to tell their truth.

When I spoke with Lorraine Goodman and Val Stephens in 1995, they were living in Inala's poorly maintained public housing. We were in Lorraine's kitchen with her husband Bill, a retired sailor, and a friend of theirs, Gordon. We spoke for three hours but there was more they wanted to say so I agreed to come back the next evening. Our conversations ranged over Lorraine's days as a tenant advocate and Val's biting criticisms of the Building Better Cities program. They talked about their grandchildren and how they were all finding it hard to get jobs. One had been in prison because he'd driven an unregistered car and no one in the family could afford to pay the fine. Another was very bright at school, but he'd been turned off by a couple of teachers who had expressed amazement that a kid from Inala might want to go to university. He did an apprenticeship but he still hadn't found any work. Val cried a little when she told me about that.

As I left, Lorraine decided to give me a hug, which was a little difficult because she was rather short and her head only came up to my chest. She was glad I'd stayed so long but she was unsure about some of the things she'd said. She and Val joked that maybe they should destroy the tape I'd just removed from the tape recorder. Lorraine stopped laughing, stepped back a bit so she could look into my face, and said, 'Look, love. Just go out there and tell them what we told you. Tell them what's true and what's real. Don't lie, don't just make it up. But tell them everything. You'll know how to put it so it sounds good. They have to know what it's like because we can't change things.'

Lorraine was right. She and Val couldn't change things. They were full of ideas, and they had worked all their lives as mothers, foster mothers, tenant advocates, neighbours and friends to make things better for other people. But they couldn't make the world change. I told Lorraine that I wouldn't lie, and that I'd do my best to tell people what was true. I told her that I shared her hope that things would change if I could capture the intelligence and the good sense of what she had said. I don't know if I've got it absolutely right, Lorraine, but I hope it is true. Most of all, I hope it moves the people who can read my words if they can never have the benefit of listening to you.

Chapter One

DESCRIBING DISADVANTAGE

Poverty news and poverty knowledge

Journalists and other sojourners sometimes talk about 'venturing' into Mount Druitt, Inala and Broadmeadows. Most, too, have learned the venturer's vernacular. The working-class outer suburbs of Australia's cities always sprawl. Country towns and rural retreats nestle. Middle-class suburbs bask. Inner suburbs hum and bustle. But outer suburbs sprawl, as if the very laziness of their hold upon the landscape tells us something about the deficient people who live in them. They are also our backdrops for despair. Scenes set, characters are found for stories about 'mounting social problems'. Surly kids slouch against walls, smokes up their sleeves, ready for another exposé of 'life on the wild side'.

Beyond the humdrum of graffiti-painted fences and gangs, each of these suburbs has also provided the chief illustration for stories about a looming social crisis. Perhaps it is unfair to judge the quality of journalists' stories by what a sub-editor selects as the headline. Perhaps the headline writers themselves regret some of the choices they have made over the years: 'The Housing Commission Ghetto' (the *Sydney Morning Herald* describing Mount Druitt, which it also called 'wasteland, wantland'), 'Lonely Outcasts in an Urban Desert' (the *Australian*, also on Mount Druitt), 'The Sad Sameness of Broadmeadows' (the *Age*), and 'Broken Suburb' (the *Australian* on Inala).[1] Bidwill and Broadmeadows' Banksia Gardens were even described as 'The Bronx' in the 1980s, perhaps to make Australia's urban poverty look more like the real thing.[2]

The worst examples of these stories – found in newspapers or on television – apply the same mix of excited revelation and inexpert sociology to the city's badlands. In the words of one reporter writing for Melbourne's *Herald* in 1977, young people in Broadmeadows 'never had a childhood', because 'they puked over it years ago in some back alley after swelling their stomachs with grog'. I'm not actually sure where this reporter located a back alley in the part of Broadmeadows she described, but back alleys are a traditional location for the activities of the delinquent, so a back alley there had to be. The same report of 'brutal social problems' – two boys throwing cans at passing cars – concluded that 'every can they throw is an inarticulate cry against the society that has left them insecure, undereducated and unemployed'.[3]

Unemployed they might have been, but Ray and Wayne, the two boys she interviewed, were articulate enough to provide a few good lines. And if they were engaging in a rather mindless sort of protest it might have been because the other things their 'Olsen Place Gang' had tried – including a petition to the local council to request recreation facilities – had so far failed to achieve any outcome. Nor did the reporter make much of the fact that writing petitions seemed rather a tame activity for a 'gang' devoted to terrorising their neighbours.

In Brisbane, the *Courier Mail* published a few articles in the 1960s deriding Inala's status as a 'model suburb'.[4] In 1990, much was made of a 'riot' between police and 'gangs' of Aboriginal people (described variously as 'up to 100' or 'more than 150' or '200 men, women and children'). Trouble first 'erupted' when police attempted to make an arrest during a fundraising event, but was later said to have 'exploded when the Aborigines ran out of beer'.[5] One year later, after a Queensland Criminal Justice Commission report blamed police over-reaction and concluded that some of those arrested probably had been bashed at the Inala Watch-House, the *Australian* – though not, as far as I can tell, the *Courier Mail* – reported that the state government was going to examine Inala's 'poor socio-economic conditions' in yet another major study.[6]

Few events matched the intense coverage accorded Mount Druitt's 'Bidwill riot' in 1981. The *Daily Telegraph* reported that '1000 boys and girls from rival schools fought a bloody, no-holds-barred battle that held a Sydney suburb in terror', while the *Sun* led with '"Time Bomb" Warning'.[7] A day later, journalists quoted a local policeman's description of 'a barbarian children's army'.[8] The *Sydney Morning Herald* later offered a more reflective piece on 'teenage riots'; the *Herald* also reported Premier Neville Wran's visit to the area and his proposals to build youth centres.[9] But three years later, feature writers were still using the Bidwill riot (by now 'a two-and-a-half hour street brawl by knife- and chain-wielding schoolchildren, spanning several suburbs') and the well-worn photographs of its supposed flashpoint: a fight between two girls over a boy.[10]

The people who lived in the estate 'racked' by the 'wild brawl' had their own stories about what happened. Fran Hume, who moved into Oreades Way in 1979, said:

> That happened right near my house. I stood there, and my son came running home and said: 'Mum, Mum, there's a big fight going on'. I said: 'Where? Where?' I looked over to the park and there's hundreds of kids all over the place. The helicopters had brought the journalists in, and they gave cigarettes to kids and then proceeded to take photos of them.
>
> They made it a hundred times worse than it was. It was just a couple of kids fighting.

A local state Member of Parliament agreed: 'The TV crews actually said to these kids, "Look, before you start this, wait there until we've set all the cameras up". It was all orchestrated'. Carol Parker said, 'Oh yes, we've had our riot'. Laughing, she told me, 'I was right down there with that riot. I was watching from the end. I was quite surprised when I was standing there looking at it, the mums who were in the riot, pushing their prams in amongst the kids.' I asked if perhaps they were trying to sort it out. Carol laughed again, this time at my seriousness: 'No, I think they were enjoying themselves'.

Paul and Ella Sammler offered this assessment:

> It was basically two girls fighting over a boy, that's the view around here. And, you know, whenever there's a school fight you always get their friends and kids hanging around. So these two girls had a fight, and I think it just spilled out of the schoolyard onto a traffic island. So they congregated there, and of course the crowd was around, and one of the local neighbours called up someone, who called up someone else, and before you knew it the Channel 7 helicopter was there. And all the local kids, nothing to do on a weekday afternoon, saw this helicopter and thought, 'Wow, what's this?', and just flocked to it.

Everyone in Bidwill had their explanation. My best guess is that a small-scale fight was made into an event by some unfortunate decisions taken by people who should have known better and who should have predicted their serious consequences. Someone contacted a newspaper journalist and the newsroom at Channel Seven to report the likelihood of a brawl: some said it was a school principal, others a local shopkeeper eager to publicise his concerns over juvenile crime, still others the Mount Druitt police who were embroiled in a battle with the Police Department for more constables.

The actual fight was, by most accounts, contained or even over before any journalists arrived, but they had come a long way and they needed a story, and someone – again, it is hard to know who – suggested that the flashpoint be re-staged for the camera. In my view, this is the only way to explain the stage-managed photographs of wrestling, hair-pulling girls. Add to this the decision to land a helicopter in the middle of a housing estate in which perhaps two-thirds of the population were less than 15 years old: it is not surprising that every boy and girl decided to come and take a look. Photographs of children waving sticks and running between houses may also have been staged for the cameras, according to the people who were there; at the very worst, it is possible that there were incidents on the edges of the crowd they didn't see. It is a strange kind of riot, brawl or battle, too, that apparently produced no injuries serious enough to require medical treatment, no reports of property damage, and no arrests; local police claimed at the time to have warned six young people but this claim was not repeated or verified in later accounts.

It wasn't just Bidwill. Stephanie Todd, who had lived in Broadmeadows most of her life, remembered a conversation with some friends who used to hang out around Olsen Place:

> The *Age* came out. I think it was the *Age*. It was in the late 1970s or early 1980s, and they said, 'You don't look rough enough. Pose better'. They did the fags and everything and said, 'Well, how bad do you want us to look?'
>
> So they're doing all this, and when I was talking to them later on about these beautiful photos in the *Age* they said it was just incredible, they really wanted them to pose for it and really play it up. They had a ball, but it was contrived.

In the heady journalism of disadvantage each fabrication produced its own truth, mostly about uncontrolled kids and uncontrollable tensions.

Each implied a solution: resources, perhaps, certainly sterner policing. And each provided the evidence for the next, one item producing the image or anecdote that was used again and again, even if it was no longer close to the truth. In Broadmeadows, long-time resident Geraldine Cannon remembered that some young people once broke all the windows at the local railway station. 'Then, every time anything ever happened the television news would show this same picture of all these windows boarded up. It went on for years, as if they'd just been broken again. People used to think they were wrecking that station every week.' Or, as an Inala youth worker put it, 'It's not as if they know anything about what's happening here now. They just dredge out the old stuff and play it again.'

Of course, the media does not speak with one voice. Against the grain of inaccurate and irresponsible stories about these suburbs, other writers have attempted to portray them honestly, even if sub-editors couldn't resist headlines such as 'Little Hope in Suburbs of Despair'.[11] Martin Flanagan's warm, empathetic stories about Banksia Gardens are a case in point.[12] Flanagan let people speak for themselves; in one article, he even dared to make Banksia Gardens, with its mix of ethnic backgrounds, an epitome of what was best in Australian culture.[13]

Sympathetic stories remained a minor stream next to the gritty grunge that aimed to entertain more than enlighten. If it is easy enough to satirise, its impact cannot be lightly dismissed. Whatever the facts, for instance, the supposed riot had lasting consequences for Bidwill residents, even for Mount Druitt people as a whole. It was there in the sideways glances of prospective employers, or the raised eyebrows of the loan officer at the bank. The riot also generated a predictable policy response. Premier Neville Wran arrived, in another helicopter, to announce urgent new initiatives: large youth centres that local residents say were built too quickly and in the wrong places. No one really bothered to ask Bidwill people what they needed so the centres became graffiti-covered bunkers requiring barbed-wire protection from the local youth they were meant to lift out of delinquency.

The riot created a story over which local people never regained any control. Their home was turned into a 'time-bomb', a warning, and they became characters in a lurid drama of mayhem. As Martin Mowbray has argued, the Bidwill riot is an important part of our recent history because it shows in a particularly powerful way how the inaccuracies of what is said about the poor are reflected in and further amplified by the policies that are applied to them.[14] Portraits of the poor determine what we think we should do and can do about their poverty. Pictures of poor places, meanwhile, help justify interventions and penalties that could never be contemplated for the leafy streets that lie just minutes away.[15]

In that vein, more recent newspaper and television reports are likely to be just as damaging to the prospects of impoverished people. Poverty news in the 1990s featured a widening gap between negative, dismissive stories focusing on 'welfare cheats' and more careful accounts discussing whether or not Australia was producing a permanent 'underclass'. By the time Peter Putnis wrote his analysis of media images in 1999 the balance had swung decisively towards the former, helped along by conservative government ministers who were more than happy to fuel the anti-welfare fire.[16]

Earlier stories ranged from the heavy-handed to the more serious. After the Los Angeles riots of 1992, Victorian Premier Joan Kirner's simplistic warnings about an 'alienated underclass' were gleefully translated into 'Dole Queue Riot Fears' and 'Jobless Violence Warning' by the *Herald Sun*, while in the *Australian*, P. P. McGuinness managed to combine a lament that social order was 'breaking down among the underclass', with a suggestion that what the poorest people of both Los Angeles and Australia needed was less welfare.[17] The *Sydney Morning Herald* ran a special series on *Australia's Underclass* in 1993, combining expert commentary, editorial observation and portraits of those who were 'excluded ... [from] mainstream, working society'. It began with images of Mount Druitt, which, it said, 'to middle-class Australians can seem like another country'.[18] Brisbane's *Courier Mail* led with a study by the Queensland Council of Social Services and a feature article by Don Petersen, titled 'Trapped in the Cycle of Despair'.[19] Perhaps the most comprehensive study was Deborah Hope's 'Poverty Doesn't Spell Underclass'. Hope assessed the evidence, interviewed disadvantaged people, and made the important point that increasing inequality and hardship did not translate into a permanent poverty cycle for any one individual, let alone an entire class.[20] Stories about the underclass became less frequent thereafter and were outweighed by a preoccupation with the largely concocted problem of welfare fraud. However, in 1998 *Time* published Susan Horsbrough's 'Living on the Edge', a sympathetic portrait of life in Mount Druitt that nonetheless described 'an underclass beset by social problems'.[21]

All along, public debates about poverty rested on journalists' translations of competing claims from experts in universities, think-tanks and welfare organisations. The dissemination of poverty news has always been closely associated with the creation of poverty knowledge, as journalists and experts shunt information, statistics and stories back and forth. During the 1990s, for instance, the release of new research reports, such as those by labour economist Bob Gregory or incomes specialist Ann Harding, prompted newspaper stories. In turn, these generated human interest pieces featuring new quotes from the same researchers. Journalists also shaped their language to the changing concepts of poverty knowledge, most obviously in using words such as 'underclass' but also by adopting definitions of disadvantage as 'relative' or 'locational' and emphasising the idea of 'social exclusion'.

Certainly, poverty news had a deep well of knowledge from which to draw. As two recent surveys make clear, Australian researchers have made a significant contribution to the study of disadvantage in the thirty years since the famed Commission of Inquiry into Poverty.[22] A particularly rich research stream, flowing from the University of New South Wales Social Policy Research Centre, studies the effectiveness of different approaches to welfare and ways of refining our definitions of poverty.[23] For their part, welfare organisations have also produced numerous well-argued studies on the prospects of poorer Australians, based on social surveys, oral testimony and participation in actual welfare work.[24]

However, Australian research has had its weaknesses, most obviously that it has remained 'almost entirely pre-occupied with the *measurement* of poverty'.[25] Of course, it is important to measure the effect of specific policies over time: the significant reduction in poverty among aged people between 1975 and 1990 is a case in point.[26] Just as useful are assessments of whether and how so-called social wage benefits (such as subsidised housing, medical care and education) make a dramatic difference for vulnerable groups.[27] Most poverty researchers also emphasise that describing the meaning and experience of poverty must involve ethical considerations as to what constitutes 'living decently'.[28] Abstract measurements of income or expenditure do not tell us everything. Accordingly, they have studied perceptions of adequate income and defined poverty in terms of deprivation, exclusion and an inability to achieve basic standards, such as adequate heating or having enough cash to get by in an emergency.

Sometimes this has also involved asking poor people themselves what poverty meant.[29]

Australian researchers' main achievements in the 1990s, perhaps, were to insist on the continuing significance of poverty and to keep before the public the issue of growing inequality. Yet to make poverty news, some creators of poverty knowledge resorted to poverty lines and the idea of an 'underclass' as simple, dramatic ways of describing the problem. Not only were their own more complex arguments discounted and the views of poor people largely ignored, but debates over precise measurement dominated public discussion of poverty. The fact that the wealth and income gap between the richest and poorest Australians was increasing was turned into an inaccurate but more newsworthy claim that the poor were getting poorer. In a recent example, a report released in late 2001 claimed that one in eight Australians – more than two million people – lived in 'income poverty'.[30] The conservative Centre for Independent Studies criticised the report and claimed that the proportion of Australians living in what they called 'relative' poverty was more in the order of 5 per cent, or around one million people.[31] Almost absent from the ensuing newspaper and television 'debate' about numbers were moral and political judgements, such as whether the difference between one or two million people enduring hardship was in fact the most important issue.

At the same time, the problem of poverty was being turned into the problem of welfare dependency. While Australian poverty knowledge largely avoided American researchers' fascination with cultural pathology, concerns about so-called poverty traps sometimes mimicked an American obsession with the supposedly distinctive behaviour of poor people.[32] Such claims detach the problem of poverty from the problem of inequality, portray poverty as a product of the welfare system itself and suggest that poor people lack effort and initiative. In other words, we are encouraged to focus on what is wrong with poor people, and on their bad decisions, rather than on what might be wrong with the context in which those decisions have to be made.

The worst excesses of tabloid reporting aside, the major problem with poverty news in the 1990s was not sensationalism or a lack of sympathy. It was more a problem of what news stories and some poverty researchers confirmed as the way to talk about the issue. If sympathetic stories captured bravery and stoicism, few captured the real challenge of the injustices they described. They made poverty seem pitiable rather than something for which we could identify causes. Even those stories that refused to see it as self-inflicted still tended to imply that poverty was inevitable. They also tended to portray poor people as 'trapped', 'excluded' or 'powerless', rather than as people who might know something very important about the problems and their solutions.[33]

Some stories also adopted an ominous unease, using terms such as 'growing unrest and frustration' or 'looming problems'. This has always been a tactic of poverty's narrators, of course: the moral of the story and the reason for taking action is often what 'they' (or their germs or criminal habits) might do to 'us'. In other versions, poverty was becoming a threat to perceptions of Australia as an egalitarian or decent society: if we let people suffer like this, in other words, we must acknowledge something negative about ourselves. However, in both versions, the significance of poverty lay in its capacity to do moral or even physical harm to people who were not poor, rather than in its basic injustice. The debate that impoverished Australians might like to have would focus on neither the magnitude of the threat they pose nor their own culpability for poverty. It would ask instead whether their poverty constitutes an injustice and, if so, what remedies might best address it. This would demand what American writer Alice O'Connor calls 'a genuinely different kind of poverty knowledge'.[34] In Australia, and despite the efforts of poverty's expert interpreters, that seems further away than ever.

In the zoo

In 1994, the coordinator of a job program in Mount Druitt developed a support group for long-term unemployed adults. The organisation that helped fund the project asked if he would mind showing the results of his efforts. As he told me about what happened, his wife, a local teacher, joined in:

> Paul: So, we had a visit. The visit was from a private girls' school, thirty of them, and they had a walking tour of the centre, you know, 'Come and see unemployed life in Mount Druitt'.
>
> It was terrible. I've got grown men and women, as well as young kids, and it must have made them feel so low to have these two groups

of girls traipsing through and asking 'Tell me why you're here', 'Why are you unemployed?', you know.

Ella: Why were they there?

Paul: It was part of their social studies unit, to give them an idea of what unemployment looked like.

Ella: That's like the zoo, isn't it?

Paul: I was disgusted.

I have no doubt that the schoolgirls were serious and interested in what people had to say. But that hardly seems the point. What disgusted Paul and Ella, and might disgust others, was unemployed people being put on display.

Performing poverty and explaining your behaviour are hardly new features of life in the badlands. I was aware that workers and residents were mostly hardened to the continuing demands of the stage. For workers, there were always new managers to educate, or new staff to 'break in' at what were then called the Department of Social Security (DSS) and the Commonwealth Employment Service (CES). For residents, there were public meetings or community consultations, new social workers – 'You have to sniff them out, have a bit of a laugh, see what they say, you know' – and new community project teams, or new researchers like me. If anything, residents were less troubled by the performance of disadvantage than workers. They prided themselves on their ability to discomfit outsiders and took a good deal of enjoyment in stories of 'mean streets':

> People at work, some of them have had the silver spoon in their mouth all their life. They reckon they wouldn't even get out of the car if they came over here.
>
> They think we've all got knives or something. Just one big riot, that's our Bidwill.

In her 1977 story about the Olsen Place Gang, mentioned at the beginning of this chapter, the *Herald* reporter realised the pleasure her characters took in bravado: Ray and Wayne 'recognise the responsibility to "perform" to the admiring crowd'. Yet she didn't grasp, or perhaps didn't convey, the fact that she and the Melbourne newspaper readers for whom she was writing were part of the crowd too. If you live in the 'zoo' you learn to play to the audience.

Criticisms of poverty news and poverty knowledge tend to emphasise deficient policies or inaccurate public understandings. It is just as important, however, to recognise that what is said about poverty also shapes what poor people feel they can say and must say, and even the way people feel they must act. The people in this study were avid readers of poverty stories, especially in tabloids, and they frequently referred to specific newspaper articles and television reports. Those stories provided the plots and common conclusions that had to be endorsed or undermined. They also provided character sketches and stage directions that came together in a kind of disadvantaged 'style'.

It all demands an intricate choreography, a clever performance in which they must become all too expert. It starts early. Paul, who grew up in Mount Druitt during the 1970s, remembers:

> It was like that at high school. The teachers would say: 'The Disadvantaged Schools Program Coordinator is coming out, look poor'. They were joking but they weren't joking, you know.

People were tired of indulging the missionary zeal of this week's trainee social worker or today's 'social affairs' journalist. Little wonder that they relished the performance sometimes, competing with each other to ask impossibly hard questions at community meetings or give all-too-easily shocked outsiders a bit of dramatic colour. Little wonder, too, that several tested me with tales of mayhem and hopelessness. After I spoke with a dozen workers at an Inala health centre one passed me a note apologising for some of the lurid stories about depravity they'd told at the start of the conversation: 'We have had so many researchers through here,' she wrote, 'who have not listened to us and have told lies. I wanted to see what you'd believe.' At a job club in Mount Druitt, teenager Matt asked me if I would be taking photographs and was disappointed when I said I didn't have a camera. He'd just spent most of his money, he joked, on a new tattoo for the occasion.

For people living and working in suburbs such as these, describing disadvantage is always a dialogue, albeit one in which they never have the final say. The constant round of reports, consultations and news stories was and is part of life's rhythm. Every few years a caravan rumbles into town, puts up its booths, sends out a small army of consultants, asks pretty much the same questions as last month or two years ago, writes a report that you'll probably never see, then packs up and decamps. If the report is released, a journalist or two will poke around, sometimes sympathetic, sometimes just looking for twenty or thirty seconds of something that makes news. When you are asked stupid questions like 'Are there any problems?', you seize your opportunity. They won't listen to you anyway, because their answers are already in place, and their images of your life – a few used needles, tattooed teenagers and the only smashed-up house in the street – are already on the videotape. If they're not, they'll be cut in from last year's exposé. In the end it's easier just to play the game.

I found that local workers also experienced the dangers of performing disadvantage. Like the residents, they had already talked too often and with too many people about what was wrong: 'We talk and talk and we answer questions and say "Look around. What do you think?" and nothing gets done'. They spoke of Inala, Mount Druitt and Broadmeadows as 'laboratories' and 'testing grounds', even as 'zoos' for clever people who come to watch the antics of the inmates: 'Anybody who wants to try anything out, they'll usually do it out here'. As Father Patrick Nolan remarked, 'As soon as you become a problem on the scale that we're on, you become something of a museum where everybody wishes to come and see you.' Or study you. As I kept reminding myself, asking people to talk was to ask them to speak yet again about problems that hadn't changed and facts that shouldn't be in dispute.

It is remarkable, in a way, that so many reports have had to be done. Not all have seen the light of day; many sit unread on some official shelf. Most were well argued, presenting the facts and making reasonable suggestions. Some were excellent, incorporating all of the knowledge that had been produced before without asking for it again, and recognising that the task was to listen to people and trust what they said. Yet even the most successful projects were reminders of what hadn't been done last time, and local workers, even more than residents, still faced the complicated question of how to describe grim realities in ways that would attract attention.

Poverty news is based, in part, on tactical stories and statements that come from inside disadvantaged places, from welfare workers, community activists, local councils and ordinary residents. All have had to make hard choices, and it was sometimes easier to manufacture a crisis and become a prophet of despair, for instance by making the unintentionally disparaging claim that western Sydney was 'a social and cultural desert'.[35] The language of the wasteland seemed to work, at least for a while. The people who used it were well aware of its dangers. Yet if funding in the here and now depended upon attracting attention, it was difficult to cast aside a strategy that worked.

The agonising twists and turns of this language are evident in most of the reports. The Sydney City Mission's *Poverty in Mount Druitt: A Grim Reality*, is typical. Released in 1981, it begins with the claim that 'the despair brought about by youth unemployment and the insecurity caused among young people by the breakdown of the family are factors in a tragic jigsaw puzzle of poverty', and later argues that 'in many cases utter despair ... has led to wife and child abuse and bashings, breakdowns in marriages and utter hopelessness'. Then come the warnings: 'a growing problem of aimlessness and despair ... [that] is likely to grow into an epidemic'; a second generation that 'faces a seemingly unrelenting wall of hopelessness'. At the same time, however, 'by isolating Mount Druitt as the subject for this report, it is in no way suggesting that the people of that area are inferior in any way to any other area'; indeed, 'there are thousands of families ... who function well in the community ... and [are] providing a loving environment in which their children will grow into well-adjusted young people'.[36]

Describing disadvantage from the inside remains a tortuous mix of reputation-saving, claim-making and storytelling. It must balance different arguments that all too easily undermine each other. You need to talk up problems, tackle outsiders' misconceptions and show the long-term consequences of inaction, all the while being reasonable, of course, about the limits of what can be achieved. All of this in a report that must be concise, easily accessible and written in a way that respects the local people who participate as characters in its narrative. It is a dangerous form of storytelling. What is most impressive is not the frequency of lapses into melodrama but the skill with which workers negotiate such a demanding genre.

Community worker Janet Sagemore, proud to call herself a 'Broady girl', described how 'Broadmeadows was "discovered" in the late 1960s as "the deprived Broadmeadows"'. As she said, this figurative description became stuck in the minds of those demanding action and those from whom action was demanded. A worker in the Western Sydney Area Assistance Scheme also referred to the danger of using the language of despair: 'It's all very well to try to attract funds by pointing to all these terrible indicators, but this is where people *live*'. A veteran worker in western Sydney argued, 'You can claim disadvantage and try and jump on the resources bandwagon, but you pay the price', and a social planner was just as unsure about how to address both sides without wearing two faces:

> Obviously a crisis, even a false crisis, will attract a lot of attention, but then a lot of people are going to see that as extremely negative attention and are then going to turn on the people who organised it, you know, 'Why are you putting down our area, when we've just spent years and years trying to make it more attractive?' or whatever.

These workers were angry. The problems they saw had not changed, and they were still calling for action that they shouldn't have needed to justify. They felt that injustice should be argument enough. As one Broadmeadows social worker said, 'Again and again, the community has to stigmatise themselves to achieve anything', while a youth worker from a nearby centre added, 'Simple arguments are never enough. It has to be dramatic.' Elaine Cummings, then principal of a Mount Druitt primary school, let out some of her anger:

> For so long, and still, we have had so many people who come to 'save the children'. We've had missionaries, we've had people come from all sorts of angles, and they've come to save the poor people and they've come to save the children ... We don't need people to save the children, we just need some bloody good teachers.

Talking about powder kegs or flash points or people who need to be rescued might elicit guilt, sometimes even sympathy. It brings a few dollars, a visit from an appropriately concerned government minister and another from an appropriately outraged Opposition spokesperson. Everyone has their roles, and everyone is trapped in the same game. But this game has real costs, not least a skewed general knowledge about poverty that makes it hard for poor people to speak honestly about their problems. For many years they have faced a harsh choice: talk up the needs and perhaps receive some help but risk the very real perils of making your street look like a war zone.

Yet escaping from the game is difficult because you can end up with no words to describe real problems. One response was to simply blame unknown troublemakers, normally from 'better' suburbs, as in this exchange between two Broadmeadows residents:

Geraldine: There were a lot of ideas that Broadmeadows teenagers and people were not only poor, or working-class, but were also deviants. That was untrue, because quite often it was good fun for people to come into the area, vandalise, do whatever they want and then disappear back into their own neighbourhood. It was Broadmeadows youth and people who were blamed, when it wasn't them at all. Deviant acts such as graffiti in trains, and causing havoc in the neighbourhood, weren't actually done by our lot at all. Therefore, a stigma has always been around Broadmeadows, but often it's been people from elsewhere.

Rhonda: And the newspapers blew it up.

Geraldine: That's right. They did. They said, 'These terrible people in Broadmeadows'. But when the truth came out we found out they were from the Toorak area, thank you very much. They wouldn't do it in their area, but they'd do it in ours, and we were getting blamed.

Getting a little of your own back on Toorak was an enjoyable reversal of outsiders' perceptions, even if the details weren't always certain. Another strategy, particularly common among local councillors, Members of Parliament, and small business owners, was to deny that there was disadvantage. As one Mount Druitt councillor said, 'I certainly wouldn't like to be saying now that we're such an underprivileged, disadvantaged area that we need this special treatment'. Another local politician told me that Bidwill didn't have any problems: 'It's all tied up in image', he said. Well, it isn't. It's tied up in a long history of real deficiencies and real injustices; in problems that have been fitfully addressed and just as often ignored. To say everyone in Mount Druitt or Inala or Broadmeadows is disadvantaged is obviously incorrect. But to say that injustice is a matter of image and perception is no solution either.

There are other losers too: those who saw themselves living in a dangerous slum and who sealed themselves in their houses waiting to be moved; young people who took on the performance of angry alienation and made it into their only way of responding to everybody else; and people who assumed that they were 'the million unemployed' and the 'bludgers' and had come to the conclusion that there was no point even trying.

Sophie, a young sole mother in Inala, said she was happy enough living there because she knew people and was involved in a social group for other young mothers like herself. But she was very worried about her daughter. Her two-year-old, as bright-eyed and bushy-tailed as any toddler could hope to be, was at that moment creating an abstract design out of a jigsaw puzzle by refusing to conform to the pattern cut into the pieces. 'I have to leave, though. Because they say it's inherited, you know. That there's this generational thing, something like that. I don't know. It's good here, but maybe I'm doing her in if I stay, you know, making her just like me.' Imagine that as the anxiety that interrupts your days and troubles your nights. Imagine being one of the unemployed people in that job centre in Mount Druitt, on display for earnest schoolgirl day-trippers. Imagine what the descriptions of disadvantage, those loaded and often vindictive words about fraud and helplessness and incapacity, strip away and then put in its place.

As long as outsiders continue to demand that such stories are told, residents and workers will have to participate in conversations – and prophecies – that veer out of their control. What we know about poverty traces conversations that have been occurring for a long time; tactical stories that distort the present and darken the future. All along, the stock of common knowledge about Inala, Mount Druitt or Broadmeadows is refuelled. Reports build upon reports, action plans criticise past inaction. The most common refrain is the imperative to overcome deficiencies, again framing these suburbs with words of warning about dire consequences should this or that proposal be ignored. It is a delicate business and it can come unstuck.

Descriptions of disadvantage provided people with a limited and skewed set of resources for local talk about poverty. By focusing upon threat, poverty news invites either rejection or confirmation. The worst examples of sensation-seeking were easy enough for people to dismiss, but the emphasis on fraud, hopelessness and threat was harder to dislodge. These had to be denied and refuted, or deflected onto those who 'really' deserved them. It is not surprising that people said, 'I'm not like that, but some of those single mothers (or Aboriginal people, or recent migrants, or young unemployed men) are'. Poor people often want to distance themselves from what is taken for granted about poverty. Little wonder, then, that most of the people with whom I spoke refused to call themselves 'poor' or 'disadvantaged'. Those words were too loaded. Little wonder, too, that the people who had most reason to claim such titles were most vociferous in their rejection of them. It might free them from other people's fictions but they still ended up trapped, this time without the words to explain situations that, by any measure, can be described as desperate.

It's very easy to ask for yet another performance of poverty. It's much more difficult, and takes more time, to seek out the words and the ideas that are rarely requested and hardly ever heard. I'm not suggesting that the people of Mount Druitt, Inala and Broadmeadows are somehow responsible for a common knowledge that portrays them as inhabiting slums or some textbook landscape of compound disadvantage. That responsibility belongs to others. But I do want to emphasise that describing disadvantage is a dangerous game, for their stories, tragic, despairing, heroic or humorous, may come to be all that is known about their places and all that is true about their lives. Maybe it would be better if the hardest-pressed people never again had to tell these kinds of stories or risk making news. It would be better still if what we wanted to know about poverty was not the strange antics of its victims but what they can tell us of its injustices and its remedies.

Chapter Two

HEROES

Fantastic stories

There were some stories I heard often. Relished in the telling, these were local legends in which everyone could find their part. Inala's favourite story concerned the devastating floods of 1974, which had badly affected some of the 'better' suburbs along the Brisbane River. At a local housing cooperative, Jenny Baker and Rosemary Judge told the story:

Jenny:	I mean, my husband, when we had the 1974 floods, he helped rescuing people, you know. And there were boatloads of people coming from Jindalee, and when they found out they were coming to Inala, they would rather go back and sit on their rooftops.
Mark:	Really?
Rosemary:	That's true. That's as true as I'm sitting here. They would rather go back and sit on their rooftops than come to Inala. And Inala was giving them food and clothes. You watch any telethon, it's always people from Inala giving.
Mark:	But sit on their rooftops?
Jenny and Rosemary:	It's true. That is true.
Jenny:	There's a spirit here in Inala that you don't buy. It's like a big country town. That's the best way to describe it here. All the supports are here for you, everyone says hello to you. You go to other suburbs, nobody says hello to you.

Long-term resident Judy Owen also used the floods to make a point about Inala's superiority:

> The community spirit is very strong here. During the 1974 floods, this is what other people noticed. It's a community feeling which is very, very strong, and tight. Where other people live, they're not so quick off the mark, you know. They probably could live thirty years next-door to someone and not know their neighbour.
>
> Here, they're not living in each other's homes but they're willing to get out and help.

Kate Legge, a coordinator at a local housing project, was also living in Inala at the time:

> During the 1974 floods, because Inala is a higher area it didn't flood. We got cut off from different places around Inala, but other suburbs, more 'elite suburbs' – we may as well put them in a box as well (*laughs*) – went under, of course. And Inala people actually opened their doors and offered their houses to put these people up until the floods subsided. Those offers were not taken up. Nobody would come out here.

I again expressed amazement, and Kate responded, 'Well, it's very sad, and what an insult to people in this community'. After a pause she added, 'But what can you expect of people like that?'.

Did 'boatloads of people' from Jindalee really force their rescuers to turn back and restore them to their perilous rooftops for fear of ending up in Inala? Perhaps Kate's version is more feasible: insensitive things were said, or nervous comments were made. Perhaps the flood's victims did prefer offers of help from more well-heeled suburbs. It's hard to know. But it is not important, in a way, to the moral of the story: Inala people understand and respond to the sufferings of others. They are willing to sacrifice, even for strangers.

In Mount Druitt's Bidwill, almost everyone talked about the Bidwill 'riot'. It was such a powerful story about the stupidity of outsiders that everyone wanted to claim a part. Some of its narrators could not have been there because they had moved into the area months or even years later. Yet they could still share in the solidarity of outrage.

One group telling me the story included a young woman, Carol, who had come to 'Concrete City' in 1982, nine months after the riot. As the story built Carol joined in, spurring on the others. As the laughter gave way to sober reflections on the difficulties the riot had caused, one of her friends asked, 'Were you here then, Carol?' There was no challenge in the statement, just inquiry. 'No, not right then. Remember, I came just after, after Luke was born.' Carol smiled, then added, 'but I feel like I could have been there.' 'That's right', her friend agreed. Carol could have been there, because as a single parent deserted by her son's father, she was the kind of person for whom these crookedly intermingled townhouses were home in 1981.

Yet it also meant more than that. To know about the riot was to know about and emphasise the difficulties of the past, even when you had come to know that past after the fact. It was important to take part in telling stories about the riot because to bear witness to that dramatic event was to place yourself among Bidwill people. It was a way of recognising the place to which you now belonged and the people with whom, by belonging, you shared a past and a future.

More personal stories moved just as easily into narratives of defiance. Colleen Willis moved into a townhouse in Blackett in 1982. She was desperate for housing, knew she didn't want to go to Campbelltown on Sydney's south-western edge, and so accepted Blackett despite misgivings about her new neighbours that later made her laugh. After a year or so she became involved in the tenant participation group; twelve years on, she was working in the Parramatta Regional Public Tenants Council, where I talked with her and Fran Hume, a long-time tenant activist and community house volunteer who lived in Bidwill.

Colleen and Fran both lived in the medium-density public housing units that were the mainstay of the Housing Commission's local building program in the late 1970s:

Colleen: The architects in those days should have been shot.

Fran: Shocking. Yes, shocking. No room to move.

Colleen: The funny thing is that the townhouses I moved out of won an award.

Fran: You must be kidding.

Mark: Did you get a vote?

Colleen: No. (*Laughs*) It was before I moved in.

Fran: Bet you were so excited when you heard that, weren't you? (*Laughing*)

Colleen: Yes, so excited. (*Laughing*) Anyway. So what happened was that we wrote a letter to the Department of Housing and asked if they could track down the architect and ask him if he could come out to a presentation we wanted to do because we heard that he won the award.

Mark: Did he come?

Colleen: No. But we were ready. Four by twos, everything. (*Laughing*) I mean, my comment used to be: that architect wouldn't *live* in something like that. They built it, and I reckon they should be made to live in it.

This story also surfaced in other conversations. In another version I was told that he had actually come to the townhouses but had driven off very rapidly once he realised the tenants were there. One consistent thread was that the architect was a man and the protestors were local women, adding to the story a much-enjoyed confirmation of men's basic stupidity about the realities of domestic life.

Whether the architect ever knew of his possible fate is beside the point. Nor is it important to ask whether such a fate was ever actually planned. The larger point of the story is not shaken by its possible inaccuracies. What remains true, in Bidwill and elsewhere, is that public housing tenants are put into cheap houses and poorly planned neighbourhoods in which their architects and builders would never live. One Bidwill resident, who had moved in just a year before I spoke to her, told me 'they wouldn't have put their bloody dogs in these places'. Another said, 'These were OK for us, for our kids, you know, because we're not as good as other people, are we? We don't deserve decent homes. We're just the ones at the bottom of the heap.'

Others stories told at the Housing Commission's expense stressed its lack of respect for tenants. There were tales of ill-maintained houses and incredible delays in repairs. If such stories portrayed residents as the victims of neglect they also showed an ability to turn a situation to their own advantage. In one tale, residents of a street somewhere in Mount Druitt had been requesting the installation of security locks on their doors. Unsuccessful for a number of months (or years according to another telling), they decided to create a crisis by breaking into each other's houses and stealing small items, all of which were then returned after the police had done their reports and the maintenance department had finally installed the locks. In another, people living in townhouses that bordered a recreation ground had ill-made fences. They couldn't get an inspector to come out. Someone found something large enough to do some damage – in some versions, it was a car, while others, with a keen sense of pantomime, described using a horse – and spent the best part of one night 'encouraging' the fences to fall over. The inspector came.

In Broadmeadows, stories recounted residents battling the same kinds of problems. Roger Randle moved to a low-deposit sale home in Coolaroo in 1971. By the mid-1970s he had helped create the Broadmeadows Progress Association (BPA) and worked as a community development officer. At the beginning of his activist career, he and other BPA members decided to tackle the local council in very direct ways:

> I mean, we did do some radical things in those days. The snakes issue in the big paddock around the school: one weekend we went up there with spades, hit a few snakes over the head and killed them, came to the Council Chamber early, all sat in the front row with brown paper bags on our laps.
>
> When all the councillors sat down and got on to this issue, which was on the notice paper, about this complaint from a ratepayer about snakes, two or three councillors said there were no snakes in Broadmeadows. They started hammering in, saying, 'This is stupid. There are no snakes', and all that.
>
> So we flicked open the bags and all these snakes fell out into the middle of the council chamber. You've never seen a council chamber clear so quickly in all your life – literally. (*Laughs*)
>
> But it got attention. The very next day they had the army there with flamethrowers all over the place. (*Laughs*)

Broadmeadows' favourite legends were more often than not tales of direct action. One was the campaign to expose the ferocious debt repayment policies of Waltons, which had been sending its salespeople out to sign up residents of new estates for furniture and appliances:

> Then we took on Waltons, because Waltons was this nice store that was there to help everybody, and it didn't matter how much you borrowed off them they'd always loan you more. A system of enslaving people for life.

> We beat Waltons. It took fifteen, twenty years, but we beat Waltons. We beat them in Broadmeadows.

Another fondly recalled BPA campaign forced the Target chain stores to reinstate lay-by in 1972, after the company withdrew the service to encourage payment by credit card. Merilyn Langford, one of the key activists, recalled how 'we organised a big petition to keep the lay-by, because they were forcing people onto [credit] cards. We said that wasn't right, because people can never get into debt on lay-by.' The petitions were ignored:

> So we organised a boycott of Target one Friday. Well, that took a lot of people. People stood outside and every time someone came into Target they'd have a discussion about why not to go in. They had stooges with trolleys and the whole thing. But they only got one-third of their normal business. We won that one too.

The lay-by campaign, as well as a successful campaign to prevent the Housing Commission from building an estate under the flight path of Melbourne Airport, had become something of a rite of passage for Broadmeadows' older activists. These were places you had to have been even if you actually came to the suburb a little later. As in Bidwill's riot, or Inala's flood rescue, you wanted to be there, and you would have been if fate had brought you to Broadmeadows in time.

The antagonists in Mount Druitt and Inala also included the state housing authorities and other government departments, though stories there recalled more sporadic actions. Broadmeadows stories were just as likely to be embellished, but the frequency of specific political campaigns there made its stories of heroes and battles rather different from those in the other suburbs. Broadmeadows groups also maintained stronger links to trade unions. Several BPA activists were union leaders, and the group's tactics – boycotts and black bans, for instance – owed much to the factory and workshop.

Yet there were strong similarities in tales of battle and defiance. Stories pitting residents against their enemies commonly began close to home, in the everyday frictions of life for renters, welfare beneficiaries and unemployed people. Their immediate targets were the local housing department workers, the social workers and the people on the DSS counter. There were stock characters: the worker who wouldn't listen to you, the welfare centre coordinator who treated people with disrespect, or the housing officer who wouldn't help you if you didn't show enough gratitude for what you got: 'You know, not enough gravel rash'. In Mount Druitt, there was a worker renowned for 'crinkling up her nose' whenever she came into your house. Another insisted that her clients not smoke in her presence, even in their own living rooms. There were even tales of social workers 'gone feral', including one who had allegedly fathered numerous children among his clients and then claimed illegal benefits as a single parent, a pointed inversion of the widespread belief that welfare clients are the ones prone to cheating. Many stories began with a rookie worker, some 'la-de-da lady, you know, believes all the shit she reads in the newspapers; can hardly wait to get back to the bloody North Shore', or a 'missionary who's come to save us' and 'just about falls over you trying to tell you how sorry she is. Then she drives away again.'

These stock characters represented a more generalised stigma and disrespect; like those people from rooftops in Jindalee they invariably head back to where they belong, to the places where they learned to look down on Inala, Broadmeadows and Mount Druitt. Stories moved beyond the local war of words to reveal the larger problem: that disrespect and neglect are all you can expect when you come from a poor area. The disdainful tenancy officer and the uncaring social worker were larger than life characters, composites of real people moulded into caricatures by their dramatic function: to express what impoverished people had learned to anticipate and to fear from everyone. Their paths through each suburb were plotted against those of the 'good workers', who had names and faces and more concrete histories. The good workers stayed, worked long hours and were always there. The bad workers expressed their distance from you in their clothes and their words and their faces. They didn't want to listen, or to learn. 'You'd think', a Broadmeadows woman said to me, 'that they came here with blinkers on. You really would. Blinkered, just like horses.' In their humiliation and defeat, of course, the bad workers also stood in for all of the people who needed to be taught something about Inala, Broadmeadows and Mount Druitt.

One of the most surprising discoveries for unprepared newcomers is that the people who live in these suburbs actually think they are better than people who live in 'nicer' areas. Unlike those who have received everything 'on a platter' and 'with the silver spoon', they had to earn whatever they have. They are more supportive of each other, more generous and resilient, and more willing to sacrifice for others. They are much less likely to cheat, hurt each other or deceive. As Judy Owen insisted, 'The people here, they're pretty genuine. We care about each other. They're not false.'

While numerous jokes and anecdotes revelled in the ignorant prejudices of people crossing over into the 'badlands', other stories took residents across that boundary. They dramatised what happened to people who moved to a 'better' suburb. While men and women told these stories the mover was invariably a woman with children. She was commonly portrayed as someone who never accepted her neighbours, who kept her distance behind closed blinds and refused to pitch in at the school or the childcare centre. One such character sported Hollywood-like 'sunglasses and a headscarf' and 'scurried from her car to her house without looking sideways'. After moving to a better suburb these mothers would always find that the people there were unfriendly and cold. There was a crisis: a child fell ill with asthma or a baby was eager to be born. The new neighbours failed to lend a hand and made clear that in their kind of area people were expected to look after themselves. Shamed by their abandonment of real friends, the movers then returned, often to the same street or estate.

Such stories reinforced local knowledge. They asserted the crucial importance of neighbours and friends in a world of potential misfortunes, and described a rhythm of reciprocal support whereby offering help guaranteed its return. They highlighted the particular dangers of isolation for mothers. They also inverted the assumption that poor people are deficient and rich people are better. Struggling people care for each other and will always help in a crisis, while rich people care only for themselves. As a woman concluding one of these stories told me, the people who live 'over there', a dismissive gesture away, 'won't lift a finger, you know, wouldn't give you water to put you out if you were on fire. Unless you paid for it.' This was not a joke, and she had no smile. It was sharp, bitter fact. This was her experience of an unjust world, revealed to her through the small acts of denial at the welfare counter or the housing office.

Stories about the benefits of ordinary know-how over expertise, or about the benefits of living in a 'real' community, are not the sole preserve of poor places. But they have a particular edge there because the urge to be respected is especially strong and especially unlikely to be fulfilled. The inversions are more extreme, and the ridicule harsher, because there is a much greater threat that you will – in fact and not in fantasy – be treated badly, ignored, accused, perhaps even punished. When you're sure most people think you don't count for much it's all the more reason to make yourself count, in a story that you can control, told with and among people who know how hard you try and how difficult it is to get along.

Stories such as these can redeem all kinds of questionable local characters. Joy Round, a volunteer for St Vincent de Paul in Broadmeadows, told me about some alcoholic men she'd been helping in a shelter. Most had lived on the streets or in refuges, and the shelter was their last stop. Joy painted them as lonely figures, with nothing and no one really to live for. One Christmas Joy did her usual collection of money to buy presents for local children. It was 1993, a hard year in Broadmeadows, and she gathered less than usual. Somehow the men at the home got wind of the fact that Joy was struggling for funds, so between them they sacrificed their smokes and got together $1300. 'They told me it was because they wanted all the kids to get a present at Christmas. These are homeless alcoholics, and they gave me $1300. I just didn't know what to say'.

These were fantastic stories. But they were not fantasies because they referred to real experiences. They were not a completely accurate narration of events; flourishes were added after the fact and stories were shaped to a desired conclusion. But that doesn't make them untrue, because the stories of our lives are always in some sense strategic. We often remember ourselves saying the things we wished we had said, finding the right words for the right moment when really we didn't know what to say until later. So in Mount Druitt the impossibly naïve social worker stumbles too easily into the trap and the wily client's triumphant one-liner is tailored just a little too well. Broadmeadows' victory over Target is telescoped into an inevitable triumph, despite the long afternoons when the boycott faltered and maybe came close to breaking. The Inala boatmen row towards Jindalee, only to be rebuffed and turned away.

People knew their stories contained inaccuracies. They sometimes offered wry assessments of their own legends or bit players who had taken themselves to the front of the stage. They always tempered tales of evil social workers by reminding me that these were the 'bad apples' and most workers weren't like that at all. They knew there were exaggerations and that details had been embellished. But like all legends, they spoke a truth that people wanted to be heard. They didn't so much narrate a particular event as appropriate it, making it the core of a morality tale; in this case, that in disadvantaged suburbs people are decent and generous.

Behind all of these fantastic stories lay a powerful sense of injustice. Residents recorded a past in which they had struggled to be recognised as good people. To understand the sense of the world shared by any group of marginalised people you must listen to such histories, to their folktales, jokes and legends, or what anthropologist James Scott calls 'the "offstage" conversations of the repressed'.[1] In his study of the ways in which Malay villagers used fanciful stories to emphasise the social obligations of more powerful people, Scott makes the very important point that these stories become 'a kind of social text on the subject of human decency'.[2]

In Inala, Broadmeadows and Mount Druitt, people also used stories to reflect larger truths. Local legends used ridicule, irony and dramatic inversions to accuse those who so often accused them. They turned the stigma on its head, charging the rich with moral poverty and selfishness, and adding a few more insults besides. They turned their own poverty and hardship into a story of heroic endurance. Most of all, they merged themselves into a self-respecting and steadfast community, an enduring body that was larger than any of them alone and within which each of them could not only find a place for now but a path into the future.

Origins and battles

Not everyone who shared in the story of heroic endurance was badly off, and those people often acknowledged that they were stretching things a bit to still call themselves battlers, at least in their understanding of the term. Though more recent residents were not excluded, these legends were told to me by people who had, for the most part, lived in Inala, Mount Druitt or Broadmeadows for ten or twenty years. Few, however, were unjustified in claiming firsthand experience of hard times. Those who had become more comfortable remembered the privations of the 1960s and 1970s, and they could find more than a few children, grandchildren, neighbours and friends who were really struggling. Most of all, these stories traced the continuing lessons of what it is to be poor or powerless. People expressed a truth about the world they had learned from experience and had not forgotten. They still saw plentiful evidence that the aspirations of people like them would be ignored. They possessed a very acute appreciation of how power is used, most especially of what happens to ordinary people when it is used badly. As American anthropologist Elizabeth Janeway put it, their everyday lives 'rubbed' that awareness into them. It might have faded but it hadn't gone away, and it was just as troubling to see it being repeated for the people around you.[3]

For all the implausible details of some of their stories it is also important to see that the problems on these estates were neither fictional nor temporary. The people of Inala, Broadmeadows and Mount Druitt had good cause to picture themselves as the resourceful opponents of uncaring institutions. It is important to consider what they had to fight for and keep fighting for, as the careless mistakes of the first estates were repeated. The stories about heroes and battles traced the struggle to force the Housing Commission or other authorities to fix the manifest problems of what they had created and promise never to make such errors again.

Such struggles have something in common with those of other suburban pioneers in privately built estates. They too had to demand street lighting or footpaths, and raise money to equip raw new schools with playground equipment, books and even chalk. But the struggles of people in these public housing estates were different in their degree and longevity. As renters, or to qualify for the low-cost housing built and offered for sale by the housing departments in the 1950s and 1960s, they had to have very few resources. From the first, Broadmeadows, Inala and Mount Druitt also endured the inexorable logic of not wasting money on the poor. In the minds of hard-pressed Housing Commission authorities, houses had to be built quickly to meet demand. They had to be cheap in order to spread limited resources as far as possible. That meant providing very little: in Broadmeadows, for instance, a new Commission house in the 1950s included a gas water heater and copper, a concrete wash trough, a gas stove and an open fireplace. Strict allocation policies restricted already spartan homes to people who could not afford such luxuries as linoleum, blinds or heaters, let alone the community services and facilities the Housing Commissions themselves could not or would not provide.

The estates became very crowded very quickly. In Broadmeadows in the 1950s and 1960s a rough rule of thumb was that you needed twice as many children as there were bedrooms: five or six children for a three-bedroom house, eight children for a four-bedroom house. They didn't build many that were bigger, so families of eleven or twelve made do with four bedrooms, a living room, a bathroom, a laundry and a kitchen. Geraldine McCartney, who moved into old Broadmeadows in 1956, joked that you were lucky if you had a big back garden, because it was somewhere to put the kids. Many of Broadmeadows' first residents came from the emergency housing camp at Camp Pell in Royal Park, while some of the later arrivals were 'decanted', to use the Housing Commission's unfortunate term, from declared slum areas in Fitzroy and Collingwood. They came with a rush; in Geraldine's words, 'They were moving us out here in droves'.

Broadmeadows' first ten houses were built in 1953; the Housing Commission built 740 brick veneer, concrete and timber houses the following year, and more than 1100 the year after that. They were building 2000 houses a year in Broadmeadows by the end of the 1950s, and more than 4000 a year by the 1960s. That meant around 12,000 or 15,000 new people a year; in the busiest times, perhaps 300–400 new people – more than half of them children and teenagers – arrived each week.[4]

Broadmeadows tenants quickly learned the problems of poor design: in some streets, shifting ground prised apart the prefabricated concrete houses and rain poured down the walls. Mildew covered everything in cold weather, as Geraldine recalled:

> I dreaded the inspections, and the power they wielded. I had mildew growing in this room, the walls were actually black, and there were five tenants asked if we would take part in a program to allow the Commission to paint the inside walls with certain paints to see if it would stop the growth of the mildew. If the mildew grew I was not to touch it but to get in touch with the Housing Commission, because they wanted to estimate the rate of growth of the mould. This I duly did.
>
> On a Saturday morning, someone from the Commission came out to see me, and dear heaven, a few days later I got a letter to say that I'd made no attempt to wash this mildew off the wall and if it wasn't done in so many days then they would provide the labour and I would have to pay for it.

Stan Butcher helped neighbours deal with the same problem:

> Well, the best we could do out of the Housing Commission at the time was 'if people would open their windows and let the air in, that would solve the problem'. In the middle of winter when you've got the fire going, how do you sit there with the windows open to get the air in? They said, 'Oh, yes. You didn't ask us that. You asked us how to solve the mould problem'. They treated us as a bunch of bloody hillbillies.

Mount Druitt's first home was completed in 1966, and within ten years there were 9000 homes and 45,000 people. Here, too, hundreds of people would arrive in one or two days, following close behind the last builder's truck. Many of the residents of the first estates – Whalan, Tregear and Blackett – were people from inner Sydney who couldn't afford anything back east. If they rented or bought from the Housing Commission at least they had sewerage and paved streets; residents in nearby private developments had to wait until the 1970s for those luxuries.

The Bidwill estate was built in the late 1970s, and from the beginning was a place dominated by rental housing for the most disadvantaged. As local worker Anne Neilsen said, 'Bidwill has never really been a working-class area. It's the class who used to work, if I can put it that way.' As house sales and private building reduced the proportion of rental properties in the other neighbourhoods to 50 or 60 per cent, Bidwill and Shalvey, with 90 or 95 per cent public housing, became increasingly different from the rest of Mount Druitt, let alone the rest of Sydney. Built according to planning vogue, many of the Bidwill townhouses proved less successful as actual buildings; Carol Parker, a tenant who later became a volunteer at Bidwill Community Support, remembered that 'some of them were flooded just after they built them. Water used to flow through them, about two foot of water in the lounge rooms. You had your own water feature'.[5]

Inala's origins coincide with those of Broadmeadows; its first houses were built on an old wartime ammunition dump and were occupied in 1953. Within three years, around 7000 people lived in 1400 houses, none of which had sewerage. Plans to sewer Inala 'by 1965' were still being detailed in the Queensland Housing Commission's *Annual Report* in 1959. By 1963 there were more than 2500 houses and 13,000 residents. Inala's neighbourhoods still bear the record of changing fashions and priorities: the shift from timber to concrete and brick veneer or from the small houses of the 'flower' streets in the northern part of the suburb to the slightly better-equipped houses of the 'star' streets further south.[6]

In every case, and despite stated intentions, the Housing Commissions always privileged rapid construction over the timely provision of important services. They could not always provide those services themselves. But the decision to set aside areas for recreation or sites for community halls, churches, schools or health centres meant little if no attempt was made to cajole government departments into filling those sites with actual buildings. The South Australian Housing Trust managed to do this in its estates, especially at Elizabeth, suggesting the problem elsewhere was mostly one of ingenuity.[7] The New South Wales Housing Commission, already criticised for its estate at Green Valley, certainly recognised 'the need for civic, commercial and industrial establishments at Mount Druitt on a scale commensurate with the proposed residential development'. Its response, though, was to highlight the primary role of the State Planning Authority: 'the provision and location of these amenities is not the Commission's responsibility', it argued in 1966.[8]

The Housing Commission also held the line against the Blacktown Council; in 1967, the Commission reminded two separate deputations that its funding agreement with the Commonwealth government precluded 'providing civic buildings or making cash contributions' and that 'in any case, expenditure incurred by the Commission in the provision of facilities … could only result in the construction of fewer dwellings at higher rentals or instalment repayments'.[9] Strict interpretations of who was responsible for what, of who should be criticised for any delays, and of the narrow bounds of possibility, would remain a vexing problem for the residents of Mount Druitt and the other suburbs.

In Inala, shortages of funds encouraged the Queensland Housing Commission to ask the Brisbane City Council (BCC) to organise water, electricity, stormwater drainage and sealed roads, placing Inala within already long queues for such services. The BCC faced its own financial constraints, especially during the mid-1950s, and the Commission was eventually forced to take back road building and drainage. The Commission's statement in 1955 – 'The township has been planned to give all the modern facilities required by a community of such size' – would still seem optimistic ten years later, with around 17,000 people already living there. A 1966 report on Inala's history suggested that 'sewerage reticulation is well under way', and noted that 'communal health services, including maternal and child welfare, dental and other services are also proposed'. Alongside narrow interpretations of their responsibilities and duties, the Housing Commissions also tended to highlight proposed rather than actual development.[10]

The Housing Commission of Victoria, too, made agreements for the provision of railways, roads and schools that came to nothing or came too late, and told the readers of its annual reports about steps being undertaken or nearing finalisation. In all three suburbs reports about services and facilities were always written in the future tense. Residents of Broadmeadows might have agreed with the Housing Commission that 'a unique opportunity exists here to plan a city from its inception' but would conclude, with some justification, that this was an opportunity lost before it began.[11]

The various Housing Commissions claimed to be undertaking modern planning exercises. Not surprisingly, this created a sense of expectation in the suburbs they were constructing. Yet this expectation was always out of step with the Commissions' own much more limited sense of what was possible. Some of these battles were predictable enough: local councils had their own reasons for protesting about the absence of facilities they didn't want to provide, while conflicts between different government departments and authorities were hardly novel in Melbourne, Sydney or Brisbane. The Commissions were more surprised by how quickly local residents and their advocates complained about the 'dumping' of people in 'paddocks'.

Some of the best examples of these battles involved the Broadmeadows Welfare Advisory Committee (BWAC). BWAC emerged as an advocacy group and then as an advisory committee to the Broadmeadows Council in the late 1960s. Its first members were ministers and social workers employed in church welfare agencies but it then drew a large number of residents into local activism and employed its own community workers before being supplanted by a new body, the Broadmeadows Development Committee, in the early 1980s. BWAC and the Housing Commission soon developed a testy relationship. BWAC argued that 'the causes of many of the problems lie in the original inadequacies in State planning'. It seems a fair point, but not one that the Commission would accept, at least not until the 1980s.[12]

Again and again, members of BWAC urged that the past not be repeated, and a coordinated effort made to tackle the crucial deficiencies.

Shortly after BWAC's demise the new Cain Labor government did create a Broadmeadows Ministerial Group, finally bringing together the various departments and authorities to coordinate the servicing of new estates. Unfortunately, previous mistakes were not so easily undone, and every government authority, not least the Housing Commission, was trapped by the failures of the past. Not that the Commission retreated from its defensive lines. Stung by criticism, successive housing ministers and senior officials seemed almost hurt by the idea that they were careless. They wavered between irritated statements about their own inability to do anything and an insistence – sometimes almost snide – that community facilities 'rely on voluntary efforts by the local population'.[13]

Some responses were frostier: during a meeting between a BWAC deputation and Housing Minister Vance Dickie in 1974, he stressed the 'accepted interpretation' that the Housing Commission was not a planning authority and had no responsibility for providing transport or other services. The deputation then asked him to explain which part of this interpretation allowed the Commission to succumb to pressure from the Minister for Transport and partly finance a railway overpass at Broadmeadows from funds supposedly reserved for housing. The Minister's reply was not recorded.[14] Later, during Jeff Kennett's reign as Minister for Housing, a worker from a local agency involved in BWAC suggested that 'trying to communicate with those responsible for decisions in these areas can only be described as like trying to talk to a dead elephant'.[15] A couple of former members of BWAC to whom I spoke unkindly suggested that on becoming Premier of Victoria in the 1990s, Mr Kennett took his revenge.

There was one point residents constantly made, with the support of local advocacy groups, councils and researchers: as a 1985 report on Western Sydney put it, this 'did not happen by accident'. If these were places of 'harshness and restriction', this was not some inevitable product of either public housing estates or working-class tenants. In other words, these estates were not 'social disasters'. They were 'planning disasters', in the middle of which local welfare groups and residents were doing their best to pick up the pieces with whatever resources came to hand.[16]

Local advocates and residents, whether in the 1960s or the 1990s, looked towards the future and insisted that the kinds of mistakes made in their own neighbourhoods not be repeated in the next. They urged the Housing Commissions to develop the same sense of responsibility they were applying as volunteers and workers in neighbourhood houses, welfare groups and social clubs. Instead, they found themselves being blamed for the failures: not enough initiative, too few 'natural leaders', no real effort. Or they were accused of 'expecting everything to be provided because they are public tenants'. Pam McShane's characterisation of the situation in Mount Druitt in the 1990s can just as easily stand as a description of the past thirty years:

> The response isn't appropriate anyway. You know, to throw some money at the problem, and not accept any responsibility for the creating of that problem. All the money that is thrown is from people coming in and saying, 'This is what we are going to do for you', or do *to* you, actually, (*laughing*) and then if it fails it's because 'they' won't let it happen, or 'they' won't accept this opportunity. They make assumptions from no experience of the place or the people, from very great distances.
>
> The community is still held responsible for its failures. Nobody else is accepting responsibility for that. That's a very savage thing to do to a community that really doesn't deserve it.

As Patrick Nolan added, 'In Mount Druitt you always have to wear the sins of "the wise men from the east", the people who live in the leafy lanes'.

Those sins didn't stop as each suburb passed from its pioneer stage into a kind of premature ageing. During the 1970s the insistence that public rental homes be restricted to the very poor gathered momentum. It was further strengthened by the Labor government in the 1980s, and reached its apogee in the 1990s under a federal Coalition government minister who insisted that public housing could only ever be a 'housing of last resort'.[17] Accordingly, the problems of vulnerability and meagre resources in these areas just kept getting worse; as the eligibility criteria for rented housing tightened so did the virtual rule that each new tenant would be poorer or more desperate for housing than the previous one.

The targeting of public housing was perfectly rigorous and undoubtedly intended to be fair. Yet it made less sense in a real world where that housing was concentrated in certain neighbourhoods. Perhaps it is better to say that targeting responded to one problem – ensuring that limited resources were delivered to those who needed them most – by ignoring another problem: that any such policy, given the location of the housing, would increase rather than decrease the concentration of poorer people. It would also cement the association between public housing and poverty. The bad name of targeted public housing, the bad name of the kinds of people – especially single mothers and the unemployed – who were becoming a greater proportion of its tenants, and the bad name of the places in which most of it was located, became locked together in a stigmatising spiral that proved very hard to stop.

One 1970s measure to improve targeting was charging so-called market rentals. Essentially, the Housing Commissions attempted to make rents for their houses roughly equivalent to rents in the private market, with tenants charged a proportion of that market rental up to a fixed percentage of their household income. So, if a family contained two earners, or if one person earned a reasonable wage, they might pay 100 per cent of the rent, while those with no wage-earners might pay 50 per cent. The point of the policy was to reduce the advantage of public over private rental housing, encouraging those who could pay full rent to vacate public properties and provide space for people on the always burgeoning waiting lists. In a refrain that would be repeated in the 1980s and 1990s, the so-called 'rich tenant' was the main target. The Victorian Minister for Housing told the *Sun* in 1976 that some people had been 'riding the gravy train too long' and would have to be 'weeded out'. The Minister didn't seem to notice that the people to be 'weeded out' were often the very same people that the Commission was insisting should be taking the lead in developing community facilities and spirit.[18]

Market rents encouraged – indeed, to some extent, forced – families with workers to leave neighbourhoods such as Bidwill or Dallas. And it wasn't difficult to become relatively well-off: a regular weekly wage for an unskilled worker could take a family to full market rental. Sister Elizabeth Newsome worked for years in Inala and Carole Park, and remembered the clumsiness of the policy. In Queensland, rent was tied to what the Commission called the 'gross income' of the household. Everything was counted: family assistance payments, child endowment, wages, even the five dollars earned by a child doing a paper round. The rents were pegged to a figure based on the entire Brisbane market, rather than to the going rate in Inala or nearby suburbs. In one case, a family in public housing was charged $155 a week in market rent when private rentals in that street were around $80. A campaign finally forced the Commission to cap its market rents in Inala at a still inflated $120 a week. A policy that made perfect sense to its inventors worked in unexpected ways:

> I remember one family in particular who came in. They had been working in some sort of rural community. They gave up their job there and came to Brisbane in the hope of improving their situation down here. There was a break-up of the relationship, I think. That's right: she came down with the kids, and he stayed up there. She was on the lowest rent because the rent tied to income is very low for single parents with dependent children and no income; it's lower than in any other state.
>
> So that was the first thing that happened. The next thing is, he decided he would return to them, so then they were on an unemployment benefit, so the rent went up marginally. He gets a job, doesn't he, and the rent goes up further. The kids start to get into secondary school and start to get Austudy, so it goes up further. She got a job, so it went up further, and they were up to $145 a week at that time. So they moved into private rental in Inala, and they got it for $80 a week.
>
> OK. But, he lost his job, didn't he. She lost her job because the jobs they had were not secure jobs. So they were trapped: there was no way back into public housing, even though now they needed it again.

Kate Legge and Liz Hinkler were also tenants at the time:

> Liz: There were lots of families who maybe would have stayed together for longer, except for the fact that they had to pay such high rents. Once their children began to get income it meant that their rents went up so much that it just became unaffordable or impractical for them, so kids were moving out, especially once they got a job, because of the income test.
>
> Kate: And that was part of the impact, those dynamics: large rent increases, they moved out to whatever suburb, then their children slowly left home, which left them on a smaller income but paying exorbitant rents, so they actually needed to come back.

Most amazing of all, the Queensland Housing Commission assumed that tenants would charge all visitors for board, and included this completely invented figure in household income:

Elizabeth: There was also, during that time, fairly draconian measures about looking after rent. There would be government cars outside people's houses at night, and the reason was that because rent was tied to gross income, if you had anybody stay overnight, that person should in fact be paying part of the rent. Their income should be assessed.

This is true. They would follow a person leaving a house in the morning to his place of work, they would find out his income, and they would bill the woman back at the home for his portion of the rent. Two dollars fifty a night. It was just the most extraordinary thing. (*Laughs*)

Single mothers were the main target because it was assumed they were all living with men on the sly. In the late 1980s Val Stephens had no children at home but she continued to provide shelter and help for foster children or neighbours:

I had a man come to me one day, and he said to me, 'I'm going away. Can I leave my suitcase of clothes here with you?'. I'd known this young fellow for quite a long time. I was in my fifties at the time, and he was in his twenties.

So next thing I know the Housing Commission inspector comes and knocks on the door and says, 'You've got a man staying here'. I said, 'Gee, I wish I did'. (*Laughs*)

He said, 'You've been seen hanging men's clothes on the line'. I said 'Yes, I have. This young fellow came to me, asked if he could leave a suitcase full of clothes, I opened it up, it was all filthy, so I put it through the washing machine and hung it on the line, stuck it back in the suitcase and it's there waiting for him.' But the inspector honestly thought I was having it off with this young bloke.

In Inala, the policy also had a dramatic effect on Aboriginal people, who often provided rooms for relatives and friends visiting from Cherbourg and other former missions.

People in these communities grappled with the consequences of poor decisions from the beginning. Many residents concurred with long-time activist Rose Sinclair: 'We all felt that we were just dumped here and left to get on with it. Just dumped'. They remembered how little was provided, and the bareness of the houses. They shook their heads, remembering the mud and the dust. They thought back to their own arrival as they visited new tenants and found them living without electricity because there was no money for the connection fee, or huddled in one room because the Salvation Army had run out of spare beds. No matter where they had ended up, as activists or community workers or as people buying rather than renting a home, they remembered those times and remembered themselves 'coming to nothing'.

It was an experience they could share, not just with others who had been there a long time, but with some of those who had come just a month or a year ago. It was still hard; the Commission was still draconian and even in the 1990s, after the Commission became the Housing Department and started talking about client service and customer relations, you still had to struggle for the things other people took for granted. You still had to struggle for respect, and to think of yourself as someone other than a passive victim of other people's decisions. There were clumsy experiments and cost-savings in the past, and there would likely be more in the future. In the places poor people live that's the way it was and the way it still is.

Heroes and villains

Remarkably, perhaps, stories about continuing injustice didn't lead into the dead ends of despair. Helen Laplace, who was a social worker in Broadmeadows from the mid-1970s, talked about 'Broady' as 'a place which always had things happen to it'. This is an excellent description of how most people felt. Yet from the failings of the powerful came the outlines of an alternative story, which emphasised how local people had taken a place to which things happened and turned it into a place where they made things happen. They expressed a patient conviction that the world could be changed, if only for a time and in small ways. It was an important part of their stories, for to believe otherwise was to accept that things would never get any better.

Marianne Carr, who moved into St Mary's in 1969 and worked as a welfare officer in Mount Druitt during the 1980s, told me about a host of small campaigns. At one point, she began to cry:

I'm getting very emotional about this, sorry.

It's very hard. Just give me a minute.

It's hard to remember it, because those people had so little. They were so generous, and they had nothing. It was very humbling. If you could only bottle it. It was like, well, they had so little, and they were so gracious and generous. And they had some weird people in amongst them, and they were gracious and generous to them. They really taught me. I thought I was a tolerant person, but they really taught me.

Marianne, like many others, remembered a tremendous generosity of spirit and a resourcefulness that, at its best, forged powerful bonds between neighbours and friends.

This was a collective project, largely led by women because the men were at work earning a wage. It was a project dominated by thoughts for the future: a better future for children but also a better place for those who might move in later. People told stories about how they created – sometimes literally – neighbourhood houses and community centres. They formed preschools and fought for the funding to hire good teachers. They turned dusty lots into playgrounds. They volunteered to work at the health service or the legal rights centre and sometimes ended up managing them as well. They campaigned for footpaths so they could take the pram to the bus stop or the shopping centre. They organised meetings to argue against steep rent increases and draconian inspections. If there were new opportunities, or new policies, they seized them too: women's refuges, youth clubs or tenant participation. When the wheel turned and government departments came to take things away, they defended them with words and, if necessary, with actions.

In stories about their own successes, people included the outsiders who came to help: the good social workers, or the nuns and the priests who built a mission but never became missionaries. In the pantheon of heroes, no public figure had a higher status than Gough Whitlam, especially in Inala and Mount Druitt. Whitlam was a symbol for all of those who came to listen, and who actually did some good. Everyone could point out the signs of Gough's progress: streetlights and sewers, community houses, legal services, health centres, even footpaths. Everyone remembered the Australian Assistance Plan, the Regional Employment Development Scheme and the first attempt to provide free medical care through Medibank.

Many Australians, not least nervous Labor politicians, have become convinced that Whitlam's was a reckless government that almost steered the ship onto the rocks. The residents of Inala, Broadmeadows and Mount Druitt remembered Whitlam as a different sort of captain, someone who cared for and listened to the real battlers. During one trip to Inala, a group of people discussed what the Whitlam government had done. Marilyn listed almost every institution that surrounded the Inala Shopping Centre; Carole wasn't sure about the Legal Service, and Doug wondered about the Aboriginal cultural centre. I asked, too, about a couple of the institutions that I was pretty sure had been built in the early 1980s, well after Whitlam's fall. They discussed this, and Carole responded: 'Well, I think he did build them, or maybe he put the money away to build them later'. Gough Whitlam might be pleased to know that services built by conservative governments or state authorities in the 1960s or years after his dismissal have been gathered into the pantheon of his achievements. Vengeance, it might be said, takes unexpected forms.

Gough, however patrician he might have seemed, was remembered as someone who respected ordinary people. He spoke as if he understood their aspirations. He wanted to do away with the impediments that should have been removed years before: the houses without sewers or the schools without money and decent buildings. He knew that people needed decent health care, even if they couldn't afford it:

> Gough Whitlam has a great following here, and that would be from people of all political persuasions, because we saw Gough Whitlam as a man who saw problem areas and tried to do something about them, tried to solve the problems.
>
> We had a library built at the high school; there was no library. How can you have a high school without a library? It was just great. We had our footpaths put down, our parks upgraded. This all came through the RED [Regional Employment Development] scheme, the employment scheme. That took up the slack of unemployment, it employed a whole lot of people here. I'm sure there were other things happening too.

How can you have a high school without a library? If you lived in Inala, the answer to which you'd become accustomed was 'because it's not the Commission's responsibility', or 'there are no funds and we have yet to complete our feasibility study', or 'you people have to learn to do some things for yourselves'. What you heard from Gough was, 'You're right, you can't have a high school without a library. That's ridiculous, and your government has a responsibility to provide you with one.' In Mount Druitt, Jack told me:

> Well, if we're talking about Whitlam, the guy's brilliant. The founding father, sort of thing. (*Laughs*) People say he went too quick too soon. Whitlam got me my first home. He had vision.

Three other people in Mount Druitt told me that Gough got them their homes, while others said he had built the sewerage connections.[19]

In Broadmeadows some people expressed resentment that the suburb did not participate in some of the more innovative Whitlam programs. Broadmeadows was defined into the north-western rather than the western region of Melbourne; the western suburbs of Sunshine, St Albans and Braybrook saw most of the new initiatives, while Broadmeadows remained more reliant on church-based agencies. Still, Broadmeadows benefited from the Australian Assistance Plan and other programs, as Merilyn Langford said:

> Yes, during the Whitlam time it was good, because that was real consultation. When he set up the health centre it was actually to give the health centre to the community. The same with other community services: legal aid, grants to self-help groups. Yes, a whole host of things, very good initiatives at the time. And he got persecuted for it. (*Laughs*)

Here was a political leader who gave people health centres and houses and who reaped a harsh reward from the rich and the powerful. The most significant memory of the Whitlam years is not that what was delivered was all that great, nor all that lasting; after all, as Pam McShane said, 'I don't really think anything got a chance to take root'. What mattered was the spirit in which resources were given, and the way in which local people were trusted to come up with ideas and solutions. What mattered, too, was that Gough – and by Gough, people meant all of the politicians and community workers and activists who made up his cavalry – talked about rights, and about justice and equality. He talked about what needed to be done if ordinary people were to have real opportunities and a decent life. That's what they remembered, and that's what they missed.

These stories of the Whitlam years meshed with a longer history, produced by the older residents of Inala, Broadmeadows and Mount Druitt and shared, at least in part, by some of the newer arrivals and some of the long-established workers. Their stories carried them into the present and the future. They described their world as a battlefield, with allies and enemies, skirmishes and uneasy truces. They told of disaster avoided because they took action, banded together, and cared for each other. And because powerful people would continue to make mistakes, and poorer people would suffer the consequences, continuing vigilance was essential. This is how the stories could be shared: the fact that Inala or Broadmeadows and Mount Druitt were still vulnerable could bring older residents and newer arrivals into the same drama pitting 'us' against 'them'.

Looking back into the past or forward into the future, the stories of heroes were both hopeful and fearful. This was a history of particular places, but also a working-class chronology of Australia. Some of the older men and women looked back to Depression or wartime childhoods, to the 1940s as a time of promise, and to an uncertain 1950s, when it was hard to find decent housing, and when illness and bad luck could still bring terrible consequences. The symbolic victories of the Whitlam years were a marker for what followed: a time of relative security and safety, when they built a better world for the next generation. If the adults remained close to hardship, many of their children did not. They could point to the clever daughter who went to the teachers' college or did well at university, or the hard-working son with his own plumbing business who could afford a nice house two suburbs away. Happy and successful children dominated this story, just as their pictures – marrying, graduating, apprenticed, or holding grandchildren – covered walls, bookcases and the top of the television set.

However, others could add only a darker conclusion. They looked at the newer estates and saw the same mistakes being repeated. The housing departments were talking about renovation and rebuilding but tenants didn't know what that meant for them. They looked at their grandchildren and saw young men who couldn't get jobs and young women bringing up children in hardship. They looked at the services they built in the 1960s and 1970s and saw them closing down for lack of funds. The good workers were burning out and not being replaced, and even the ones who stayed never seemed to have any time.

Most of all, people felt left behind. The stories were meant to come to a fruition, prove that they changed the world, or at least their part it. But the conclusion they sometimes came to, nervously and uncertainly, was that the world had not changed. The story they wanted to tell – of success and a permanent change in the fortunes of people like them – was starting to unravel. They would keep struggling, and they would never give up. Yet there was a fear that the hard times were back for good, that the time of full employment and better prospects for the poorest Australians had been a false dawn. It might seem a pessimistic prediction. But nothing that the people of these suburbs were hearing in the middle of the 1990s, whether it was from 'their' Labor Party or the other side, was convincing them that it wasn't going to come true.

The limits of heroism

There are reasons to question and even challenge local legends about heroic endurance and strong communities. Not because their details were sometimes inaccurate or tailored to dramatic or comic needs, for that is the nature of storytelling. Instead, they might be questioned for the divisions they forged, and because, in a way, they created the circumstances for their own undermining. If you looked around and things weren't really any better, then perhaps it was because the people like you, the heroes, were a diminishing force. Perhaps it was because new people in the public housing estates in Inala, Broadmeadows and Mount Druitt were different. Perhaps they lacked your urge to help others, kept to themselves too much and didn't share with the people around them. For all of its attractions as a local history, the story of heroes could have hard edges. It was a vindication that could become vindictive.

This issue of blame certainly surfaced in some conversations. In most cases the villains came from the outside: politicians, the government, the bad social workers, the Housing Department. Those villains hadn't changed much. But others had been added, people who were set apart because they were recent migrants, Aboriginal or young. People wanted to remember Inala or Mount Druitt or Broadmeadows as places in which everyone helped everyone else, where they were 'all in the same boat'. But if they only remembered that strength by inventing its decline in the present and blaming newcomers for destroying it, then a powerful story about heroes started to produce its own victims.

Workers in the community centres and welfare agencies had a very strong sense of these dilemmas. They recognised the pride in these heroic claims but they also saw their defensiveness and occasional aggression. Advocates for Aboriginal and ethnic communities, and the people with whom they worked, were particularly aware of the ways in which the heroic story could all too easily turn into an angry, denouncing lesson about 'our Broadmeadows' or 'our Inala' being under siege. In Inala it was the young, the 'transient' renters, and the Aboriginal 'gangs'; in Broadmeadows, it was the Turks, with their mosques and their separate schools and their supposedly insular ways; while in Mount Druitt it was the single mothers, the Aboriginals and the Pacific Islanders.

The divisions were, I think, mostly a matter of when a person had arrived. Older residents were automatically included, and that meant the Aboriginal people who arrived in Mount Druitt and Inala in the 1960s, or the first groups of Turkish migrants who came to Broadmeadows and worked at the Ford factory in the 1970s. The primary line of division was longevity. This distinguished the different kinds of people who were moved into these suburbs at different times, as public housing allocation shifted over the years from slum clearances and housing for largely Anglo-Australian workers in the 1950s and 1960s, to financially restricted but less homogenous welfare housing in the 1970s and 1980s, to housing of last resort in the 1990s. In other words, divides of culture, age and lifestyle were understood in terms of the shifting nature of public housing itself, both the changing composition of those most in need and their increasing concentration in certain estates.

These relationships were very complicated. Whenever I had a conversation with longer-term residents about the story of heroes and villains, they swung back and forth between rejection and acceptance of newcomers. The most common point of view was that the 'new people' were not all that different from everyone else. Indeed, some argued that things were much harder now for the young or for new migrants because of unemployment, or they insisted that common concerns still brought people together across cultural, language or generational divides. They would point to new heroes, who echoed their own remembered struggles: the young girl down the street doing her best with two little children, the Aboriginal family next-door who were having the same old problems with the Housing Department, or the Turkish mothers who were coming to the school to help with children's reading, just as they had in the 1970s. There were many different stories and many variations, and there was always a capacity to reflect upon heroic stories in a critical way and include people who were different or new.

To share these stories means telling them honestly, with an eye to their hard edges and their occasional censures. Of course, the older and more established residents of these three suburbs were hardly alone in the way that they would sometimes turn a nostalgic sense of the past into something more like a denunciation of the present. The past is always being repackaged as a safer, better, happier and more agreeable place: it is a time before thieves, when you left the doors unlocked, when everyone respected older folks and people always meant well and there weren't the tensions and divisions that we have today. The past is a resource for all kinds of stories, something into which people always reach if they want to cast today in a negative light.

Yet the stories of heroic endurance in Inala, Broadmeadows and Mount Druitt were not a form of that generic nostalgia for better days, because they also talked about hard struggles and continuing privations. If their stories were sometimes the stuff of legends, and if they made heroes out of themselves, it was because they had a much greater and more reasonable need to tell each other and everyone else that they were heroes, that they were successful and did endure, that they were not the inferior, incapable, lower-class people they knew others assumed them to be. Theirs was not so much a rosy regard for an invented yesterday as the defence of a tradition of activism that had made their lives better.

What I heard from people in these suburbs was not nostalgia about the past but mourning for the loss of whatever security and certainty they had found there. As Beatrix Campbell discovered during her tour of working-class England in the 1980s, people did not claim that the past was better, because it wasn't; instead, they were frustrated and angry about a future that seemed to offer little real improvement and some chance of steep decline.[20] In Broadmeadows, Mount Druitt and Inala there was also a memory of vulnerability and a fear that it might return. For all of the pleasure in what had been achieved there was a pervasive melancholy at how fragile it might turn out to be. And in the end, the great majority of people – whether they arrived in the 1950s, in the 1980s, or just a year or two before I talked to them – didn't turn on the newcomers. They turned on those who really bore the blame: politicians and outsiders, the rich and the comfortable.

Stories about the courage and strength of the heroes of Inala, Broadmeadows and Mount Druitt made the very important claim that ordinary people deserved better. I enjoyed hearing them as much as people enjoyed telling them. We laughed knowingly, conscious of a shared pleasure in dethroning the powerful and celebrating the wiles of the powerless. I don't reject their legends. Nor do I want to call them untrue or divisive or nostalgic, because by and large they were not. Instead I want to challenge their dominance because they do not exhaust what people wanted to say and what everyone else needs to hear. However important they were and are in local life, they cannot have the last word.

It is imperative to capture the capacities, inventiveness and ingenuity of these people, but not by calling them heroes or demanding more heroic stories. Magnifying their heroism and their endurance is to continue speaking about the wrong thing. It must not be all that is said, because if it is we end up trapped in a language about strong and weak characters, the heroes and the unheroic. It will mean endorsing a view of the world in which the powerless have to prove themselves worthy by their capacity for struggle and sacrifice. It is to ask everything of them, and nothing of the powerful. Most of all, it is to ask impoverished people to be satisfied by memories of past endurance, and the fading afterglow of social democracy, rather than claims for a better future in the here and now.

Chapter Three
SUFFERING

Losing ground

The welfare workers of Inala, Mount Druitt and Broadmeadows sometimes struggled to describe what they were seeing. They wanted to talk about poverty's damage without reassuring me, or themselves, that it was all going to get better. Helen Croydon and Patricia Stephenson, who had both lived in Broadmeadows for twenty years, said that 'people feel more powerless now than at any other time since Broadmeadows became a suburb'. Patricia paused, and then added, 'I don't know what else to say. I think people are just starting to feel powerless to affect what's going on.' Helen offered support: 'Oh, yes, that's true. It's all "what's the point?"'. Patricia continued, 'Yes, people say "it's all hopeless"'. After a pause, Patricia raised her hands, gesturing out of the window, and added, 'I despair a bit too, I guess'. With a consoling half-laugh, half-sigh, Helen agreed. Theirs was a struggle to find words to describe despair that were not in themselves despairing and dispiriting. It was a conversation they'd had before and a conversation I heard in almost every welfare centre or neighbourhood house I visited.

If it is difficult to imagine the dimensions of need present in Australia's poorer places in the middle of the 1990s, an example from Broadmeadows gives as good an illustration as any. The CARE mission on Camp Road was one of the area's first welfare agencies, providing counselling, financial help and emergency relief to people in old Broadmeadows and Dallas. During the early 1990s it also helped people from newer estates in Coolaroo, where mortgage repayments were so high that almost every week carried the possibility of someone losing their home. When I spoke with the coordinator, I asked whether needs were decreasing, increasing or changing. He thought for a moment about how best to answer. He said that at that point, in May 1994, the agency had been forced to impose a two-week waiting period for its emergency food parcels. In other words, if you came to CARE looking for help you put your name down for a parcel in two weeks time. Only the most desperate people could be helped immediately. So people did what they had to do. They planned ahead. In two weeks time if the electricity bill was due and you had to pay the rent or the mortgage, you put your name down for the emergency parcel. 'It's absurd', the coordinator said.

Again and again, workers talked about communities that were 'absolutely battered and broken' and had 'been kicked one too many times'. April Stewart first worked at the Mount Druitt Family Welfare Centre in 1981 and 1982. She left to go to another job and then returned in 1991. She saw troubling differences:

> I think people are perhaps a little more aware now of the losses, of what they don't have, and their expectation is that they should have an equal cut of the cake, of resources.
>
> And there's, well, a lot of pain.

Elizabeth Newsome, the veteran Inala nun, said:

> I would see three generations of a family, and of course the generations are short because the children tend to be born to younger mothers. I would see the first generation lose their jobs and fight to try and get back in, the next generation would say, 'Well, if we don't get it, our kids will'.
>
> Well, not now. I think. There's no hope. There used to be hope, and they would work for that hope. But the kids know there's no hope.

Most workers were in unison about dashed hopes. Anne Neilsen talked about seeing 'basic despair':

> My sense is that years of frustration and inability to do anything have bred a despair which is actually one of the things that you've got to really work against. And it's hard too, because there's no point in trying any more.

> I think there would be many people whose real focus in life is survival, and they can't do anything more than survive. If they try to get out of it they get sucked back into it because something goes wrong.

Iris Delen, of the Parramatta Regional Public Tenants Council, said 'people really haven't got a chance. It's like their feet are in quicksand'. Asked to describe the people he saw, job centre coordinator Paul Sammler thought for a moment; 'I'd say scared. If they read the papers they know what's going on and they're not very hopeful.' He searched for the right words: 'Scared. Overwhelmed sometimes.' In Broadmeadows, Jenny Krause described being 'inundated with people in absolute distress; families who were never in distress before'.

Workers also shared residents' perceptions that they were increasingly part of 'little worlds' that people outside neither understood nor cared much about. About half had come to Inala, Broadmeadows and Mount Druitt as trained social workers, while the others had also been, and in most cases still were, residents, entering paid work in neighbourhood houses or welfare agencies after years of volunteering. Those who lived elsewhere talked about struggling to find the words that would honestly capture the world they went to each morning and left each evening. Jenny Brearley, who went to the Banksia Gardens estate in 1987, remembered: 'I didn't realise that people lived with such insecurity until I went to work there … It was a multitude of dilemmas. It was almost like movie stuff.' A worker in Bidwill described it as 'like their own little world. They've got their own rules, and that's their life, and I don't think many people can come in and understand it.' Other workers used terms such as 'lost world' or 'the forgotten world'.

Whether they had been there two years or two decades, workers shared their fears and misgivings. They wanted to speak about poverty and deal openly with very hard questions about the nature of their work. They endeavoured to translate what they were seeing every day into an analysis of what might lie in the future. Some seemed almost burdened by the weight of what they knew and by the fear that they might become overwhelmed. There was always a temptation, they said, to take on too much of the struggle, perhaps losing the distance you need in order to handle each new person with the care and attention they deserve. There was a persistent anxiety that you might exacerbate the problems by making mistakes, or by being tired and inattentive and driving away a vulnerable or difficult person.

Some had so often worried about their effectiveness that they had, in their own terms, 'burned out' and left their jobs behind. They had struggled to remain true to their principles, and as far as I could tell they had done a remarkable job. But they were exhausted. Many workers agreed that you could cope with four or five years in one role, but it wasn't easy: you needed to stay long enough to see something done but you had to avoid becoming the person upon whom everything depended. A few had found that they could no longer resolve those anxieties, or live with the contradictions between what their experiences told them to say and what it was possible to say to the funding bodies and in the annual reports.

It wasn't a dilemma for everyone. A few workers, who were mostly new to the area and working in government departments, pretty much repeated what I read in their brochures, mission statements and strategy plans. Two Commonwealth government workers told me that I would hear nothing but the 'party line' because they were not permitted to discuss policy questions with members of the public. Two workers from the DSS were told that their responses would have to be written down and approved by a senior manager because I 'couldn't be relied upon to ask appropriate questions in accordance with policy principles'. I cancelled that interview.

All but these few spoke freely, however, and their caution stemmed from careful reflection rather than anxiety about party lines. They shared the dilemmas of speaking about poverty, particularly the difference between what they wanted to say and what they felt obliged to say, especially to outsiders. Their dilemma was how to show respect for local people while speaking honestly about the limits of their capacities to overcome difficult problems. The tension between assistance and empowerment, acting for and alongside needy people, always preoccupies good workers. They were just as concerned about how to acknowledge truths about what poverty does to people without endorsing a whole series of fictions about neediness, dependency and inadequacy.

It was a very hard task that we set these workers. There was an ever-growing insistence on accountability, efficiency and provable outcomes, in places where standard measurements of success – the number of people 'cured' of dependency, perhaps, or the number of people trained for jobs that don't exist – were and are bizarrely inadequate. But in an atmosphere one worker described as 'shit-scared about outcomes and wasting money', they were constrained in what they could say. They wanted to talk about loss, pain, despair, and their sense that the most vulnerable people in Inala,

Mount Druitt and Broadmeadows were losing ground. A long-time worker in Sydney's ethnic communities said she was seeing 'the sort of thing that happens when people have been really traumatised and turned into victims'. I asked her what that meant, and she said:

> Well, they like to feel that people in power *are* looking after them and have their best interests at heart. They want to be rescued.

But how do you describe something like that while maintaining your belief in your own capacity to make a difference, and in the capacity of local people to attain the self-determination that workers attempt to nourish?

Their greatest difficulty, in a way, was finding words to acknowledge the limits of what they could do to 'fix' the problems that poverty was creating for their clients. Life in Inala, Mount Druitt or Broadmeadows was not always heroic, even if people's willingness to keep fighting was a source of inspiration. Some people were ineffectual, even helpless. They didn't endure so much as survive. Some had become dependent, relying on workers to help them carry out the simplest tasks because they were scared they'd get it wrong. Some wanted the worker to make decisions. Some just wanted to be rescued. A welfare coordinator talked about those for whom the agency was 'just part of their world. They just wander in here, and we become part of their social world. They'll chat to the person at the desk about everyday things. It's sort of like going to the grocers or going to the milkbar.' This agency helped some clients by paying their bills for a short period. Often, attempts to give back such responsibilities were resisted:

> That really distresses us. We sometimes get their kids, too, as they grow up, young girls, late teens, with a baby, and we find we're doing the same for them.
>
> Now the younger ones, we tend to have more hope of changing direction with. But some of the older families, you see little glimmers of hope that something is going to happen, but I imagine some of those will be with us until we bury them. That's horrific work.

The workers and volunteers for agencies like St Vincent de Paul, who often went into houses in response to reports from the police of abuse or neglect, were similarly troubled by the problems of hopelessness and dependency. They recognised the same fear of change, and of rapid alterations to the rules, even if the rules were disliked. In the lives of impoverished people, few changes had been for the good.

Priests, ministers and church-based workers seemed most able to worry out loud about this kind of passivity:

> When I came here I knew all the theory of leading from below or from the rear and so on, but I doubt that it works because people just can't go with it.
>
> On the other hand, I'm still committed to that, not only temperamentally, but because I see all the damage being done all over the place by high-profile authoritarian leadership striding off into the wide blue yonder. If that happened here, and you looked back, there'd be nobody following you.
>
> In a sense, though, the saddest thing about the place is that nobody wants it to go anywhere, they don't want anything changed. They can't be happy with what they've got but I guess the fear of change is worse.

Another minister said, 'If we are all the time providing services that make it easier for people to survive without struggling, maybe we'll have more people who give up the struggle and come to rely on you as a service. That's the dilemma.'

Of course, the workers who reflected on these issues did so because I asked them and because they felt it was important to show their recognition of very real dilemmas. And those dilemmas were always put into a context, bracketed between a recognition of how hard things really were and, as Inala community worker Pam Wilson put it, the discovery 'that people are amazing … I'm amazed every day when people walk through my door, at the kind of stuff they've been through, at the fact they've got the guts to even come and see somebody and tell them what they've been through.' If it was important to recognise the potential pitfalls of their work, it was just as important to maintain perspective and to recognise how capably so many of their clients made their way.

The frustration that workers expressed can be summarised in the following way. They were aware of the importance of being very, very honest about poverty. It is important not to pretend that all poor people are heroes or battle successfully against the odds, and it is important to stress the endemic anxieties that wear people down. They wanted to portray poverty for what it really is: a form of injustice that can and does wear away at people, perhaps even breaking them, but slowly and unevenly. Like

Irene Simmons, a resident of Coolaroo West and a member of the local neighbourhood house committee, they wanted to shout out the harshness of the mundane:

> I know families who, after they've paid everything, live on twenty dollars a week. How do you survive? How do you feed even one parent and three kids on twenty bucks a week? What do they eat? Boiled potatoes, maybe. I don't know.
>
> It's terrible.
>
> There are people who live day-to-day, you know, I'll feed the kids tonight and hopefully something will come tomorrow. People who can't survive without visiting the service providers and getting a food parcel every fortnight, just to feed their kids. People who put the kids to bed at seven o'clock at night because then they don't have to have the heater on. Bath them every second night because it's cheaper than bathing them every night. That sort of thing. It's just criminal.

They also wanted other people to know something of the degradation they saw and had often felt themselves, what it meant to feel inferior and to have to ask for 'handouts'. At the Women's Activities and Self-Help House in Mount Druitt, Julie Laidlaw, Jane Stewart and Kylie Brown talked about the humiliations of poverty:

> Julie: It's dehumanising, that's the thing. You're meant to be humble.
>
> Jane: Oh yes, the deeper the gravel rash goes in, the better they feel. (*Laughs*)
>
> Kylie: I've been a single mum on and off for the past nine years, and people just don't realise how hard it is. Not until you've lived through it. Getting handouts and asking for help is hard, especially when you want so much to be independent and want so much to get by, but on the other hand you want your kids to have what they need. It's very hard.

Marc Calvino had been working in a community health centre for almost four years. He could draw upon his experiences of working overseas, as well as with Spanish-speaking people and other clients in Broadmeadows. He talked about how two migrants from El Salvador described the cuts to services introduced by the then relatively new Kennett government in Victoria:

> The story, which a couple of people told me in their own language, goes something like this: now we've kind of adduced the idea that Australia wasn't going to turn the corner very quickly and that Australia was going through a tough time, and we've pretty well adjusted to saying, 'OK, we'll get through this and we hope we can carry our family through it'.
>
> Along comes this government which kicks us in the guts and now we're sinking; it's just knocked the stuffing out of us. That's the sort of story you hear, that's the generalisation … [and] that is how people perceive it: that they've been kicked in the guts, they're just managing to stay afloat … [They say] they've lost the ability to control their own lives, albeit in a limited way, but at least that sense where 'even though it's tough, we think we can hold our family together'. But now, no. The budget's blown, the money just doesn't go around.
>
> That's the one that really hurts me, too, because a personal philosophy is always to try to respect the freedom of people and affirm them in being responsible for their own lives and making choices. I think they're losing that. That capacity is incredibly deficient.

Poverty means a loss of capacity to make decisions, a loss of any real sense of choice and of movement towards a future. Kevin McDonald, in his study of young people in Melbourne's western suburbs, talked about 'the destruction of the capacity to become an actor'.[1] Political economist Amartya Sen wrote of poverty as 'the limitation of the *lives* that some people are forced to live'.[2] Living at the bottom of an unequal society means living with all kinds of limitations that others do not have to accept. What's more, it means living with those limitations when other people's freedom from them – and their freedom to do things you cannot – is constantly paraded before you: 'avoid the rent trap', or 'it's time you spoiled yourself with a new car or a family holiday'.

In some ways it is worse now. One change that has heightened the clash between expectations and experiences for younger people is that television provides a constant reminder of what they can't have. Parents and social workers often referred to *Neighbours* or *Home and Away* or American sit-coms as major sources of tension. Of course, everyone knew that the cheery landscapes aren't real, but workers described impoverished mothers and fathers feeling diminished and sometimes even blamed by their children's implicit comparisons between their own lives and life on Ramsay Street or in Summer Bay. The problems in fictional places are dramatic and always solved. It isn't like that in Bidwill or Dallas.

To understand what poverty is, you have to be able to imagine worrying about money all the time. Many of us experience the occasional anxieties of three bills coming at once, or the tight January that follows an indulgent December. When you're impoverished that is what you wake up with every morning and struggle to sleep against every night. You have to choose between paying the electricity bill or risking another power cut and buying milk and cheese and bread for your children. This is the world the workers were seeing, and within which they struggled to maintain their faith in responsibility, choices and self-determination.

Those with harder hearts will insist that very few people go hungry or cold in Australia and those who do probably bring it upon themselves. They point to the money spent at the pokies or on cigarettes, or wasted on snack food and the latest must-have sports shoes for the kids, without really thinking about what it might be like to go without everything that's special or done for pleasure. Volunteer Joy Round, herself from a disadvantaged background, let go of her usual calmness to weave her own remembered privations into those of the people she now helped:

> But I know why, why they do the 'wrong' things. Some people do judge them, that they spend their money the wrong way. It's hard to explain but when you're always poor and you've never got enough to eat and all of a sudden you get some money, you splurge it, you enjoy something just for a day. And then people say 'Oh, look what they've done with the money, they've gone to the Show, and spent all that money on those kids'.
>
> But those kids will remember that one day they went to the Show. They won't remember all the times they went hungry, that will come and go, but they will remember that day, because I do, I remember those days. It's hard to explain, but when you've been through it, it's very easy to accept.

Early in 1993, just before the federal election, the federal Keating Labor government made a special one-off bonus payment to people living on pensions. All around these suburbs workers noted a sudden increase in spending. Not on pokies or alcohol, but on ice cream, sweets, children's clothes, bikes, toys and trips to the movies. For one week, at least, the poorest people in Inala, Broadmeadows and Mount Druitt permitted themselves a few luxuries. Mostly, they spoiled their children.

Poverty grinds. It rubs away at confidence and capacity. It must be measured but can never be understood through snapshots and indexes. If workers in welfare agencies and those who advocate for the poor stand accused of occasional overstatement it is because they are forced into that strategy. Knowing what is there, they are compelled to seek more resources by playing for sympathy and describing their clients as people who don't deserve what happened to them, and who are brave and unflinchingly cheerful besides. When your funding demands evidence of dramatic need and proof of efficient outcomes there is little to be gained by talking about chronic suffering and hopelessness and the long haul. What counts, after all, is the extent to which the poor have suffered and proven their endurance. In any event, your funding submission will have to boil down to five dot points, an executive summary and an outcome that can be measured. Nowhere are you invited to describe the complexity of poverty, or the problems that only make sense if you know something about hardship.

The battle for resources had inured workers to tactics they found galling. Broadmeadows youth worker Natalie Phillips gave this example:

Natalie: I rang a philanthropic trust who told me that, yes, they'd funded us in recent years but they weren't giving us any more because the kids only broke everything. I didn't bother saying, 'Listen, we have hundreds of kids through and we don't exactly buy the best quality'. I just thought, 'I'm not going to tell you out in [a middle-class suburb] what life is really like in Broadmeadows'. I mean, they are good persons. Jesus wept, (*laughing*) they are good persons. And you get into all sorts of creative ways of trying to present something so it fits their middle-class 'ideal'.

Mark: And how do you do that with some of the problems you see here?

Natalie: Oh, well. You know. Lie. (*Laughs*)

Workers wanted to say that poverty is neither earned nor unearned. The truth is that it's both, for any one person and over any one period. There are people who take charge of their situations and struggle to overcome them, and those very same people have other days when it's all too much and they just want someone to come in and wave a magic wand. Most of all, they wanted to say that poverty doesn't have innocent and guilty victims. You can't drop from the sky into Broadmeadows, Inala or Mount Druitt, take a quick survey, and say 'she's deserving, she isn't, he isn't trying, and that boy over there just refuses to take responsibility for his life'. Poverty does create hopelessness, and on the bad days it can make people feel helpless and dependent. It makes people suffer, and some of them can't always see a way out. But how do you say that? How do you say that without pandering to a fantasy of self-inflicted poverty? As Joy Round wondered, 'How do you get people to see?':

> People are blaming the poor again. And people don't know, they really don't know what's going on here. They've got no idea. How do you get them to look at the everyday struggles of families?
>
> I don't know how to get that changed. But I wish some of them would just come around with me for a while and see what's going on, especially here.

Listening to the workers of these three suburbs, a good number of whom had lived in poverty themselves, the most crucial lesson you learnt was that poverty is a matter of injustice, no matter what its origin and no matter how ineptly some people struggle against it. There are great difficulties involved in designing good welfare or employment policies in ways that address demoralisation and lift people out of ruts they have partly made for themselves. We need the best minds in public and private welfare working on those questions. The need for careful planning is not the real problem. The problem is that we always start from the wrong direction, by assuming that only a certain kind of undeserved hardship merits our help and that we can quickly judge the causes of someone's poverty without knowing much about them. And with work tests, huge caseloads, a mounting obsession with fraud and an ever more stern emphasis on what the poor must do to earn and maintain our help, it is only going to get worse.

Perhaps this is too bleak. Our political leaders tell us that our aspiration-driven economy is booming. I don't know for sure how that is playing out in these suburbs. But I did ring Broadmeadows CARE in 1998 to speak again to the coordinator. He wasn't there but I took the opportunity to ask the receptionist about the waiting periods for emergency relief. In 1998, there was no longer a two-week waiting period, she said. In Broadmeadows, because of cutbacks and reduced donations, the waiting period for emergency food parcels was now three weeks.

Deserving and undeserving lives

If the dilemmas faced by welfare workers are relatively well known, those faced by welfare recipients are recognised less often. It was often very important for people to tell me about their 'mistakes'. It was almost routine, an expected moment of confession and contrition. At one meeting with unemployed men, for instance, my ambiguous question drew out a reflex response:

> Mark: And what you would do about unemployment?
>
> Tom: Well, there's not a lot I can do. I do try to find work and I've applied for things, but all those years in one place, you know, I don't have the skills they want now. And I'm too old. But it's very hard.
>
> Mark: Right. Sorry. I see what you're saying. I was interested in what you would do about the general problem of unemployment, you know, what needs to be done.
>
> Tom: Oh, OK. I mean, a lot of people don't have jobs that want them. There's training and all that, but there's no jobs. It's the jobs at the end of it that matters.

People were used to telling the story the right way. They had come to know what people want to hear. As Broadmeadows Aboriginal worker Ron Kenjarra said, 'People get sick of telling their life story in half a dozen different places to achieve one end. If you're short on tucker, you've got to go to all these different joints to get a reasonable food voucher and a bit of cash. You've got to go through the story over and over and over again.'

Telling your story is part of a performance, and a number of people talked about having to 'act poor'. People in hardship must describe their lives all the time, often to someone who has the power to give or deny them something they need. This emphasis on proving need creates its own kind of convincing stories. First, you must establish that you are actually suffering. It is best if that involves some kind of crisis or a dramatic absence that merits immediate attention. Then you need to show that your suffering is unearned because you have not brought it upon yourself, say through drink, bad decisions, reckless spending, or poor budgeting. If your impoverishment is a result of bad behaviour, you must show your determination to break the cycle. You need to suggest that you have learned from your mistakes, point to the episodes in your past that demonstrate your capacity to persevere, and make an effort to change yourself and your situation. You must accept that no one else can be blamed. You must be weak enough to have suffered yet strong enough to prevail.

Perhaps even more important to a successful performance is what is left out. Hopelessness and despair have a place, but only at the beginning, and they must be reduced as the counsellor or social worker helps you come to an understanding of the true situation. It is particularly important to avoid anger. Poor people are not allowed to be angry. They are not allowed to suggest that their problems are not of their own making or that someone or something else – the government, the system, the rich – is to blame. If anger simmers it must never begin to boil. It must be vented where it can't be heard and can't be seen because anger has no place in a welfare system designed to sift the entitled from the unentitled. Suffering must be quiet and patient, earnest in its entreaties without ever expecting too much. You can't expect the world to change just because that world has made you poor.

There was a lot of anger in Broadmeadows, Inala and Mount Druitt; an anger born of frustration, distrust and fear. Much of that anger also reflected what residents and workers described as a renewed determination to blame impoverished people for poverty. Government services, in particular, were being driven back to an emphasis on policing the poor. If that version of welfare work was suppressed and to some extent supplanted by a focus on social justice, advocacy and community development during the 1960s and 1970s, it was never entirely dismantled. The workers with whom I spoke were just as angry as the residents. This was not the work they wanted to do and it represented a hard-felt retreat from their best principles.

Social workers often reported increasing levels of humiliation:

> The humiliation that people go through these days, because before, OK, you had a problem and you came to get some food and that's it. Now people

> have to confess everything, get through all these bureaucratic systems, and if you come here three times you can't get any more food, no matter if you're starving.
>
> I think with some organisations, the way that the government is now, we have to go back to the old welfare system.

Many were unnerved by the return to a kind of social work where advocating on behalf of poor people took second place to policing their entitlements. This was the bad old type of social work based on the careful examination of people's stories for falsehoods, about which they had written passionately critical essays during their training. Its most important symbol is the ritual of confession: clients must talk about their suffering, then workers investigate the truth of their claims before assessing which of the limited remedies they have available is actually deserved. Of course, the real problem is never really known to the clients themselves. This is welfare based upon the conviction that rigorous investigation will always reveal their self-deceptions as well as their lies.

Disadvantaged people themselves were just as dismissive of the emphasis on suffering and patience and the silences that were imposed:

> Anne: So, what do you want to hear?
>
> Mark: I want to hear what you think about the welfare system, your perspective on whether it works, if it might work better. That sort of thing.
>
> Anne: But do you want to hear the truth? That's what I mean. Or do you want to hear the, well, what would you call it … ?
>
> Sheila: Like in community consultation, hear what *you* want to hear? Or like at the counter in Social Security?
>
> Anne: Yes, hear what you want to hear. The story. I mean, we can tell you the *story*. All the usual stuff about why we're down the bottom and how it's nobody's fault and we're ever so thankful. Ta very much for all the help and isn't it great that someone's come to save us.
>
> Mark: I want to hear what you want to tell me, what it's important to know. The truth?
>
> Anne: (*Laughs*) Well, *that's* different.

Sometimes, their anger boiled over into bitter recrimination. Some also trapped themselves in the logic of blame by pointing to cheats and people using the system; 'I mean, it's not fair, I'm doing my bit, but I'm struggling and her children are wearing Reeboks'. Yet, as was typical, Carol Hills followed that remark with, 'I am so angry that we are forcing our people to do that to get more money'. The anger was directed at a system, at the way the world was working. Those who used that system could hardly be blamed for its inadequacies, and she could understand why people did it.

Yet for all their rejection of a suffering performance, people living in poverty were nonetheless trapped within it. After all, it worked, at least in the here and now. You might mutter under your breath, and you might know that the worker was just as unhappy as you were with the limits and the rules. You might know that more money or a job was what you really needed, and the worker would probably agree with you.

Impoverished people always maintain a kind of moral independence from the system by revealing their knowledge of how it really works. Challenging its presumptions, puncturing its logic and showing up its cruelties and idiocies, they build what American philosopher Nancy Fraser calls 'alternative narratives' of entitlement.[3] But if you need something, if your benefit has been stopped because the welfare department suspects you of cheating, if you need to get into a training scheme, if you have no food in the house or enough warm clothes for the winter, what then? You might lose a little dignity, you might have to spin out a story that isn't absolutely true, but that way you stand some chance of getting help. That's the game. It was also the game in Broadmeadows, Inala and Mount Druitt and everyone knew it was. It had to be played because the other options were too difficult. For the busiest emergency providers the alternative was to make desperate people wait while you fought a battle to change rules you didn't invent and certainly didn't endorse. For the desperate client, telling the truth as you saw it, or making demands rather than requests, just wasn't going to work. The suffering story, the deserving story, was a better risk, and it was best to become very good at it.

Some weren't all that skilled. Men, according to their female partners, slid too easily into anger. They got the story wrong, yelled at the social worker, blamed the government. Bravado is all very well, but you're not going to get anything if you can't play the game. These women said they had to do the talking, and preserve the precarious balance between truth and half-truth, secrets and stories. They regarded themselves as better tacticians than men: they had more experience and they knew which stories worked and which didn't work. At the same time they saw themselves as more durable, more able to separate themselves – and their dignity – from what they knew was a performance.

Men's inexperience and inability posed very real dangers. A woman in Mount Druitt shared with me this experience of dealing with her husband, who was retrenched in his late thirties:

> It was terrible. Shocking. We were so used to having the money, and it's hard too, when you have to run around filling out rebate forms. It's very degrading.
>
> For my husband to stand on a dole line: he would stand there and say 'Let's go home. I don't want to do this'. He had to declare every single thing and he'd never had to do that in his whole life. He said, 'This is shit, I don't want to do this. I'll go and look for another job'. I said to him, 'We've got no money'.
>
> And that was hard for me to say, you know: 'You have to stand there. You have to tell these people everything'. That was very, very hard for him. Just as well I was with him this day because he would have gone, and without any money.

Other women talked about accompanying husbands to the Social Security Office, or making sure that they dealt with the police or the tenancy officer, to keep control over the family's story and the family's reputation. As one Inala woman told me, 'God, no. You'd never let him go and speak to the welfare people. He doesn't have a hope.' Two other women who were there laughed in agreement: 'What would he say, I wonder? Probably something I've been keeping a bit quiet.' Anne agreed, 'Yes, or he'd start on about the politicians and the bosses'. Judy remarked that she always tried to prepare her son for the interviews:

> You know, I have to get him to see that he has to say some things and not say other things. I told him, last time I think it was, that it was no good telling the person on the desk to piss off. I think he still did though. I had to go down and smooth a few feathers, you know. Dear, dear.

Some men let their shame get in the way. They brought their children to the welfare centre because children can't be denied, or they brought their partners because only their partners knew what to say. Workers in the emergency relief centres said they hardly ever talked to these men:

> I'm a great fan of many of the women that we see. I believe that we have some incredibly strong and resilient women who survive and cope with really horrible situations.
>
> One of my real problems is coming to grips with a lot of the guys who seem, almost, well, it sometimes seems to me that there's a body of men who move around this community in and out of relationships with all sorts of women and they take no responsibility. Their kids are fathered here, and then the fellas disappear and turn up somewhere else.
>
> Now in some of these cases you find these very strong women who actually mother the father as well. Mum and Dad will come to the agency to get help, and in some cases you'll find Dad will wait out in the carpark there, Mum comes in and weeps and does all the stuff to get what she needs, and you say 'Can I carry this out to your car?', and she says 'No, that's fine. He's out there.' You go out, and he'll be shy: 'G'day. Thanks for the help.' Meek, sort of useless little guys.

In part, this reflects a working-class tradition in which women have always acted as the controllers of family histories as well as family fortunes. It also reflects the very different relationships impoverished men and women have built with the wider world. Men's contributions to family and neighbourhood life were limited by their preoccupation with work. If they were not working, few took on the responsibilities they saw as belonging to women. One of the most important was controlling exchanges between the family and outsiders. Women, especially mothers, also understood themselves to be much better performers of the stylised story of suffering that was often still crucial to a successful outcome. They shared with each other a strategic knowledge about how to describe poverty and maintain your entitlement. Of course, they were highly critical of the need for such tactics and justifications. Yet the fact remained that it had to be done.

The real dilemma of these tactical stories is that they can mask real suffering, deprivation and neglect. Life had been very hard for many of the people with whom I spoke. They wanted to share that, describe how it was that they had stumbled into disadvantage. It was important for them to talk about who was to blame. That often meant shifting back and forth between a well-rehearsed story about suffering and a more tentative account of what was 'really true' and the things that had 'really gone wrong'. They wanted to tell the story shorn of the burden of proving entitlement, and respond to my statement that I wanted to hear what they wanted to say. But it was difficult to know how. As I listen to the tapes, I can hear myself trying to offer reassurance by talking about the structural causes of disadvantage or the long-term impact of neglect. I talk about the recession and what economic downturns do to people. I try to console without shifting the story back into heroism or undeserved suffering. It didn't always work, because the problem of finding the right words was mine as well as theirs.

Nothing better shows the power of a story that has to be learned and repeatedly told than the difficulty both men and women experienced in disentangling their lives from its conventions. For instance, Tom, the man who misinterpreted my vague question about unemployment, had worked in a low-paid government job for twenty years, saving what he could. In the late 1980s he decided to strike out on his own, taking a redundancy payment and buying a fruit and vegetable business. Five years on, the business had failed. He walked away because it was all he could do, and in 1994 he was living on unemployment benefits and looking for a job. But he was too old for the unskilled work he could get. He had ended up poor.

Three or four times Tom talked about how stupid he was to leave a steady, secure job. He blamed himself for risking everything. He didn't talk a lot about his family but I got the impression from his friends in the group that his wife and children had left and he was living alone in a public rental flat. His intent was to prove that he knew there was no one else to blame, that he had brought the world down upon his own head. I remarked that a lot of small businesses don't survive recessions like that of the early 1990s and that it must take a lot of courage to walk away. He replied, 'But you can't say that, can you? You can't blame anyone else.' Tom was a successful product of an understanding of poverty in which the first question is what you did to cause your own suffering.

Another unemployed man, Keith, had driven trucks and done labouring for about fifteen years, but he'd fallen ill with kidney problems and could no longer do any hard physical work. In 1995, he was living on sickness benefits. One of his kidneys had been removed and he was very pale and thin. He talked about his illness and said that the doctor wasn't sure that he would last long without a transplant. Still, he'd given up smoking and the booze.

Keith had a plan. He was trying to win custody of his youngest son, who was living with his mother and a new boyfriend for whom Keith had little regard. He didn't like his chances in a custody case if he just had his sickness benefits. So he had volunteered at the neighbourhood centre to clean windows and gutters for elderly people, partly for something to do and partly to develop a bit of a business. The centre had bought him a window washer, Keith had bought a bucket and some cloths, and he already had a ladder. He wasn't charging anything; instead, he was trying to make a bit of a name for himself, and save money out of his benefit for materials. Eventually, he thought he could keep up the volunteer work for his 'old ladies' and maybe get paid by people who could afford it.

Just before I spoke with Keith, someone at the DSS had confronted him about his 'window-washing business' and told him that his sickness benefit was going to be cut because he was earning fraudulent money. Keith was a nervous man, unsure about the rules. He showed me a sketch of a brochure he'd wanted to get printed, and it was clear that he found writing difficult. He told me he'd always been a 'problem child'. He had missed a lot of school, and been to the doctor a lot when he was young. He told me, too, that he'd learned that it's best not to stand up to people at the DSS because he could never talk like they could and they would always win the argument. So he'd given up on the idea of washing windows. It wasn't going to work, he said, because it was just too hard to earn a little bit of money when you're on a benefit. 'I'm just not going to work any more, that's the thing', he said.

Keith was not the most capable person. He was ineffectual, and not all that good at talking. But Keith's problem was that he got sick and lost his job. He'd become broke, and then broken. He was struggling, unhappy to rely on his benefit but unable to come up with a plan. At his age and with his illness he would probably die unemployed. He had stopped trying, but not because of some innate inadequacy or some predisposition to laziness or fraud. Keith had made been into a 'loser' by the very system that was supposed to help him.

In Inala, Lorraine Goodman and her husband Bill lived in public housing. They'd taken good care of their home, though now their children were gone they were worried they might be forced to move into a smaller flat. They had always struggled, because Bill didn't earn a lot and then started having problems with his back and his legs and had to stop working early. They'd had to support their children too: one son was unemployed for five years after leaving school, and then kept getting short-term and part-time work so he couldn't afford to move out. Lorraine had been ill, and that ate up more money.

Lorraine's biggest problem, though, stemmed from her childhood. Her father was a bit of a 'wanderer', and kept moving the family from town to town. Lorraine didn't do very well at school. For a start she was at a new one every six or so months. But she was also very deaf, and couldn't hear what the teachers were saying. In country primary schools during the 1950s the classes were too big for anyone to notice, and Lorraine just assumed she was stupid. When she was nine her mother died, and her father made her stay home to look after her three brothers and a ten-month-old baby. He remarried when she was 13, so she got another year at school, but she still couldn't hear anything. 'I couldn't read when I met Bill', she said, 'I just sort of bluffed my way through'.

Unable to read, Lorraine couldn't look for decent work. The few jobs she got she lost because there always came a time when she had to read something or write something down. She didn't really have any help for her deafness until she was nearly 30, when Bill helped her understand that she had a disability. It was only then that she learned to read, mostly with Bill's help. Seeing them together, I could imagine the gentle way in which he must have helped Lorraine understand that she was not stupid. Yet she still found it hard to talk about. Twenty years of raising a family, organising tenant groups and taking part in neighbourhood activism hadn't removed her sense of shame. Nor had it overcome the financial penalties she and her family had borne as a result of her inability to read and write.

Such stories will be depressingly familiar to anyone who works or has worked in social welfare. What stands out is the importance of misfortunes – accidents, illness, retrenchment – in the context of long-term deprivation and insecurity. As they didn't have much protection, these people paid and kept paying a harsh price for those misfortunes. This should at least give pause to the notion that you can call poverty 'earned' or 'unearned', or that there are innocent and guilty victims. Freeze any of their personal histories at one moment, and you will probably find what you are looking for. There will be a moment when Lorraine did something she wasn't meant to do, when Tom made a foolish decision, when Keith didn't take his chances. Forget that impoverished people get very few chances and find it very difficult to succeed. Forget the incredibly heavy price they pay for their failures. After all, everyone gets what she or he deserves. One outcome of that cruel commonsense is the self-delusion it encourages among the successful. Worse, many impoverished people, unable to disentangle their own life stories from its embrace, end up wondering when and how they brought this upon themselves.

Tragedies

If they were hesitant to share the details of personal deprivation, people could convey something through local tragedies. Some were very recent, and others were shifted into the present tense. The characters in these stories were strangely ambiguous and yet known by everyone. Few people knew their names, while in other cases names were not revealed because the ripples of the tragedy might yet be moving back and forth across the neighbourhood.

Most depicted people brought to destruction by fate and the harsh cruelties of the system. One I heard from April in Mount Druitt concerned a young man who had been in prison. Like many others, he was drifting, staying with a mate and spending his time in the pub. He didn't have a job because he'd given up looking for one after a couple of months of rejections. Because he didn't have a job he couldn't move in with a woman: in his own mind, and those of his potential partner, a man had to provide for his family. April remembered the day he had broken down in the welfare centre. He'd struck up a relationship with a young mother. He thought that it was going to be fine because he'd started looking for work again, and she'd let him stay. He loved the children and enjoyed being in a family. But the job he got didn't last; his partner had kicked him out and told him he was useless.

April's story concluded with the young man crying in her arms, because 'all he wanted was to have a family, that's all he wanted in life, to be a father, and he didn't know how to be one'. A few months later, I spoke with two young women who lived in the same area, and heard what I think was the same story about the same man, but with a different conclusion. Maybe they knew more of the story than the worker, who may not have been told everything. Or maybe these events had transpired in the interim. What they told me was that a young man had been going around talking about a local woman's children as if they were his. She'd thrown him out, and then he had come back and taken one of the children, claiming that the child was his. They weren't quite sure of all of the details, but the child had been returned safely; 'He didn't want to hurt the kiddie, he wanted to be his father. It's sad, isn't it?.' The man had threatened to kill himself but had been arrested and charged – with kidnapping they thought – because the child's mother was scared it might happen again. He was back in jail.

Fears about the loss of children were repeated in other stories. Peter, a Broadmeadows community worker, told me about a client who was once told by an insensitive social worker that she had to keep lots of food in the house if she wanted to maintain custody of her son. As time went on, Peter was puzzled because she seemed increasingly unable to manage. One day, she made him a cup of coffee and opened a cupboard to get the sugar. Every cupboard was stacked with cans and packets of food, even baby food she didn't need. There were boxes of cans in the laundry, and packets of pasta and cereal in a cupboard in the living room. So fearful was she of her child being taken away that she had stockpiled 'enough food to last three winters, or a nuclear war'. She had spent so much money on food that she had fallen behind in her electricity and gas bills and was about to be cut off. 'But if there's enough food', she told the worker, 'they won't take him away. She told me that. She told me I had to have lots of food or I would lose him.'

A story told by another worker emphasised the impact of changes in child protection. At the time, she said, the 'service cuts [had] just been horrific … the band-aids were all back on. Let's go in and grab kids and all that stuff.' For several years, she had been helping a young single mother, slowly moving her towards stability by treating her with respect. The young mother had found a job, and was trying to break away from an angry and sometimes violent boyfriend. Because of him, and for her past indiscretions involving minor drug use, the family was under watch by a state welfare department. In comes a new manager for the local office of that department, who has been directed to take a more interventionist approach on child protection. The person telling me the story arrived at work one day to find the young woman sobbing on the agency's front step; 'They took them last night. I didn't know what to do. They just took them.' She wouldn't be consoled, and she wouldn't believe she could get them back because she couldn't understand what she had done to merit losing them. She stopped going to work, and disappeared into her house. Two weeks later she was dead from an overdose.

The identity of the characters in these stories is significant. Invariably, they were young adults, almost child-like in their inexperience and their inability to cope. The young men were almost always unemployed; the young women were mothers living alone with their children. A few stories described other victims: one I heard in both Broadmeadows and Mount Druitt involved a family's destruction through gambling. By and large, though, the stories were about young people and their frustrated expectations: women who wanted to be good mothers and men who wanted to be providers.

The point of these stories was to attack the system, not all of the workers within it; after all, workers themselves often told the stories, or were included in them as people who tried to help. Instead, the villain was often a misguided 'do-gooder', an interferer who hadn't taken the time to understand and to learn, or the system itself, unforgiving, clumsy, even brutal. Nor were these stories morality tales in which incapable and flawed characters got their comeuppance. Their more common conclusion was 'there but for the grace of God'. These young women and men stood in for the older storytellers' own children or grandchildren, or were the friends and peers of the younger ones. The mother betrayed by a gambling son might be you, not because your son gambles but because there is no one who will look after you if such a disaster occurred. The children seized from the next street might be yours, if you didn't do the right thing by the social worker.

In the way they shaped the details, workers and residents made these stories into statements about everybody. They pictured a world that could turn malevolent, a world in which even the most hopeless and helpless people were treated badly and held in contempt. It wasn't you, but it could have been. Some of the people who shared their stories with me would then tell me about their own unemployed grandsons or brothers, or their daughters and cousins struggling – and sometimes failing – to give their own children a better life. They would cry, tell me about a son who had died, a daughter lost to heroin, a father so long unemployed he'd given up trying. They could find words, but only often broken and stumbling ones. Father Patrick Nolan, with a vocabulary drawn from a religious vocation and years of care, could say it a little more easily:

> You know, a lot of our young people have died. They're gone. They've actually given up. They've just packed it in, got out of it. That's the very sad voice of a large number of people who died unemployed, who never experienced work at all.

Died unemployed. How can people die unemployed? The hard-hearted will find answers quickly enough. They probably weren't trying. They were probably a bit hopeless. Talking to some of the people most like the characters in these tragedies, especially the young unemployed men, you hear hopelessness. One told me he'd be dead soon, and maybe not soon enough. They were broken, in a way. They could fix themselves, according to those who listened to them every day, but this was risky and would take a long time. They wanted to be 'good dads', and that meant having 'real jobs'. But they couldn't see how that was going to happen.

No one argued that people shouldn't be accountable or take responsibility for themselves. I doubt they would have any particular problem with a concept such as 'mutual obligation', so long as that meant the rich, as well as the poor, were obliged to share. They wanted to live in a world that was really fair, that recognised vulnerability as a shared problem and saw protecting people from disaster as a common responsibility. If this was the world that might be, stories about local tragedies illustrated the world that was and most likely still is.

It is easy to understand why impoverished people shared stories about the tragic destruction of vulnerable and almost child-like characters, or talked about poverty in terms of self-infliction and shame. They lived on the lowest rung of an unequal society and they heard constantly that inequality measures skill and talent rather than power and advantage. They struggled to argue that those rewards weren't just. Workers, conscious of the need for more resources, reasonably added their support to the conviction that what they were seeing was tragic and unmerited. These more tragic stories, like the stories of heroes, helped prove that disadvantaged people deserved something better. They conveyed telling truths about the meaning of deprivation, and people's capacity to keep battling. Most of all, an emphasis on heroes and victims was a tactical decision, made necessary by the dominant frameworks for understanding poverty and inequality within which poor people must survive. Stories about courageous struggle, perseverance and suffering have been created, at least in part, by the people who demand them from the poor. Impoverished people and overburdened workers have had to learn how to tell certain kinds of stories, and they know better than anyone what must be disguised and discarded.

But it is not enough. If the insistence that poor people must be heroes makes no adequate response to poverty, neither does the argument that they must be the innocent victims of harrowing circumstances. This makes the intensity of their suffering the reason for caring, as if it is only when poor people have suffered, really suffered, that some will merit our compassion. Such a position is easily punctured. You can always find someone to drag in front of a camera who will confirm what everyone wants to be true: that there are good poor and bad poor and the most important task of social policy in a rich twenty-first-century nation is to sort the truly needy from those who don't deserve our compassion. Worse, it helps to make each poor person the subject of a moral investigation, a test of their responsibility for their situation, without ever demanding a similar investigation of the structures that manufactured their poverty in the first place. If compassionate responses to poverty depend upon the heroism of poor people, or the depth of their suffering, they are left with a knowledge of poverty's injustice and dreams about justice no one wants to hear and no one asks them to share. An entire dimension of what they know, of what needs to be said, of the truth, is lost to those who say they want to listen.

Chapter Four
ANGER

Angry battlers

I managed to stumble into the middle of one Bidwill family's argument. There had been trouble in the street that morning, the lingering aftershocks of a noisy gathering the night before. Don, injured at work, was living on sickness benefits. The husband of his daughter Sheryl had run off. She had lost the house they were purchasing and had come back to her father's home with her three-year-old son Kain. Kept awake by the party, Kain was in an unforgiving mood. Both of Don's sons were unemployed, and the eldest, Craig, had been arguing loudly in the street most of the morning. Primed for a fight, they battled to control the microphone attached to my tape recorder. Don and Sheryl made weary responses, while Kain struggled to get near enough to record *Baa Baa Black Sheep* onto the tape. Craig and brother Darren shouted invectives about politicians and bosses and said all such wankers should try living without a job for a few years and see how they liked it. Before joining a fresh eruption of neighbourhood conflict outside, Craig yelled into the microphone, 'They should fucking come here and live like we fucking do before they fucking crap on about how easy things are'.

Anger also simmered beneath the surface of another conversation, a few streets away and a few nights later. A couple renting a townhouse, Vincent and Karen Villar, had invited along four of their friends and neighbours who had also spent much of their adult lives in Bidwill and nearby estates.

We shared a long and enjoyable conversation. They joked about the abandoned car at the end of the court being a signpost: 'Here we don't tell you to turn left at the nice big tree; we tell you to turn left at the burning car wreck'. It was a Sydney February evening, balmy without the sweaty dampness that made me yearn for Melbourne. Vincent and Karen's four children drifted in and out to claim a parent's lap or a biscuit, or to listen. There was banter between friends, and serious discussions of unemployment, low wages and the Housing Department's new program to renovate Bidwill. There were also flashes of bitterness. At Christmas the year before a charity had donated toys and clothes for Bidwill's underprivileged children. Darren said:

> It was very nice and everything, and thanks very much, but the whole estate still looks like shit and we're all still fucking poor. How are they going to fix that?

Their anger was directed in part at the Department of Housing, but it was also a more general statement about the stigma of being poor:

> Vincent: They forget that just because you live in a Commission house, you live on low income level, doesn't mean you're not as smart as Kerry Packer. Or somebody like that.
> Graeme: They're all the same, those people.
> Vincent: Actually, I don't reckon Kerry Packer's that smart, he's just rich. (*Laughs*)
> Karen: Rich and lucky.

There was anger, too, about expectations of gratitude:

> Louise: My area manager, when I asked him for something to be done about the house, he said, 'You should be thankful we're letting you live in our house'. So I said, 'Yeah, right. Thank you very much'. You have to be grateful.

Most of all, though, there was anger about being abandoned and left behind, and then made to feel that it was your fault. 'It's as if', Vincent said, 'we don't deserve any respect'. Graeme nodded agreement, and added, 'It's like we're sitting here waiting for something to happen. Someone to come and say "We've got a positive program. This is what we want to achieve. We need your help."'

It wasn't always easy to hear or to speak about anger. People softened it with irony and humour, or simply pulled away. It took me a while to realise how to let them speak of their anger rather than deflecting it automatically with a reassuring word or gesture. It was not a matter of unleashing anger or encouraging bitterness, but allowing it to come when it did. The difficulty, of course, is that impoverished people – and the workers who assist them – are not meant to be angry. It's not reasonable for them to say harsh things about 'bastards sitting there with a cushy job and a BMW', or 'Australia the great egalitarian society, what a load of bullshit', or 'middle-class wankers who don't give a damn about people like us and should just fuck off'. If you are poor, you're meant to be grateful and patient. If you work among the poor, you're meant to be reasonable and recognise that only so much can be done. Impoverished people are acutely aware of the fact of their need. In many ways, that made them more wary of their anger than I was.

Nor was their resentment focused on what outsiders might expect. I was in Inala, Broadmeadows and Mount Druitt shortly before the rise of Pauline Hanson and the One Nation Party, but some commentators were already predicting she or someone like her would find rich soil in such communities. After all, Hanson claimed to voice feelings of exclusion among Anglo-Australian 'battlers', who were fearful of further change and wanted migrants and Aboriginals put back in their place. A local Labor parliamentarian in Sydney nervously told me his constituents felt that 'governments of whatever persuasion have deserted them'. Surely, these most disadvantaged neighbourhoods were the angry tinder for One Nation's fire.[1]

To an extent, Hanson captured resentment towards politicians – though I would argue that this waned quickly as the nature of One Nation's own political machine became apparent. She may have attracted some support in these areas. That would have stemmed in large part from a deep dislike for the two main political parties and for politicians, and the fact that Hanson could be understood, at least for a time, as a stirrer. She said things that others didn't, and even if they were stupid things it was amusing to watch the reactions of the real politicians. The fact that she stumbled over words and didn't talk the clever talk would have only increased her appeal. People could vote for Hanson, or say they were going to, from a sense of devilment more than anything else.

Certainly, fears of battlers lining up to vote for One Nation turned out to be somewhat inaccurate. A study of voting patterns in local polling booths suggests that One Nation did not do well in these suburbs, not even in Inala during its Queensland high tide in 1998. As essayist Mudrooroo predicted, Inala people seemed not to have felt that Pauline Hanson – a small proprietor and home-owner and not a working-class woman – spoke for them.[2]

At the 1996 federal election, in which Pauline Hanson won the seat of Oxley, Inala lay in the neighbouring seat of Rankin. Two years later, however, an electoral redistribution had made Inala part of Oxley. While Hanson stood for the seat of Blair in that election, the voters of Oxley still had One Nation candidate Colene Hughes, and 18 per cent of them voted for her. Looking at polling booths, however, it is clear that the One Nation vote came largely from Ipswich and surrounding areas, not Inala. The lowest vote for One Nation, 7 per cent, was recorded in Forest Lake, a new middle-class housing estate south of Inala. At the four Inala booths, the One Nation vote varied between 9 per cent and 12 per cent. In the booths serving Riverview and Ipswich, just 10–15 kilometres down the Cunningham Highway, 20, 25 and even 35 per cent of voters supported One Nation. In 2001, at the next federal election, One Nation's vote fell to 12 per cent in Oxley, but in the four Inala booths it fell to 4 and 5 per cent, in most cases trailing the Greens, the Democrats or the informal vote. Perhaps even more telling, for the 1998 Queensland state election – when One Nation had its best electoral performance – the party did not bother standing a candidate in the state seat of Inala.[3]

Taken in isolation, a vote of 12 per cent for One Nation in an Inala booth might indicate significant support. Aboriginal people and migrants from Vietnam, Latin America and the Pacific Islands make up about one-sixth of Inala voters, so the level of One Nation support among white Anglo-Australians was plausibly even higher. Yet in booths in other parts of the seat with relatively similar proportions of Aboriginal or migrant voters, such as Goodna and Redbank, One Nation attracted more than double the share of the vote it achieved in Inala. Also, in these three elections the federal Labor vote in the Inala booths remained fairly stable, rising a little between 1996 and 1998 and then falling slightly in 2001. It is difficult to know for certain but a reasonable conclusion would be that Inala's One Nation voters were people who normally voted for conservative parties: in every Inala booth the decline in the One Nation vote between 1998 and 2001 almost exactly matched the number of votes returning to the Liberal Party.

Much the same case can be made for Mount Druitt, in which the One Nation vote can be measured over two federal elections in 1998 and 2001, and a state election in 1999.[4] In 1998, 9 per cent of Chifley voters made One Nation their first preference, and this was true of 11 or 12 per cent of voters in the Mount Druitt booths. The highest One Nation vote – 15 per cent – was in the Mount Druitt neighbourhood of Emerton, yet one of the lowest – 8 per cent – was in Bidwill. One Nation's vote declined in each subsequent election: 8 per cent in 1999 and 5 per cent in 2001. Federal Labor also did best in 1998, when it gained 65 per cent of first-preference votes in the Mount Druitt booths. In other words, the Labor Party and One Nation both peaked at the same election, and then fell, with the Liberal Party picking up voters from each.

Of course, it is dangerous to draw too many assumptions about political beliefs from voting statistics. However, they do offer little support for the view that disenchanted working-class voters in these suburbs turned to One Nation. The most convincing proposition is that the real losers in recent economic and structural changes – the retrenched, the unemployed and the poor – did not look to Hanson for their political voice. In their careful study of political attitudes, Murray Goot and Ian Watson emphasised that One Nation voters 'didn't think of themselves in class terms', were oriented towards right-wing populism, and had much more in common with Liberal and especially National Party voters than the traditional Labor voters living in places like Inala, Broadmeadows and Mount Druitt.[5] I would agree with Mudrooroo that most people living in hardship still regarded the Labor Party – albeit after a sigh and a forlorn smile – as their only likely voice.

During my interviews some people talked about recent migrants and Aboriginals being favoured, or about bludgers cheating the welfare system. It would have been relatively easy to make a few people talk about nothing else. If this was the only kind of anger you wanted to hear, you could certainly find it. But it was not the dominant issue or the first thing people wanted to say. I don't want to diminish the problems that racial and cultural bias cause here, or the possibility that some people might be drawn towards the sense of threat and loss that One Nation expressed. What needs to be remembered, though, is that these suburbs are unlike the kinds of areas in which One Nation did best. Inala, Broadmeadows and Mount Druitt were and still are very diverse, and each has a large and long-standing urban Aboriginal community. Anger here was muted by contact, cooperation and closeness. There was shared ground, the possibility and often the legacy of common cause. There were complaints and grumbles, but there was just as often recognition that the real problems, the things that made people really angry, couldn't be blamed upon migrants or Aboriginals. In fact, they were shared with them.

As Stephanie, a member of a support group for long-term unemployed people in Broadmeadows said, 'It's money that counts. Things you haven't got. We haven't got it and other people have. I don't care if they're white or black or Asian or bloody purple. Doesn't matter.' Around her there were nods of agreement from a man who had fled Poland in the 1950s, a woman who came from Echuca in the 1970s, and a man who had emigrated from Indonesia in the 1990s. In a Koori organisation in Mount Druitt, Marlene said, 'When you're here, it's not being Aboriginal that matters all the time. It's where you are, you know, on the ladder. It's not just about being black.' People in these suburbs were angry, but their anger was drawn directly from the concrete experiences of being poor and insecure. It stemmed from the injuries of class; the resentments, in other words, that no one else really wants to hear.

Distrusting welfare

Joe: You'd think it was their bloody money, the way they treat you down at DSS. Like they really resent you getting it and want to take it away because everyone knows you don't really deserve it.

Lyn: It's just awful a lot of the time. If you make a mistake, you're trying to get something you shouldn't have, you know. They jump right on it: 'You're not telling the truth, what else are you lying about?'

Mari: Look, you are guilty until proven innocent at the DSS these days. That's no joke. You really are. I'm not saying all the workers are like that. Some aren't. But a lot of them treat you like you're a bloody criminal if you're on a single mum's pension.

Elena: It's all test, test, test. All the questions. And it's not like the people on the counter understand all the rules anyway.

Pam: A friend of mine lost her pension for a while. It was their mistake but they wouldn't admit it. Not for a long time. Probably meant nothing to them, but what's she supposed to do with her bills and buying food and everything? 'Sorry' doesn't put food on the table, does it?

Amid growing concern about the disaffection felt by those being ruled for those who do the ruling, perhaps too little is made of how governments themselves help to produce a sense of disengagement and distrust among particular groups of citizens, especially the poor and the young.[6] The people with whom I spoke had very good reasons for their angry distrust of a government that so often manifested its distrust of them. The very fact of their entitlement to help was a matter for constant and often intrusive investigation. Theirs was not an inchoate anger directed at anyone in authority but a specific resentment about real experiences.

People described being caught in a kind of war with the welfare system, especially the DSS and the public housing authorities. During the 1990s they described two versions of that system, which from their perspective produced pretty much the same outcome. First, Labor spoke about social justice and overcoming disadvantage while assuring everyone that any such assistance would be strictly targeted. Then conservatives spoke about waste, the burden on the taxpayer, and the importance of bolstering the self-sufficiency of low-income Australians. Both approaches relied upon the conviction that limited funds had to be spent more wisely; in turn, a lot of money could be saved – for debt reduction or other programs, depending on your politics – by more rigorously policing people's entitlements.

This was hardly a surprising outcome; a passing acquaintance with the history of this same debate in the United States would have shown the inherent dangers of a focus on efficient targeting. Well-meaning American liberals, conscious of scarcity, tended to 'accentuate the deservedness of the chosen and the undeservedness of the rejected'. However, 'these justifications [tended to] outlive the period of scarcity' and were turned against the poor.[7] As historian Alice O'Connor laments, 'Liberal poverty analysts not only acquiesced but actively participated in what they hitherto had been trying to avoid: they re-pauperised the poverty problem'.[8] Australian discussions just as inexorably turned into a debate not about reducing inequality but about the need to reform certain kinds of welfare and strengthen the obligatory contributions of their recipients.

Residents, activists and workers described the consequences: government agencies dominated by a distrust of their clients and an obsession with possible waste. The delivery of welfare has always contained a tension between compassion and control, service and suspicion. Yet the practical experience of welfare targeting in the 1990s, among those being targeted, was of workers driven more or less readily towards control, suspicion and an ever more punitive surveillance. People also stressed the costs of this approach, especially the suppression of novelty and self-determination. The mania for obedience and the emphasis on testing people's entitlements, they argued, helped create the very lack of initiative and reliance on social workers that some consider impoverished people's chief deficiency. People terrified of being punished for mistakes were rarely willing to take chances. Suspicion did not generate a determination to avoid so-called dependency, but a fear of doing anything that might jeopardise what people already had. As a community worker in Broadmeadows argued, 'Once you have fear, fear will not drive change. You will never have change, because fear will not make change.'

People living on welfare described a ponderous structure of unreasonable obligations and irrational sanctions. They knew the government system distrusted them and encouraged its workers to treat them as potential cheats. There was a culture of dobbing in 'frauds', but also a feeling that insensitive decisions justified clever evasion. Most felt that they couldn't win: urged to avoid dependency, they nonetheless found that independence, especially the skills involved in managing on a low income, could be interpreted as using the system or breaking the rules. Any opportunity to earn a little money meant entering into a complex procedure of reporting that would defeat most of us; indeed, its complexity for both beneficiaries and administrators almost guaranteed that errors would be made. Effectively, people wanted to be innocent until proven guilty. Several of them noted the difference between tax evasion, in which surveillance is tempered by the need to protect an honest majority, and welfare cheating, in which the honest majority are sacrificed to a tiny fraudulent minority.

In their accounts of poor treatment, the issue was not how much they received. The indignity of the investigation was much more painful. They also resented having to passively accept someone else's interpretation of their problems. Glenys described a recent argument during a DSS interview:

> I've had a terrible run-in with them just recently, when I said to them, 'What do you want from me? Tell me what you want, because I am giving you everything I possibly can, but obviously it's not the right stuff.' They cannot tell me. They won't tell me, and then they send me another form for me to fill in.
>
> I screamed, you know; they're wasting my time, making me full of anxiety. They won't give me an answer because they were told they weren't allowed to tell anyone anything. I said, 'Can I have a look at my file?' 'Oh no, you've got to go through the *Freedom of Information Act* to see your file.'
>
> That's my file. I snatched it off the poor lady. I grabbed it, and I looked through it, and she didn't know what to do with me, so she raced out and got someone else, who demanded it back, so I said 'No, it's my file, I'm going to read it because I want to know what you people are doing. This is my life. I want to know what you are saying about me.'

The workers and agencies that people valued were not those who had the most to give, or gave without question, but those who treated clients with basic respect:

> I mean, it's not the good ones who say 'the tenants can have everything'. That's not what we're looking for. We want a fair go.
>
> All we're asking for is … [to be] treated with respect … [not] as 'that lower-class person'.

Most people had learned to have very low expectations; as one worker said, 'They've lived their lives constantly being put down, so you get to the point where [they think], "Here comes another one", you know'.

Nor was their anger simply a matter of bad personal experience. Individual and collective histories were gathered into shared stories of a people besieged by a common enemy. As Carol Hills, a young single mother, told me, 'What they do now, the government, is that they keep us poor to keep us at a certain level … They keep Broadmeadows down, so you're not living, you're just surviving. That's the way they like it, keeping us down.'

Shared experiences of being distrusted and treated with disdain generated strong bonds between neighbours and friends, along with an immediate identification of government – whatever its hue or rhetoric – as uninterested, uncaring and unresponsive: 'The government is constantly the enemy, I think, for these folks'. This was a commonsense guide to what had happened in the past, and a way of anticipating what would almost certainly happen in the future. As Inala community worker Pam Wilson remarked, what was passing down through families was not dependency, but anger:

> That comes through in families where they've felt that they are hard done by anyway, and the system is up the creek, and they hate the police and they hate the government departments and they hate everyone.

It is best to prepare yourself for being distrusted and for being disappointed, despite the occasional good worker. As Inala activist Rose Sinclair said, 'People are apathetic, simply because for years people knew that no matter what we do, nothing ever gets done. Maybe that's not apathy; maybe that's realism.'

In some of the recent writing on citizens' apathy and alienation, political scientists such as American Robert Putnam emphasise what is called 'social capital': the shared associations that need to be nurtured if people are to feel they are part of a larger community from which they draw benefits and to which they owe responsibilities.[9] But for people living in hardship, feelings of being distrusted by an uncaring and punitive system are the basis of their social capital. Their experiences pull them together by pushing away strangers, do-gooders and governments.

Even the productive bonds built between workers and residents remained very fragile, and were easily undone by an insensitive remark, a poorly explained decision, or an unfair procedure. Gaining the trust of local people, many of whom had been damaged in the past, was described as a very slow process:

> I wrote in the daybook yesterday about one particular woman who's been scouting around the edges the whole time, you know, and she actually asked

> yesterday if she could do something for the centre. That's been a long time. It's been about a year's work.

As another community worker put it, 'It takes time to be accepted' and 'to win the approval of the people. They test you, they really test you.' The great difficulty for many workers was that they had to prove themselves respectful, and trusting, in a situation where neither was predicted and neither was expected to last. Indeed, they often found themselves the brunt of antagonisms they played no part in creating and had spent years overcoming in their own ethical dealings with their clients.

Of course, government departments did not ignore such problems. In all three suburbs, schemes such as the Jobs, Education, Training Program for sole parents, or the tenant participation and client service projects of the state housing departments, had promised and sometimes delivered real alternatives to this culture of distrust. Sadly, however, such reforms were rarely given the time to take hold, and few survived the cost-cutting enthusiasm of 'new broom' conservative governments during the 1990s.

It is very important to see that these complaints were not about the quantity of payments, or the fact that benefits were so low as to make weekly budgeting an exercise in heroic assumptions. The problem was punitive and disrespectful treatment. Governments were not just at fault because they didn't deliver but because what they delivered came at such a heavy price in terms of self-respect and dignity. People did not expect to receive the world on a platter. As they said, only the rich presume that as their right. They did not expect immediate changes in their situations. But they did expect to be listened to, to play some part in defining what they needed, and to be treated with respect. They resented being treated as idiots, as potential cheats and liars, or as victims who needed to be saved.

What impoverished people saw reflected in the myriad rules, countless forms, intrusive investigations and the culture of suspicion was not an endorsement of their right to help – a right they knew better than anyone else carried responsibilities. What they saw instead was the shame they were meant to feel about needing that help, and the presumption that because they were in need they were probably either incapable or fraudulent. If they could sometimes joke about outwitting a cumbersome system, they also knew they were becoming trapped in its depressing theatre of exposure and punishment:

> DSS is a great place to learn just where you belong – down the bottom. They call out your number, not your name, your number, like a prisoner, like you're nobody, and then you're on show. Answer this. Check that. Yes sir, no sir, three bags full sir. You know what it's about.

In this theatre, poor people could see what everyone thought about them, and what they sometimes struggled not to believe about themselves.

Shitting themselves about accountability

An obsession with efficiency and accountability was not restricted to relationships between government departments and individual clients. It also poisoned the interactions between the central offices of those departments, their own local and regional branches and the wide array of organisations – from church missions to job-training schemes – upon which governments relied to actually deliver their services. Over the years, friction had waxed and waned but everyone agreed these relationships were becoming more difficult. Workers remembered the growth of a community development and client focus during the 1970s and 1980s, when there had been a transfer of power and sometimes money from the central to the local, along with a belief in collaboration and taking the client's perspective. The trend in the 1990s was in the opposite direction, away from collaboration and trust and towards closer surveillance and control. The most consistent complaint was that governments increasingly refused to listen: 'They don't have any trust in the community. We talk about the community not having any trust in them, but they don't have trust in people at the local level.'

Government departments were also said to be ignoring reasonable arguments, and demanding fresh evidence about needs that, as Broadmeadows youth worker Natalie Phillips put it, 'haven't changed since yesterday or last week or last month. It's almost like they're hoping the needs will just go away, like magic.' Less and less trust was being placed in the initiatives of the system's own employees, let alone the knowledge and ideas of disadvantaged people themselves. José, a Western Sydney migrant worker, argued that 'this is disenfranchising a substantial number of people, and it becomes a top-down approach towards providing a solution to a problem that *they* see, the problem as *they* see it'.

For workers, and for the many residents doing volunteer or paid work in local agencies, the easiest way of describing these changes was in terms of the rapid emergence and solidification of a 'managerialist' model, especially within the DSS and the state housing and community welfare departments. Advocacy, empowerment, rights and listening were out; efficiency, measurement, accountability and telling were in. Looking back, workers and residents said they could see it coming. But it arrived very quickly, and was promoted with disarming confidence by its mostly business-trained advocates. While the extent of these changes varied, the most vulnerable areas, such as community services and public housing, were those lacking powerful defenders. In health, the easiest targets were community-based initiatives and services rarely used by the well-off, such as free dental care.

This managerialist model was and is driven by a concern to ensure that scarce resources are not wasted, and by a conviction that important decisions cannot rely upon local knowledge. In other words, the experts at the top are best placed to make an objective assessment of needs and the best strategies to meet them. It is also a model based on targeting and delivering pre-defined services. One of the best descriptions came from Helen Croydon:

> It's all about unit costing and direct service, bums on seats and numbers through the doors. It's about 'quick through-put', quick fix, come in, we'll fix you up, and after six weeks you're gone. It doesn't matter about the past thirty years.

It was also becoming clear to workers and volunteers that some activities would no longer be supported, and indeed might jeopardise future funding. Some had received an explicit direction that they were not to take on advocacy, especially if that meant embarrassing the department or the government. In Broadmeadows, the coordinator of one neighbourhood house had been told that her 'core business' no longer included 'helping clients make trouble'. At another, the department ruled out welfare advocacy on behalf of migrant families in favour of more language training, on the grounds that this was what the clients really needed. Not suprisingly, no one making this decision bothered to ask the migrant users of the centre to define what they really needed.

It was also very common for major changes in the demands made of an agency to coincide with funding cuts. Helen Laplace and Fusun Bakir were meant to do community development work. As the cuts hit home, all they could manage was individual consultations:

> For us, it has meant that we are increasingly isolated in our work. We have to spend more and more time seeing clients.
>
> Look at our diaries. Both of us are trained not only in social work but also in community development. We're spending more and more time working in a clinical, diagnostic, intervening role, individualising the problem.

In health, there was the same pressure to focus on direct medical interventions, when, as community nurses in Mount Druitt argued, this didn't tackle the real problems:

> Part of our role is actually advocacy for people, but it's becoming more and more difficult … because we're so short-staffed and filling gaps all the time. There used to be twenty-five of us, and now there's fifteen.

Or, as a doctor at the Mount Druitt Polyclinic said:

> The accountability factor is weighing more on clinicians and people who perhaps shouldn't be concerned about that. I accept the fact that we're not here on trust, we're being paid good money for providing good services, but I think when it gets down to the paperwork being more important than the person, there's something wrong there.

No one argued against efficiency measures, or more effective coordination among different agencies to prevent duplication of services. No one argued that change was bad, and all could point to sensible, practical reforms that would help ensure, for instance, that new needs could be identified, or that services were responding in the most effective ways to changing problems. Neither were workers and local activists concerned about accountability. They had spent years worrying over their accountability to the impoverished people they helped, and how to best use the few resources at their command. As one veteran activist said, 'That lack of trust really stings. I mean, the community would know if you were stealing money or doing whatever. There is not a thing that goes down in these centres that the community doesn't know about. The grapevines here are better than a telephone.'

But managerialism provided few answers to those problems. According to those at its receiving end, it largely meant providing a minimum service at the least possible expense. There was no time to tackle complications or larger issues, no time to try and understand the often tangled histories of clients. Meaningful consultation was impossible. Ever more complex compliance strategies surrounded each benefit and how it would be used. Perhaps the most damaging aspects were the focus on avoiding risk, and the obsession with controlling how funds were spent. Avoiding risk, of course, also meant suppressing innovation and preventing the kinds of mistakes from which people might learn what actually works. In this model, change is driven from the top, by strategic planners and efficiency experts, and is then carried out at the bottom. Change is developed out of abstractions and ideas that work in theory. These are tied up in neat packages of regulations, rules and service agreements, and then delivered to the real world, where they quickly unravel. The whole approach rests on a profound distrust in the ability of either local workers or those actually suffering disadvantage to define needs and design programs to address them. In the 1990s, as governments became convinced of the political dangers of welfare, they lost a terribly important resource: ideas based on experiences.

Like nurses, teachers and university lecturers, welfare workers also found themselves spending large amounts of time keeping records and performing appraisals:

> They're shitting themselves about accountability, to the extent that they're going to extremes which make workers totally robotic in their approaches to things. They're so scared of issues being taken up by the media and blown out of proportion that they put in accountability mechanisms which basically leave you no time to do work, because you're too busy filling out forms.
>
> They are going to the extent of being totally paranoid about their accountability, about wasting resources.

In a world of bullet points, budget criteria and flow charts, the conversation about what might work was overpowered by what it might cost:

> It's like talking to an accountant, I suppose. They think with this really pragmatic, rational approach, and you're trying to justify a community

> development project, something that you think has real benefits for health, but you can't, there's no argument because you never meet on any plane.

So much was under threat, especially the most effective programs for drawing in new people, developing links between different cultures, and meeting unexpected needs. The cooking classes, playgroups, informal language classes and sports teams were much less threatening to new residents because they did not force them to publicly acknowledge a specific problem. But they weren't core business. Workers wondered how novel methods would emerge, when everything was ruled by service contracts, pre-packaged programs and performance quotas. Real client participation was becoming another risk few could take:

> I think this is getting much harder, and it's getting more professionalised and … the community is losing the ability to actually be involved.
>
> Apart from lack of time, my committee members were just attending so many meetings to try and keep things together. They're voluntary workers. They're unpaid. Why should they be slogging over pages of bloody submissions and stuff?

These pressures were further intensified by the call for increased competition between agencies: 'We've got to run around saying "We're better than that organisation over there", so that we can get our money, and they've got to do the same to us'. Leaving aside the bizarre juxtaposition between demands for competition and calls for more cooperation, this created a further series of dilemmas: 'You've got the most disadvantaged fighting with one another for meagre, meagre resources'. Or, as one Inala resident put it, 'Departments coming into a community blunder in, set up a fight, and they couldn't give a shit what happens next'. In Western Sydney:

> it could be the case that to obtain a worker in a place like Mount Druitt might well mean that one gets defunded in Fairfield or Liverpool … It just means that somebody shows a greater need and bang, that's where the money goes. The fact is that a lot of these areas have a very great deal of need, and to start ranking them, to me, is really quite wrong.

Certainly, workers argued, if the goal was to reduce dependency it was difficult to see how strict controls and an obsession with accountability would achieve it. Clients had become outsiders to the definition of needs. They were becoming consumers of solutions they were not trusted to define. Managing welfare was becoming a careful, politically safe operation, dedicated to counting effectiveness by bums on seats and simplistic 'one-off' solutions to complex problems: 'They come in with preset programs; like Daleks. They come in to "save Inala".' Or, as Patrick Nolan argued:

> What are the outcomes? What are your throughputs? It's not measurable. I mean, with most things it takes you three or four years to get it on the drawing board, to get to the starting line and get funded. By the time you get funded the need that you've actually applied for has shifted considerably. Then you get funded, and when you should not be funded they can't stop.
>
> I've watched that dynamic, observed it, for a long time. It's extraordinary. You're not supposed to stop, you see, nor are you supposed to change, move one degree from your objectives and all that stuff and your target groups. All those games you play about your stats. It's just too much. It's hard to get on, it's hard to get off, and you can't change.

For the people on the receiving end it was becoming a lot easier to sink back and accept someone else's diagnosis and someone else's prescription. We give you money, we tell you what to do, and we measure its effectiveness. You owe us compliance with rules and with plans for your future that meet our definition of your obligations, and that you may not understand, let alone accept. If we think you have broken those rules, we will punish you immediately, even though it may turn out that we and not you were in error. Because we distrust people like you, we will continually assess whether you really deserve this precious gift. Take it or leave it.

In the strongest signal of the increasing distaste for rule-bound government funding, private agencies were trying to reduce their dependence on it as much as possible. Government – the instrument of the people – was to be avoided. Five residents and workers at Mount Druitt's Pittuma Aboriginal Resources, Arts and Crafts Centre talked about the differences between public and private agencies:

> Wendy: I think that people like St Vinnies and the Catholic churches are good.
>
> Heather: Father Patrick is good.
>
> Miriam: Yes, Father Patrick, he's wonderful.

Jennifer: He's our angel.

Wendy: He is wonderful. Even if you need somebody to talk to when the day is over, sort of thing, you ring him up and he'll always find a minute for you to have a yarn. He's so wonderful, gives you a little bit of support, and when we have our people in burials and things like that. If everybody could be like him, but then you wouldn't find everybody like him, or the world would be perfect.

David: Few and far between.

Wendy: I've had a lot of goodness out of St Vincent de Paul, Salvation Army. Those people, you can't fault them. But it's the CES and the Social Security and Housing Department and places like that that you need to change.

In fact, one Catholic agency had just created a political storm by pulling out of a government-funded youth employment scheme. The coordinator spoke about their reasons:

It's only a four-year term, and the problem is ten or twenty years, and it is massive. Anything that's laid down is a quick fix, a touch and go model, or a very efficient, computerised accountability thing, where kids go off the dole, on the dole.

It was recycling the unemployed, on the one hand making people more qualified to be unemployed, and on the other hand putting people down the tube if they didn't front.

The political response was 'you can't do that'. It was shock, horror, talk you out of it, 'What can we give you? We must be able to do a deal.' (*Laughs*)

Later, he added:

The intervention must occur at the community level, not just us, but where the community begins to own all these problems, carry each other's burdens. This community is very good at that, and is getting better at it all the time, growing rapidly in that direction. But that doesn't get mentioned anywhere. And you don't want money. Sometimes, if you want to ruin something, fund it. (*Laughs*) That's a challenge, to see how you can use funding and work it out. But it can be the kiss of death … It actually interrupts the messy flow and growth that takes place at our level.

Real welfare, real community work, is messy, long-term, and liable to make mistakes before it finds the most appropriate way of dealing with single problems that are always tangled up with others. Real welfare means working with people, not working on them. Real welfare trusts impoverished people to define their problems and contribute to solutions. At the very least, real welfare doesn't apply to the most vulnerable people a series of obligations that are never applied to the powerful. But in the middle of the 1990s, real welfare was a fading dream:

> It would be governments saying, 'Look, we understand you need to have a freer rein to meet these very diverse and complicated issues out there in the community, go ahead and do it, come up with something and we'll support you when it comes time for accountability and justifying use of taxpayers' funds'.
>
> Yeah, right. (*Laughs*)

Asking without listening

There were funding cuts, efficiency drives and the heavy hand of accountability. Workers were disappearing. Clients felt punished rather than helped by the welfare system. Yet at the same time they were also being told that governments wanted to listen to them and that there would be greater participation. If Labor's favourite theme was community consultation, incoming conservative governments in Victoria and, a little later, in Canberra, began to use a bizarre rhetoric about welfare recipients as 'customers' who 'do business' with government. It was all a bit surreal.

Of course, some of this was welcome. In all three suburbs there was an effort to tackle historically bad relationships between governments and local residents, particularly in the housing departments. This was in turn linked to proposals to renovate some neighbourhoods. These were piecemeal in Broadmeadows, but Bidwill had an Estate Improvement Project, and Inala was being prepared for more intensive redevelopment by both the Department of Housing and a Building Better Cities project.

By and large, the residents to whom I spoke, along with workers in church and other private agencies, were suspicious. I think they wanted to trust and become involved. A worker in Bidwill's 'Concrete City' described her residents' views:

> My only wish with all that is that they see a result. Any little result, just so they know that something positive will happen.
>
> People out there just shrug their shoulders and think 'Yeah, right, we'll wait and see what happens'. You can only hope for their sakes that it does.

Fran Hume said, 'They are listening now … [and] if it works out the way they say it's going to go, I think it will be great'. A few minutes later, however, she added:

> I'll be an old lady with a stick before it all comes. They're always saying they're going to do things then they don't do it.
>
> You know they're not going to do anything. It's really disheartening. You know it. I get to the point where I don't worry about it, and we just get on with what we have to do here, for whoever we can help here.

In a way, people remained remarkably ready to trust that this time it might be different. But they warned themselves not to expect too much because they'd heard promises before.

Of course, consultation suggests that you have something important to say. But when people don't see themselves reflected in the recommendations they resent the implied insult that their knowledge wasn't considered worthy after all. In one community meeting in Inala, for instance, some residents tried to talk about unemployment. The response from the project team, according to two separate groups of residents who were there, was that 'unemployment is not one of the core issues being handled by this initiative' and was 'not in the project brief'. I'm sure this was an honest statement of the project's limitations, but it is little wonder that residents felt the answers, and not just the questions, had already been decided.

However enthusiastically expressed, and for all the hard work that was being done on the ground, promises to hear the community's views seemed hollow to the people who were trying to be heard. What people got was the showcase public meeting. This one-off opportunity assumed that something called 'the community' could find and articulate its authentic voice in a couple of hours. Having heard their views, the consultants could tick the box labelled community participation and move on to do what they were probably going to do in the first place. It felt meaningless:

They come to people like me, ask you to put in some recommendations, and if they've had their coffee that morning, or if what you say is what they already think, they might say 'Yeah. We'll pick up a bit of that.' But if they haven't, they'll probably throw it in the bin.

Most residents knew the place of consultation in the hierarchy of decision-making. The rhetoric of community-based planning couldn't allay the fear that Inala's Building Better Cities project, for instance, seemed much more interested in showy infrastructure and quick results than a careful deliberative process, whatever the desires of some of its workers. The people of these suburbs could also see a facile consultation process from a mile away. They were well-versed in workshops – which some rather unkindly described as 'encounter groups for planners' – and the public meeting had become one of their favourite spectator sports: 'It's fun. Especially if it's a pie in the sky thing where you know you could ask for the world and you're getting nothing'.

Workers tended to be both more resilient and more resigned in the face of botched consultations:

They don't really want to know what the community thinks, because the community is a bloody nuisance, really. (*Laughs*)

Look, they were writing this review to a brief. The agendas were well and truly set, so people's input and ideas weren't really being sought genuinely. Surprise, surprise.

In Inala, two tenant workers made similar points:

Liz: I've been saying for some time that when we have consultation, it's really what I see as they've made a decision and now they're telling us, they're informing us. They're giving us the opportunity to speak against it but it's already been set in place anyway. That's really what it is. They're selling it.

So there are lots of hidden agendas that we're not in touch with. We can see things as victories on our part, but often they're not.

Kate: And you need to ask what is driving the need for that consultative process. Is it being driven because it is a criterion of the funding dollars? Or is it that they really want to know? The researchers need

> to analyse their motivations. Are they doing it because they want to utilise what they're being given? Or are they doing it because they have to?

In Mount Druitt, numerous people told me they'd had what ethnic community workers Angie Chan and James Farrer described as a 'gutful of hopeless consultations'. As another worker said to me, 'There is a certain cruelty, I think, in telling people you're here to help and to listen, raising all the injustices, and then walking away saying, "Well, there's nothing I can do about that". Why do it? That's what I always think.'

Around the time of my visits to Mount Druitt, much effort was being put into consultations with the Aboriginal community. At the Pittuma Centre, Wendy assured me, 'There's always people up there in control', and Karen added, 'Yes. You do it their way, not your way.' At the Murawina Community Centre, local residents and workers Sandra, Liz and Barbara had been to many a consultation:

Sandra: You may say 'it was red', but they may feel the conversation related to 'black', so they make it black. It's not as straight down the line as that, but you could be explaining something to them and they're writing and they're taking notes, but it comes out differently. It never comes out as what you're telling them.

Mark: So it's almost like they're not allowing you your own explanations of problems?

Liz: Yes, it's what they want to see.

Sandra: Exactly. They're changing it around. I've been thinking greatly about this. Maybe the problem is that the people who come out to do these surveys and want to know about the culture and everything aren't *listening* to the extent that they should be listening. It's like they're hearing part of the conversation, and only taking in what they feel is being said.

Some stories described the vindication of a last word. One Inala resident, for instance, who had done voluntary work with youths on probation, talked about a meeting attended by around thirty managers and department planners:

> They decided that the reason kids stole in Inala was boredom. Nothing else. And I said, 'Have any of you ever been unemployed?', and there wasn't one person in that room who had ever been without a job. I said, 'OK, put your wallets and your credit cards, everything, in the middle of the table, and then take twenty cents each out and go home'. [They said,] 'I can't get home on twenty cents', and so on. 'Now you're thinking about why kids steal in Inala', I said.

In 1995, while I was in Inala, the pace of community consultation had dropped off somewhat after the initial burst of Building Better Cities activity. Its legacy was mixed, and included a degree of suspicion and anxiety in regard to what the 'redevelopment' of Inala might mean. Val Stephens talked about her fears that 'they're tarting these places up and I think we're going to get chucked out … And I don't know where I'm going to be exported to.' In a letter she sent me later, Val had become more worried and her humour darker:

> So we long suffering denizens of deepest darkest Inala are to be the subject of yet another REPORT.
>
> If all the previous REPORTS were laid end to end, they would probably reach right around the perimeter of our suburb.
>
> If all the recommendations of all previous REPORTS had been implemented, perhaps the REPORTERS would now be reduced to REPORTING on 'Genus Yuppie, sub-species Jindaleeus', thus allowing the REPORTEES of Inala some respite from their attention. … The REPORTEES feel they may become DEPORTEES as the direct result of this latest REPORT.

Val's arguments were harsh and rejected the possibility of good intentions. Yet what she said must nonetheless be heard. In some urban renewal areas, including the one then being proposed in Inala, consultation teams were surprised to discover that local residents were spreading stories about people being taken away from their homes in trucks. They were exasperated by people's credulity, and some of the senior staff talked about the need to educate local residents about the aims of the project. But surely the most troubling fact was that local people were able to put faith in such stories at all.

There is every reason to believe that there were benefits and gains for local people from these projects. And the desire to consult communities, to do the research one more time, sprang in part from legitimate concerns about how to discover new problems. These concerns were real enough in places that not only experienced a high degree of population turnover but were among the most culturally diverse communities in the nation. Also, there is ample evidence that well-designed and well-conducted programs can address problems of representation and achieve genuine cooperation and trust. In Australia and elsewhere, there are examples of a truly participatory process, in which people are listened to and shown respect for their honesty, capacity and integrity.[10]

Yet for all the good work, even successful community projects in these suburbs faced powerful constraints. In large part, those constraints did not stem from inadequate expertise. The problem was that while disadvantaged people and local workers were once again given a chance to speak, there was no real guarantee that they would be heard. To speak without being listened to, and then to be asked the same questions again two or three or five years down the track, erodes hope in the possibility of change. It is cruel to ask questions without really hearing the answers or to consult when pre-determined outcomes won't be affected anyway. Asking without listening is much, much worse than not asking at all. If consultation is not done for a reason, and if financial constraints and other limitations mean that what people say won't really matter, it should not be done at all. Instead, decisions should be taken and people should be told. And those who have the power to make decisions should accept the responsibility of justifying and explaining them without hiding behind a facile community consultation.

There is a long history of distrust and powerlessness in these suburbs, and everyone must acknowledge that history. People described themselves as the unwitting guinea pigs of countless experiments. Because they lived in public housing, they said, 'We're expendable. We can be moved around. It's that experimental approach. It's disgusting.' Again and again, they had been told lies:

> They said, 'This time we want to hear you. This time things would change.' But they didn't. It happens all the time, and I can't keep doing this. I really can't do this any more. I can't do it to them any more, get their hopes up.

In fact, people in these areas had every reason to ask why they were still being consulted about problems that hadn't changed and solutions they knew wouldn't work:

> People are saying, 'Well, why do we need people knocking on the door when we really want a better bus service, and how many people do we have to tell, and what do they with it anyway when we tell them?'. It's an issue a social planner confronts, because as soon as you go to a place and say 'What are some of the needs?', there's this floodgate that opens, people saying 'Well. Don't you know? We keep saying it and it appears nobody knows.'

They also had every reason to be angry. They had reason to be angry about having to wait, about having to prove their entitlements again and explain problems that anyone could see if they cared to look. But no one was really listening. Vincent from Bidwill described the common dilemma in these words:

> I think all the community is waiting for is someone to come through with a promise. One promise, made and kept. And you'll find that the people who have slacked off, given up, would come and give a hand. But there hasn't been one yet. There has not been one promise fulfilled in this place.

It's not as if they wanted all that much. Someone to make and keep a promise. Something good to happen because it was justified, not because they had 'earned' it. To be respected and to retain their dignity, and not to be treated as incapacitated, stupid inferiors.

Most of all, I think, there was a claim that was very hard to discern because it was so often submerged in bravado or in self-doubt. It struggled to surface because it was too strong, too angry, perhaps too naked in its ambitions. It was a claim that impoverished people aren't really supposed to make. What they wanted was for the world to be really fair. For the promises made about 'a fair go' to be kept. They wanted the rich to share, and the lucky to help the unlucky. They were angry about broken promises, big and small, just as they were angry about being treated like criminals or called losers and bludgers because they didn't have any money. They hated those who looked down at them, and they hated having to anticipate the put-downs and the stigma. If the people with whom I spoke were angry at the welfare system and its workers, they were more angry about what they saw standing behind them. They knew that welfare was as kind, or unkind, as it was allowed to be. If they shouted at the people on the DSS front counter, it was only because it was hard to find the people they really wanted to confront.

Much of what I heard in the middle of the 1990s was the increasing frustration of people living in hardship, the pessimism of seasoned activists, and the growing distaste of workers for a more and more punitive system. The hopeful were losing hope, those who had always helped their neighbours through the thickets of rules and regulations didn't understand them any more, and workers could see little reason to keep defending the indefensible. On top of that, in the second half of the 1990s would come the rhetoric of a conservative federal government eager to reform welfare once and for all, proffering excited press releases about the number of pathetic frauds they had managed to prosecute. We are by now so close to the language of deserving poor and undeserving paupers that we may as well bring it back for good.

Punishing the impoverished is not a particularly new idea, of course. Yet this is the future, not the past, a future being made in the name of all Australians, and a future that can only be glimpsed in the accounts of the losers. Losers do know something about the world, something winners either don't know or don't want to know. They know something about unfairness and injustice.

Val Stephens wrote me a letter in 1995, which read: 'I predict that, in a few years, to get a pension or benefit, people will be compelled to do voluntary work or forgo government assistance'. I saw Val again a little later. She said to me that as far as she could see, Australia was getting to be a cruel place. She said something else, which I wrote down:

> We won't have welfare for the people any more. We'll have lots of welfare for politicians and doctors and businessmen. We'll have welfare so rich people's children can go to nice schools and buy houses. But there won't be any for the rest of us.

It is difficult to listen to anger. If you're expecting gratitude, anger might seem alarming and unfair. The stories about heroes, or the sad tales of suffering, better suit the choices we make about poverty and inequality. The poor will have to wait and heroically endure. They will have to earn whatever help we can provide, and be grateful besides. They will suffer, which is sad, but without suffering, nothing is truly deserved. Their anger leads us somewhere else, somewhere much less comfortable. Instead of asking them to wait, it demands that we listen, and recognise what they know is being taken away. And, having listened, we might ask them what it is that all of us are losing.

Chapter Five

LOSS

Tears

When women cried, they usually cried about their men. In Broadmeadows, Brenda Longwood had spent years setting up local children's programs but was reluctant to be singled out. Uncomfortable with the tape recorder, she asked me to turn it off. 'I don't like that thing being on', she said, 'I'm sorry if that's a problem'. She said that she didn't feel very good that day. She sighed, cried a little, told me not to mind her because she was just a bit upset. It was her unemployed son. He was back home again. He was 36 but he'd never really settled down to anything. After five jobs, each lasting less than a year, and a retraining position he lost as soon as the government subsidy ran out, he had decided he wasn't going to get another job. He'd come home because he didn't know what else to do. 'What do I do?' Brenda asked, 'What do you do with a man who's not even 40 yet and says he's never going to work again? I never thought this would happen. This isn't meant to happen.'

In Inala, Lorraine Goodman and Val Stephens wept over their unemployed sons and grandsons. In 1995, Lorraine's son had been unemployed for five years, and one of her sons-in-law even longer. One of Val's grandsons had a job when he was 15 that lasted until the day before his eighteenth birthday, when he was fired rather than moved up to an adult wage. 'These bloody employers don't give a damn about poor kids', she said.

> We thought that once we'd got our kids educated, it would be all right. Our kids did better than us, by and large.
>
> Our kids were all right, but our grandkids are not. We got our kids through, and we thought 'our problems are over'. But there's no future for our grandkids.

After twenty, thirty or forty years of hard work, the fathers and mothers of Inala, Broadmeadows and Mount Druitt were bewildered. They had pinned their hopes on the expectation that if you sacrificed and made sure your children stayed in school, they would have an easier life than you did. Now, they said, 'The ladder has been pulled away. We're still stuck at the bottom and there's no way up for our kids.' They'd helped their children 'over the hurdles' and 'through the trapdoor' only to see their grandchildren fall back down again. They didn't know what they had done wrong.

It wasn't just the young. In a Mount Druitt health centre, Liz Avenel and Kylie Jones ran a support group for agoraphobic men. It was their fastest growing service, and they'd had so many inquiries that a second group had just started. Some of the men were young and had never worked, but there were others in their forties and fifties who had been made redundant or lived on sickness benefits. Some had lost their jobs – and all of their entitlements – when companies collapsed. Most were now living alone because their wives or partners had moved on. The group began as a meeting place for long-term unemployed men but the first members brought along one mate and then another. There were men who had signed up for training courses but didn't go, because to be trained with no prospect of ever getting a real job was demoralising; men who didn't attend interviews, fearing another rejection or another cynical offer of temporary work until the government subsidy ended. As Liz pointed out, most of them had gradually become too depressed to leave their homes. They 'felt they had no place in the world any more'; a man without a job has nowhere to go and nothing important to do.

People were angry about what they saw as a forgotten problem. They heard politicians talking about acceptable levels of unemployment – 6 or 7 per cent – with little thought for what that meant in suburbs where adult unemployment was double that and unemployed teenagers easily outnumbered those with work. They were angry, too, that the people who should be speaking for them no longer knew how. Stan, a retired meat worker and unionist from Broadmeadows, showed me a news clipping he'd kept. In the late 1980s, a federal Labor minister had called people without jobs 'unwillingly disengaged from active participation in the paid workforce'. 'Clever words', he snorted, 'for what a real Labor man would call being bloody unemployed. He should be ashamed.' Other people were afraid because it seemed those outside were not concerned and not ashamed any more. Mass unemployment – the unemployment of their husbands, their sons and their brothers – was no longer a shared tragedy. It was a necessary, if unfortunate, adjustment.

In Inala and Mount Druitt, people pointed out streets in which there were two or three dozen unemployed men and only one or two still working. A social worker in Broadmeadows told me about a street of fifteen houses, all with men at home, some with fathers and sons both out of work; 'They never go anywhere [and] don't know about each other', she said, 'so they suffer in silence'.

Around the edges, and in unexpected places, there were glimpses of different ways of being a man. If a new man was emerging in Australia in the middle of the 1990s, he wasn't sipping a café latte in Brisbane's West End, or considering his stock options in Sydney's Balmain, he was out in Banksia Gardens or Bidwill or Inala, out where every man used to work and where many men now didn't. He was trying to be a good father, sometimes on his own. He was volunteering at the neighbourhood centre or helping old folks with their gardens. Yet few could find solace in such slim possibilities. Instead, they mourned for lost men, a few to suicide or drugs or booze, most to the weight of a blame they had gradually turned upon themselves.

Measures

What happened in these suburbs is part of a larger story about an economy that no longer produces enough jobs for all of those who want them. Restructuring and reorganisation have wiped out many full-time and secure jobs, especially for the untrained, the young, and men aged in their forties and fifties. In a way, it is misleading to talk about job growth in Australia since the 1980s. It is more accurate to talk about job replacement: full-time by part-time, secure by insecure, long-term by short-term and casual, manual by non-manual, producing by selling, unqualified by over-qualified, public by private.[1]

Workers who lived in low-income outer suburbs were among the chief losers from these changes. Few had more than a trade qualification or high school certificate, and more than half didn't even have that. Often trained to carry out one routine task, they were ill-prepared to compete in the more demanding labour markets into which they were cast. They were car assembly workers, machine knitters in textile factories, industrial painters, electrical equipment assemblers and toolmakers. Or they were carpenters, plumbers and bricklayers, victims of one too many busts in the building trade. By the middle of the 1990s, as cutbacks bit into public services, they were being joined in unemployment by those who had falsely believed that public employment would be secure: former station guards and railway hands, Telecom linesmen, school assistants, mailroom attendants, porters, hospital cleaners and labourers for the boards of works, the water authorities and the electricity and gas departments.

Job loss didn't happen all at once. These suburbs endured more than two decades of recession, punctuated by sharper bouts of job losses. The labour market for teenagers collapsed in the middle of the 1970s. For adult men, especially in manufacturing, and for women in textile and shoe factories, tariff cuts and restructuring created a wave of job losses during the 1980s. In the 1990s came further retrenchments from struggling industries and cuts in public services. In what became an increasingly familiar process, rising unemployment brought a range of other problems, including the breaking of job networks through which people helped their relatives, friends and especially children find work.

A researcher for Melbourne's Northern Region Commission offered this apt description:

> I often say that as a region we probably could have coped with the recession; we could have coped with the recession and restructuring, perhaps, but throw tariff reform on top of that and you've got a triple whammy. A double whammy is enough. You can bounce back after two, but the third one is what has really hit us.

Hers was a common motif: a 'triple whammy', 'blow after blow'. Each recession had been more grinding than the last and took longer to loosen its grip. Each had doubled the official unemployment rate and increased the numbers of long-term unemployed. Each recovery had been less effective in whittling that local unemployment away. Male breadwinners, especially, were losing their jobs and finding it harder and harder to get another. As a retrenched factory worker in Mount Druitt said, 'It was like we had recessions and then everyone else got out of it and we didn't. So the next recession comes along and, you know, great, whoopee, we're still in the last one.'

Inala, Broadmeadows and Mount Druitt were hit by two forces. The first was a process of downturn and restructuring that detached economic growth from the creation of secure, well-paying jobs. The second was the stricter targeting of public rental housing, especially from the mid-1970s. More and more families without earners were being moved into disadvantaged neighbourhoods at precisely the time that work opportunities in those areas were already shrinking. Rising rates of divorce added a greater number of sole parents, for whom the job market has always been very unfriendly. Means testing and market rents forced out many families with a worker. Public housing estates built for low-income workers filled up with people who used to work or who found paid work difficult to get and to keep.

The transition from working to workless suburbs occurred in less than twenty years. In 1991 and again in 1996, the Australian census recorded unemployment rates in Broadmeadows of 11 per cent for men and 7 per cent for women; in 1971, they were 1 per cent and 0.7 per cent respectively. Unemployment rates tell only part of the story, of course; it is also important to examine the proportion of working-age people who are not even seeking work. Excluding full-time students, who remain a relatively small group in these areas, this gives a rough measure of how many people were falling out of the labour market altogether. Of the men aged between 20 and 64 in Broadmeadows in 1971, for instance, 6 per cent did not participate in the labour force; by 1991 that proportion had increased to 16 per cent and in 1996 it had reached 23 per cent. In all, therefore, more than one-third of the working-age men in Broadmeadows in 1996 were unemployed or were no longer even looking for work, and fewer than half worked in a full-time job.[2]

Broadmeadows was actually the least affected of the three suburbs. It is closer to major factory areas, including new industrial estates developed in the 1980s and 1990s, and to Melbourne Airport, and also nearer to the central city's job opportunities than Mount Druitt. In western Sydney there were concerted efforts to bring in more investment, and Blacktown City Council tried to lure companies into business parks and factory estates. But there were a lot of unemployed people in western Sydney, and these efforts did little to dent unemployment rates in the most affected localities. In Inala, meanwhile, the factories and the jobs that were meant to follow the suburbs out towards Ipswich never really arrived.

In Mount Druitt the picture was bleak: in 1991, 15 per cent of the men aged between 20 and 64 were unemployed and another 18 per cent were not seeking work. Five years later, 12 per cent were unemployed but a further 29 per cent were no longer in the labour force, and only 45 per cent worked full-time. Inala's situation was even more serious. In 1971, the census showed that just 1.5 per cent of Inala's adult men were unemployed. By 1976 the rate had increased to 5 per cent. By 1986, after the recession of the early 1980s, it had tripled to 16 per cent. And there it stuck, edging upwards to 18 per cent by 1991 before falling to 14 per cent in 1996. At the height of the recession in March 1993, according to the coordinator of a Skillshare program in nearby Darra, Inala's real adult male unemployment rate was 27 per cent, and its youth unemployment rate about 60 per cent. If we examine the non-participation rate among working-age men, the situation is bleaker still: 52 per cent of them were either unemployed or no longer seeking work in 1996. In other words, every second man in Inala did not have a job, while only one man in three worked full-time.

Among women, steadily increasing participation in paid work has fundamentally reshaped life in most Australian suburbs and towns, but in the disadvantaged outer suburbs of the major cities, women's participation in paid work has actually fallen since the 1970s. In Broadmeadows, for instance, 42 per cent of women aged over 15 worked for wages in 1971, a proportion that fell to 39 per cent by 1991. In Inala, 40 per cent of adult women worked in 1971, compared to only 28 per cent in 1996. One 1995 study pointed out that female earnings were an increasingly important component of household income in the poorest Australian neighbourhoods. This was not, however, because women were working and earning more but because male earnings had fallen so much.[3]

The extent of job loss in these suburbs certainly placed them among the most badly affected areas in the nation. The dimensions of the problem were even greater in some neighbourhoods. Workers and residents described particular estates as 'unemployment central' or 'dole city'. In 1991, when the adult male unemployment rate for all of Broadmeadows was 11 per cent, it was 17 per cent in Dallas and Meadow Heights, and 15 per cent in the older parts of Broadmeadows built in the 1950s. In one Broadmeadows estate, a neighbourhood worker did a survey in the early 1990s and found that only seven of 160 households contained someone earning a wage. In Mount Druitt's Bidwill in 1996, only one-third of the men had a full-time job, and one in six was unemployed.

By then, neighbourhoods such as these were being described as 'underclass areas' or even 'ghettos'. In 1995, economists Bob Gregory and Boyd Hunter concluded that 'the economic distance between Australians from different parts of the city widened to an extraordinary degree' between 1976 and 1991. The most dramatic indicator was the doubling of the income gap between households in the poorest and richest areas of the cities, the product of both steep falls in the poorest areas and rising incomes in the richest. Their speculation that poor neighbourhoods 'may be developing their own pathologies' was clumsy, but their work provided an important guide to the phenomenon of growing inequality.[4]

Boyd Hunter generously shared with me some further findings, which identified small collection districts used by the census that had become particularly disadvantaged in terms of unemployment and income. For 1976, he found only six: two were in north-west Tasmania, and the others were in Newcastle, inner-urban Melbourne, Ipswich and Queensland's Gold Coast. By 1981, there were sixteen such areas, including neighbourhoods in Adelaide's northern suburbs and south-eastern Perth. In 1986 sixty-one were identified, and Bidwill made the list for the first time. Five years later, in 1991, the number had grown to ninety-three: Bidwill was still there, along with the adjoining estate of Shalvey and five small neighbourhoods in Inala.

These figures show that Inala and Mount Druitt, in particular, have become impoverished. Some parts of these suburbs have been made into poor places. Thirty years ago their rates of unemployment were generally lower than in other suburbs. Their residents were not well-off, but they were mostly working. Children left school earlier and with fewer qualifications than elsewhere but they left to go into apprenticeships, nursing, the police force, the army, public employment or junior positions that led somewhere. The single most crucial factor in the recent history of these suburbs is the disappearance of the kinds of blue-collar and public service jobs that once sustained them.

It seems strange, in a way, to have to insist that entrenched unemployment was a product of economic changes and decisions over which working men and women had no control. Or that the people of Broadmeadows, Inala and Mount Druitt were right when they argued that unemployment was their single largest problem. They were right because they knew and because they lived with the consequences. They knew that you wouldn't see a lot of men in the streets. You might even think they'd disappeared. They were there but they were sitting at home, waiting to work again. Some of those men knew that would never happen because at 40 or 45 they were too old. They would tell you, and tell you quietly and sadly, that they had failed their families. These were the men who were paying the price of economic change, in blasted dreams.

The lost world

Work wasn't just an issue for men. There were unemployed women too; women who wanted to work but were not officially registered as unemployed and women who took poorly paid part-time jobs because they wanted to be at home with their children or because there was no affordable childcare. Meanwhile, in some of the newer estates of Broadmeadows and Mount Druitt other people were working too much. To pay the high mortgage interest rates of the 1990s, some wives were working full-time or in two part-time jobs, and some husbands were working 60 and even 70 hours a week. If wives were at home with babies and young children there was little choice but for men to work all the time. One Broadmeadows mother with three children, herself working 25 hours a week, said, 'The kids just never see him. He comes in from his day job, goes out to do his night watchman job, and he's away all weekend as well. I suppose it will be worth it down the track.'

In other families, teenagers and young adults were working to help their parents and, perhaps, save a little money for themselves. According to social workers in these newer estates, some migrant families were crowding parents, children and grandchildren – perhaps ten or fifteen people – into one house to maximise the family's income. They were also seeing a dramatic rise in outworking:

> There is a lot of outworking going on, particularly in the ethnic communities. It's been the Greek and Italian communities, but now the Vietnamese and a few others: the women are at home, looking after their kids, but they're also doing a lot of outwork. That could be fourteen-hour shifts at the sewing machine, you know, doing simple tasks, no award conditions. They're ripped off left, right and centre, and [there's] no real provision for complaints or anything like that.

Unemployed women, exploited clothing workers in their garages and exhausted mortgagees could have been a little disgruntled with the attention being paid to jobless men. Yet with very few exceptions, when asked to nominate the single most difficult problem in their suburb, everyone pointed to men's unemployment. The story people wanted to tell was in part about jobs, but it was also about a disappearing world, in which ordinary families did well because men could get and keep decent, full-time and secure work. Those who were still part of that world, however hard pressed they felt, stressed the sufferings of others. And this was something to be feared all the time: working men and women 'touched wood', said 'There but for the grace of God', and reminded each other of a nephew or a brother who didn't have a job.

What everyone wanted to emphasise was the terrible toll that unemployment was taking on men who could never have expected to become so 'useless'. They recognised a profound sense of loss and the unravelling of expectations. Something was being taken away from men that could not easily be replaced. Women had other duties and other ways of contributing. They saw themselves as more flexible, more able to adapt to the mix of paid and unpaid work and to the part-time and casual jobs that were available. But that wasn't for men. Their world was work, and without work you couldn't really be a man.[5]

Male unemployment meant different things to different generations. For older people, born in the 1920s and 1930s, unemployment was something that had plagued their fathers and was now afflicting their grandsons. They talked about wheels turning full circle and bad times coming back; some were determined to talk about 'the next Great Depression'. A few older men had retired early but most had enjoyed steady jobs all their adult lives, something they knew set them apart from the generation that had come before. They had been good providers, the men their fathers often could not be. They had been able to save money, keep their children in school, even buy a home. Their wives, they told me, hadn't had to go to work or clean rich people's houses or beg from charities.

For these now elderly men, success meant giving your children the chances you didn't have:

> I actually left school at 13 and a half, because my birthday is in March and the school year basically ended in November, so I was out working at 13 and a half. But I was determined that wasn't going to happen with my children. Fortunately, I had a pretty good job … and I was able to keep them there. If the boy had gone on to HSC too I'd have kept him there. But the two girls went to HSC.
>
> I think this applied to the large majority of families around this way: they were determined their kids were going to get a better break than they did.

They talked about 'the work I did so my kids wouldn't have to', or told me that they 'dug ditches but what kept me going was knowing that my boy wouldn't follow me there'.

This older generation was distressed by the return of insecurities they had hoped never to see again. It was very difficult to listen to people who had grown up in real hardship in the inner suburbs of Melbourne or Brisbane, or on dirt-poor farms in New South Wales and Queensland, when they talked about 'the Depression coming back'. It meant something to them it could never mean to me. Their tears were about now, but they came from a long time ago.

Men in their thirties, forties and fifties were bewildered. To become a man in Mount Druitt, Inala or Broadmeadows in 1955 or 1965 meant becoming a full-time worker in a steady job with decent wages. It meant having a trade, or starting at the bottom and working your way up, and it meant being a good provider. All of the other things you wanted to be – a good husband and father or a good mate – depended upon your ability to work. Work was your base, your everyday, the most important thing you did. Without it, as the wife of an unemployed man aged 35 said, 'he felt that he wasn't a man; he wasn't part of the family any more'.

It is impossible to overstate the importance these men continued to place on being a good provider. The expectations they learned in the 1950s and 1960s remained very powerful, and were just as strong among their wives. A man had the single largest responsibility for bringing money into the home. Indeed, the crisis of working-class manhood in the mid-1990s extended beyond the unemployed to encompass those who were working but not earning enough, those who were working longer hours or two jobs in order to remain good providers, and those who feared their days as a provider might be numbered. Job insecurity or low wages were as threatening to good husbands and fathers as unemployment. As Carol Parker put it, a man 'has to bring in enough to support a family, not just take a job'; when her retrenched husband was forced to take a casual position, 'his self-esteem went down the drain … $250 a week is very degrading for a man who used to bring home $500. He felt he wasn't doing enough any more.'

Taking work could create its own problems. It might mean sacrificing a lot of other benefits and concessions, for schools and doctors, as well as the asthma medicines it seemed almost every family I visited had on their kitchen counter. Once he got a job, Graeme Kingston found himself paying a higher rent to the Housing Commission than his neighbours paid to private landlords:

> It was leaving me with no money because after I'd bought the food and paid the rent that was virtually it, I was wiped out. So then I lost my job, and I was on social security for a little while, and I found I was much better off than when I worked. I had more money than when I worked, which is strange. You'd think it would be the other way around, wouldn't you?

Darren Domenico, a storeman, was fearful he might receive a pay rise. If he did, he would lose his family income supplement, and it would be better, in a financial sense, for him to leave his job and go back on unemployment benefit.

Such issues have registered in public consciousness, in the use of such terms as 'the working poor', or in the conviction that welfare creates too many disincentives to paid employment.[6] But few of these men concluded that it was better not to work. Paid work brought all kinds of rewards to the hopeful provider, not least an escape from a hated welfare system. The importance of work for men, even if that work was only a little more remunerative than the dole, was unquestioned. Yet Graeme, Darren and men like them were trapped in a difficult position: on the one hand, the labour market in which they competed could not provide them with what they defined as a proper job. On the other hand, the welfare system was being re-oriented around their obligation to work, regardless of how insecure or low-paid that job might be. Because low-paid jobs often brought in less real income than the dole, and wiped out other benefits as well, men were caught between their self-esteem and their desire to provide the best income they could. One solution, of course, was to attempt to remain on benefits and earn 'on the side', but everyone knew about its dangers and no one thought it was the right thing to do.

Their real problem was low wages and the insecurity of the jobs they could get. For people caught in so-called welfare traps, one approach is to either coax or force them into jobs, even low-paid and intermittent ones. Certainly, it is sensible to change taxation levels and allow people on low wages to earn more without losing other benefits. But low-income earners themselves went a little further: they wanted an increase in wages and a guarantee of full-time and secure work, so the incentive to earn would not be undermined by the futility of never getting ahead. Most of all, as Darren argued, 'We're meant to be keeping our families, you know, not just working. It needs more than just shit wages and a shit job.'

The destruction of the link between manliness and providing among these working-class men is a profound problem, and is confirmed in every study of the women and men who live with this crisis. British writer Beatrix Campbell, for instance, concluded that 'men's tragedy is that unemployment makes them feel unmanned'.[7] One of the most sensitive Australian studies, written by Jenny Trethewey in 1989, also captured men's sense of demoralisation. And the women in Trethewey's study also argued that a better future hinged upon men's ability to find work.[8] The women to whom I listened said that their ability to scrimp and save, to persevere against the odds, could enhance their self-esteem and give them a reason for struggling on. Being retrenched, on the other hand, shattered men's sense of moving through life and their sense of purpose. Certainly, their commitment to one path was in part an outcome of their privileges in the labour market, including the fact that they were invariably able to earn more than women. Yet listening to those women and men means recognising that joblessness was stripping men, especially if they were married and had children, of the most important and, in some ways, the only means they had of being a successful man.

Men didn't talk much about these feelings and I didn't press them. It seemed intrusive and insensitive to come back to their sense of loss and shame and ask for elaboration. Women said more about what they saw in their husbands and sons, brothers and neighbours, so I relied on them for details:

Liz: It has to be horrific for the men, because they can't support their families how they want to. The point is the work. The whole thing is work. And you don't realise it, unless you've been through it.

They feel very degraded and very down about being unemployed … Unless they're involved in the sporting things, the job gives them the confidence and the community activities. You lose the job, you lose that support and that communication, every day. You get up in the morning, and what do you do?

For some, the pain of unemployment was very close:

Jean: Well, I have a son who is 30 next month, and he's come to the conclusion that he will never work again. At 30. He's given up. I said to him on Sunday, 'Have you been looking for work?' He said, 'No. Why? There's nothing out there.' I knew [another man] who was retrenched at the age of 44, and he also came to the conclusion that he would never work again. It's horrible.

Carol: My husband had always driven a crane. He had only been trained for two years and he hadn't been unemployed in his life. His self-esteem went down the drain. It was terrible because they think that they're never going to work [again].

I had the part-time job, and I used to come home of an afternoon and he's be laying on the floor that depressed. He would just go to sleep, he was that depressed.

It was really hard, to see a man that age asleep at half past three in the afternoon. He was really depressed. That's terrible. It breaks your heart to see a man who's brought home that amount of money laying on the floor doing nothing. He didn't feel like he wanted to do anything either, because he was depressed.

The worst thing was, he felt like he was letting *me* down. That was the worst thing.

Another woman, working and in her forties, talked a little about her fears for her own sons. She stopped for a minute. I thought she was wondering how to generalise or explain her point, but then I realised she was wondering whether or not to press on. I think she wasn't sure if she could avoid crying. It all came out in a rush:

> My husband's not working, and I'm supporting him. He's going downhill, I can tell you. He's getting all these health problems. I don't want my husband to die, I don't want him to leave me. But he will if this doesn't stop, if he can't get a job.

Nicholas Browne began working at a Mount Druitt welfare centre in 1986. He hadn't expected to need his skills in grief counselling:

> We had people coming in here who were in their early or middle forties who had never been unemployed in their life. And they were totally bewildered, overwhelmed, with an absolute sense of loss. On many, many occasions, when I was doing some welfare work, so many males in that age group who were unemployed for the first time spoke about the feeling of uselessness and frustration. They had no direction, and they couldn't possibly see a way of surviving, and suicide seemed a very viable option to them.
>
> There were some suicides around here. Absolutely.

Most men, though, seemed to have entered a process of gradual withdrawal; hopes fading, they blamed themselves and drifted into a kind of numbed resignation. Losing their reason for being outside – going to or coming from work – they retreated into the home. There was little to be enjoyably shared with others in feelings of inadequacy. They ventured out sometimes, for company and diversion at the pub or the TAB, 'trying', as one Bidwill worker put it, 'to find a place for themselves'.

Men's unemployment also created powerful dilemmas for women. They recognised that the person they called the 'old man' had his disadvantages, not least a wife's dependence on his earnings. To become a woman, when that almost always meant becoming a wife and then a mother, had its pitfalls. You had a man to look after, and women were quick to point out that men sometimes took more looking after than children. But what do you do when your man doesn't work? Do you encourage him to change and become a different kind of man? How do you protect him, try and strengthen him against such a crisis, and somehow make ends meet?

Women were struggling to find answers to those questions. In a couple of the conversations I had with groups there was much laughter – a laughter of momentary relief and distraction, I think – about women's strength and men's weakness: 'Oh, women are the tougher sex. Of course we are'. Yet they were sometimes unsure if they could be tough enough. And I think they were also frustrated: 'They just don't know what to do, you know. It's hard to know what they want.' As experienced social workers noticed, women faced a delicate task, juggling their partner's self-esteem against the family's needs:

> One of the other things we've noticed with some of these women whose husbands have been out of work now for twelve months or so, [is that] they've been so frustrated by their husbands fairly quickly deciding that they have no options and can't do anything about it, that they have gone out and found some part-time job. In some cases they've never worked before. That, of course, just adds to the male feeling absolutely useless.

Women cared for and suffered with their men, but they also wanted men to take action, to do something:

> I've actually got a couple of friends whose husbands are out of work. And they're still young men. I mean, the 40-year-old who's been retrenched has still got another twenty good years of work in him, yet nobody will employ him because of his age. It's sad. And you see these men just vegetate, just lose their self-esteem, and they don't want to get up in the morning. They just sit around like couch potatoes and do nothing. It's very sad.
>
> The other thing I've heard, too, from the women's point of view, is that they hate having them around, you know, because they're so miserable. They can't get them to do anything, they don't talk, they don't do anything. I can understand that; your self-esteem just goes out of the window. They're not worth anything, they can't go out and work and 'bring the bread home', so to speak.

The problem, of course, was that 'doing something', for the men at least, almost always meant trying to find a job. And if you couldn't, the feelings of failure just kept mounting. In Mount Druitt, Paul Sammler noticed something similar at the job centre:

> I see a lot more unemployed men whose wives are working. They form a little 'boys' club' in the group that I have and talk about it, and yes, it's an ego problem, a status problem, the need to make their contribution to society. A lot of them turn their hand to volunteer work for local organisations, which is good. But there's still that desire to be a breadwinner and bring in enough to support their family, not just take a job.

Julie Laidlaw, of the Mount Druitt Women's Activities and Self-Help House, was very conscious of the need to help unemployed men. Just as important, though, was the attempt to help local women handle their own dilemmas:

> A lot of the time what's happening is that women are finding ways of changing which accommodate men's fears. In one sense that's probably a wise thing to do, but in another sense it's like we're always feeding into men's needs all the time, and that is really irritating and frustrating, to find that you have to do that.

There was a lot of tension, even irritation. Some women had walked away. At the Broadmeadows Women's Community House, the workers saw a lot of the stresses, and said, 'There's often a lot of pressure put on women to drop everything now that the husband is at home, as if it's almost like the home is the only place he has control over any more'. Yet for the most part it seemed to me that women attended to the problems of men as best they could. In the neighbourhood houses and the community centres, programs set up for women found a place for a man or two, or someone would work an extra four hours a week – unpaid – to run a group for young fathers alongside the one for young mothers.

There were flashes of anger, and explosions that other people weren't meant to see. On the bad days, almost every person seen by a social worker had a story of violence from the night before, and it might seem like every family 'can't take the pressure of poverty, and so they break up over the pressure of fighting over whether they can afford even a basic habit like smoking'. Constant worries about money fuelled the tensions between men who couldn't find work and women who could and, as April Stewart put it, some women 'certainly let the men know that this is what they've been forced to do because he can't provide. It's a two-edged sword.' Failed providers might lash out, but that didn't make them good men. There was no unbending road from unemployment to violence, and workers were as likely to be impressed by the ability of men and women to defuse the frustration and the pain.

The most difficult issue, it seemed to me, was how hard it was for men to think about other ways of being men, to find other tasks around which they could build a sense of capacity and purpose. As women largely managed the family's business, men were often inexperienced in the world outside of work. So, even if a man was unemployed and his wife was working, it was she and not he who sought emergency relief or financial support and counselling: 'the females are … the ones who do all the business … [but] then again, I suppose, if he is asking for a food voucher or for help, he's not a man any more, you know. A lot of men still feel that way.'

Neighbourhood activities 'just are not men's business', said one Inala community worker. While teenagers and those past retirement age might use recreational or health services, working-age men wanted work or job training. Their involvement in agencies usually involved something akin to the tasks they did at home: driving the community bus, gardening, doing carpentry or odd jobs at the neighbourhood house, building toys at the local school, walking groups of children to and from the childcare centre, or acting as an informal security guard for a community house. Workers were noticing a few more men volunteering to help, sometimes after hanging around for a few weeks or months. At home, some women reported signs of change: men doing home repairs, or cleaning or gardening they defined as 'heavy', though not cooking or washing. Certainly, if women were ill, men did all manner of uncustomary work. Retired men, too, seemed more comfortable performing domestic tasks, largely because they had already fulfilled the tasks of providing. No studies of unemployment, however, have found any great resort to or support for 'swapping' roles, among women or men.[9]

Women were certainly happy to see some changes in men. Yet manhood and womanhood were still based, for most, on notions of what men and women were good at, especially in a situation of persistent low income and insecurity. The great importance invested in both the male provider and the capable mother stemmed not from a rigid attachment to old-fashioned ideas about gender but from lived experience and a clear-eyed assessment of the risks of change. Women saw themselves as stronger, as better managers, as much more able to juggle the precarious balance between sacrifice and spending. Their hilarity at the thought of a man doing the shopping – 'imagine what he'd bring home, it'd be all lollies and coke and chips' – or handling the family's business at a welfare agency was a hard-edged humour about the things men didn't understand. 'I don't have time to train my husband', Mira said, to general agreement from her neighbours. 'It's hard enough getting by without having to take that on as well. Men shouldn't be in the house all day. They're meant to be at work.'

As far as I could tell, parenting was the one task open to greater adjustment. Several middle-aged women talked with pleasure about increased male contact with children as a consequence of their partner's unemployment, or as something they saw among their sons. Yet they sensed dangers here as well. Some had misgivings about men's handling of children: 'You know how it is with a man, and no offence, love, but he's either giving them sweets or hitting them'. Others feared that if men invested everything in being a good father they risked another kind of failure because of their inability to really help:

> Those who are unemployed, and really battling, who are not in connection with anything tangible about how the workplace is changing, except they know that their job doesn't exist anymore, what advice do they give to their kids?
>
> The world they've known is disappearing, so how do they talk about something they don't know? How can they encourage and support kids to stay at school when they didn't stay at school, and don't even know what this Year Twelve is all about?

Still, to be a good father is something, and welfare workers sometimes glimpsed a kind of desperation in that desire. To not work, and not have children, was to be a nobody. Those men, long-time Bidwill resident Julie said, 'are up the pub, because they have to kill the pain some way'. A few men talked about other ways of fulfilling their duties as a provider and father: undeclared cash work, a bit of drug cultivation or dealing, even the odd bit of thieving. Such illegal trade had the same ends as legal work; as local community police in both Inala and Mount Druitt told me, it was no coincidence that minor drug dealing and petty theft escalated dramatically in the week before Christmas, and again in late January when children needed clothes and books for school.

Yet this is hardly what anyone thought manhood should be. Men didn't always want to articulate their fears, though the women who knew them had more to say. Like Marianne Carr, they could recognise the struggle to find the words:

> I think that's the other thing that's very sad in working-class life, that the men are much more confined. If we talk about liberation per se, the thing that I'm discovering now is that my heart goes out to men, you know. When are men going to do something for themselves? Like, feminism to me was '*there's* the words, *that's* what I think, they've got the words, this is exciting, I understand that'. When are the men going to find the words? They already understand it. They know. I mean, if you talk to my husband, he knows he's been ground down, he knows that. What kind of shitty life is that for forty years, to leave at six o'clock in the morning and get home at seven o'clock? His whole rationale for that was, 'I've got a family to support'.

Men didn't have the words, at least not the words to lead them out of despair. Their words were still 'provider', 'a decent job' and 'supporting my family'. Those words couldn't easily be spoken when they were about a world that they feared was being taken away; a world, in fact, that many had already lost.

Changing young men

The future of children, especially boys, caused the most sorrow of all. It is difficult to understand that sadness unless you fathom the meaning of children's safety and security for impoverished people. They can take almost anything if it means their children will have a better life. As and when that conviction fades, so hope becomes fear.

Every conversation about children strayed into anxious questions. People told stories about their own children or children they knew, in part to seek confirmation from others that theirs was not an unusual experience.

One of the most common concerned a child – usually a teenage boy, sometimes a younger boy or girl – predicting their own future. This was Geraldine Cannon's story:

> I sat down with my youngest son and I said to him, 'What do you want to do when you leave school?', because he's off to high school next year, and I figured now is the time he should be working out what he wants to do.
>
> He sits there and thinks about it and he goes, 'I'd like to do mechanics, Mum, but by the look of things these days, when I get to 16, 17, I'll be on the dole'.

In Mount Druitt, Darren Domenico talked about his son: 'I mean, my eldest son is 13, kicking 14, and most of his friends believe they will never work. They'll leave school and go on the dole.'

Inala's Liz Hinkler heard the same from an even younger child:

> I've still got a child at school, in Year Five. I was absolutely shocked by this. Last week I was playing a game on the computer after school, and she said, 'Can I play the game?', and I said 'Get your own computer. You're not taking my game.' (*Laughs*) 'When you get a job, you get your own computer'.
>
> And she said 'I'm not going to get a job'. Her father, myself, everybody, come from working backgrounds, and it was just devastating to hear that.

The sufferings of your own unemployed children and grandchildren were more private. There didn't seem to be a ready-made script. You're not supposed to be worrying over sons in their twenties and thirties. You're meant to talk about them as fathers and workers, not as men who can't be men, in their eyes and maybe in yours. The conflicts that colour tales of irascible teenagers don't have a place in stories about adult sons. Joy Round had three unemployed sons, all of whom eventually found work:

> At one stage, the three of them were unemployed, and … it created so much tension in the house, I couldn't believe it at the time. After a while, you could see them getting really, you know, low self-esteem, depressed, though they'd never admit that. They felt like giving up. They'd say, 'How come he got it and I didn't? What's wrong with me? Why couldn't I get the job?', and things like that.

We're just a working-class family, my husband's a boiler attendant, and we did the best we could. We sent them to Catholic school, and I just thought 'all that money. What if they never get a job.' I really thought that that could happen, and I think it does happen now.

And I was thinking, at that time, how hard it is for one-parent families. People that were then as well-off as we were, we could have the boys at home and still support them and help them with getting the jobs, you know, buying them clothes and things like that. But other parents might not have been able to do as much as we did.

Casting around for faith, most parents still seized upon education. Like Val Stephens in Inala, people remembered everything they'd done for their schools:

We have always realised the value of education to our kids. You'd see us up here at the local shopping centre raffling chooks, and a lot of stuff that we made ourselves. If it didn't move, we raffled it.

A day later, and two streets away, Beth and Ros joked:

Beth: We made toys to sell, and sewing. And bloody lamingtons, always bloody lamingtons. (*Laughing*) I wonder if they have to make lamingtons at Brisbane Grammar?

Ros: Would they know how?

Teachers described the anxieties of uncertain expectations: parents, one said, 'want their children to learn, they want their children, basically, to do well, but there's no definition of what "well" is, other than probably better than they did, more than they did'. April Stewart, returning to Mount Druitt after several years, argued that the reliance on education had become even stronger:

April: I've also noticed that when people are relating to you the sadness of their life and their life story, and they have children, they then will say, 'but I want something better for my children'.

It's something that I hadn't noticed before. People were so busy surviving that they didn't have time to look to the future. They had to survive in the here and now. But I have noticed that people will come here from all parts of Mount Druitt, and outside Mount Druitt as well, and they will say, 'Well, I've had such a terrible life, but what I don't want is for my children to have this'.

Mark: And what do they see as the way to achieve that?

April: Education. The old way, you know ... They're not necessarily saying, 'I want my children to leave this area'; they're saying 'I want my child to be better-educated'.

So they think education will make it different. I mean, everything is in this big education 'ball'. Everything will be better. This is the panacea.

In Broadmeadows, the coordinator at CARE spoke about the difficulties of maintaining hope: 'I think a lot of people don't talk about it, don't permit themselves to think about it, other than think "if I give the kids a better education than I got, it *must* mean something". It breaks your heart.'

For all the bravado, there was a terrible anxiety among these parents and grandparents. If hard work hadn't paid off, perhaps it was their fault. They swung between blaming the government, employers or the schools, and blaming themselves. Geraldine and Rhonda agreed, 'We gave our children too much. I think it was just a rebound from having not a deprived childhood, but a childhood where things just weren't available, you just didn't have them.' Another mother said, 'We parents thought that they would be all right, that they wouldn't need to know how to struggle. I think it was a mistake, because they still need to know what to do.' In Inala, Audrey, now in her fifties, finished cataloguing her children's unstable lives and said, 'I have a real regret about that'. I asked her what it was, and she thought for a few moments. 'I didn't teach them how to be poor. That sounds terrible, doesn't it?' I asked her what she meant:

> Oh, [I] didn't teach them how to make do with whatever food you could find, didn't tell them to hand down clothes, you know, the things you have to do when you don't have any money. I didn't think they'd need to know. Well, I hoped they wouldn't anyhow. I guess I was wrong. I should have known better.

They thought the world had changed. They thought poverty wouldn't haunt them again. And they forgot to teach their sons and daughters how to be poor.

People working with local youth all noticed 'a sort of collective depression'. As one experienced worker put it, there was 'a feeling of hopelessness at the age of 20' and a 'feeling of no prospect of ever becoming a good earner, therefore not being able to have a family [or] own a house'. In the middle of the 1990s most workers could point to households containing two or even three generations of unemployed men. While all argued that young men were demoralised, only a few concluded that unemployment was something being transmitted through families. Most were ambivalent, unsure if they were simply extrapolating from a few cases or seeing a definite and troubling change. Those with a lot of experience didn't want to describe the situation in stark terms. It was fluid and changing:

> It's quite normal to be unemployed, whereas in their parents' generation, if you're unemployed you're a bludger. There's a lot of conflict in the people I work with on that issue alone. There's also issues about whether you should marry someone or live with them. It's very confusing. That's the message. They know right and wrong, but they don't who to believe, because there's so much information out there. They just don't know the path.

I don't think this is a simple problem, and we should be wary of easy conclusions. The most searching investigation into the experiences of young working-class people in Australia, by sociologist Kevin McDonald, stresses powerful tensions and dilemmas. McDonald argues that there has been a profound rupture in the nature of identity; youth 'is no longer lived as a project defined in terms of the future, but more as a "condition", no longer associated with images of the future'.[10] He is particularly interested in the struggle to develop solidarity, and argues that the most significant problem was that while the young people he studied felt excluded, they did not know how to turn their exclusion into a conflict with an identifiable foe. They angrily refused to accept their apparent destiny but they were unsure of what to put in its place.

In my conversations with about twenty young unemployed men and women, and a dozen young mothers and fathers who were bringing up children by themselves, there was a mix of anger and uncertainty. They also used stories about heroes and participated in the identification of their communities as unjustly treated. They created strong moral divisions, between good and bad social workers, for instance, or the agencies that helped them and the 'bastards at the DSS', or, as one Inala teenager put it, between real people and 'private school wankers'. Their uncertainty, it seemed to me, was about the journey, not the destination. The problem for the young men, in particular, was not low expectations, but how to find a way forward. They had a future they wanted to reach, but unemployment stood in their path. For the young women, becoming an adult could rely on being competent in a variety of roles, especially as a mother. But for a young man, as one Inala youth worker put it, 'everything is still hinged on his job and the fact that he doesn't have one'.

Even more than their parents, these younger men and women were also acutely conscious of their exclusion. They watched a lot of television, especially soap operas, and while they knew life didn't imitate art for anyone, they also knew the discordance would be greater for them. Fantasies of rescue and love ever after were particularly strong among the young single mothers, according to those who worked with them: there was always 'some knight in shining armour coming to rescue them. Being with a man will make it all better and they'll live happily ever after and stay home and have babies.' I think the young men had their own forlorn dreams. They knew that consuming – fast food, fast cars and a good time – is the fun part of life, the part that makes you attractive and fulfilled and successful. But they also knew that when you're not rich, consuming comes after working, not instead of it. In that way, their problem was similar to the one identified among British working-class children by Carolyn Steedman: unlike their parents and grandparents, they had never learned not to expect anything.[11] They thought they had a right to the things other people have, or at least to the work that means you can afford to buy them.

Certainly, few accepted unemployment as their destiny. Family memories were not that short, and their aspirations for a better life were still tied to an income the dole would never provide. The unemployed teenagers at a job club in Mount Druitt wanted to get a car and some money of their own, and as quickly as possible. Most saw a good future as getting 'hitched' and having a nice house. And, like most young people, they faced the fact that getting the car and the house meant working. They joked about robbing banks and doing drug deals but they knew people like them had to work.

Without work, many faced being trapped in a kind of prolonged adolescence, an uneasy half-life between childhood and manhood in which some adult responsibilities and freedoms could be grasped, while others – especially economic independence – could not. These young men did get work now and then, but it rarely lasted beyond the end of the government subsidy. At 18, some had been told they were too old to get work because their wages would be too high. Some were or were about to become fathers. Some had a car, though only a few could afford to register it and keep it on the road. They lived with a series of women: their mothers, girlfriends, partners, aunts or sisters. They would find it difficult to ever settle down because without a real job they couldn't provide for the family most wanted to have. Even more than their fathers, they were trapped between expectations about men's lives that depended upon them getting decent jobs, and the realities of a labour market that didn't provide those jobs any more.

Of course, there are other ways of being a man, and some were taking them up and trying them out. There were the kinds of 'hyper-masculinities' portrayed by R. W. Connell, including the often suicidal drug culture and the frantic manhood of car theft and police-baiting.[12] Three boys, one perhaps 12 or 13 years old, told me that they had no wish to become adults, and expected to be dead by the time they were 20. But these were not the most common inflections; like the anti-Asian racism described by McDonald, they were sporadic expressions of anger, not a coherent and dysfunctional 'culture'.[13]

The unemployed young men of Inala, Mount Druitt and Broadmeadows were not pathological, and for every would-be street-fighter there were dozens of others trying out more constructive paths, including those who circled around the edges of the parenting groups or shyly asked to join the cooking class. In some of the community centres younger men were running holiday camps for children. At one centre in Inala, a young man had completed two literacy classes and a computer skills program before he finally summoned up the courage to ask if he could help in the kindergarten where his little girl spent each afternoon.

If there is a way to build an independent adult identity without work perhaps it is through fathering, occasionally alone, but normally with a partner. I spoke with a couple of single fathers at a neighbourhood house in Broadmeadows, and other young fathers with partners at groups in Inala and Mount Druitt. Taking the advice of Pam McShane, I also spent time at local shopping centres to watch how the young men spent their time. At

Mount Druitt, I watched one group of ten young men in one of the carparks. Half were playing that game where you try to keep a tennis ball up in the air for as long as you can. They had their cans of coke and their cigarettes. With the group were six toddlers and a couple of smaller babies, one being held, the other being rocked in the pram. Two other young men were watching the toddlers play on the small piece of lawn and making sure they didn't run onto the road. Every few minutes, one would break off from the game to be given a baby or to take his position by the toddlers, and the man he relieved would join the circle of ball-players. One left the game and took a baby, perhaps his, gave it a bottle and rocked it back and forth. If they wanted a smoke they went off to one side, away from the babies. After a while, young women started to come out of Coles and McDonald's, their shifts finished for the day. Each joined the group and greeted her child, and then she, her young man and the child walked off.

I met similar groups of pram-pushing and toddler-tending young men in Inala. It was at once a difficult and a hopeful thing to see. Their tenderness and care was very moving. So was their obvious love for their children. They were doing their very best. They treasured their children in that impossible to deflate way new parents do. Yet what had they really found? A way to be a man? the kind of man they wanted to be? or simply another way to feel frustrated and powerless? Could they be good fathers without being providers? I don't think these are easy questions to answer, and of course their ways of being men would always depend upon decisions made by women. Perhaps these carpark carers were new kinds of men, fathers who took on childcare while their partners worked. But other single or unemployed fathers still said giving their children what they didn't have would be impossible without a job.

Whatever re-inventing of manhood was taking place here, it was taking place in a context of loss. It was being driven by hardship and not by opportunity. Despite the shortcomings of a version of manhood based almost exclusively on providing, and however narrow were the life paths it demanded, the pain of its loss was real enough. To speak to a young unemployed man in these suburbs in the middle of the 1990s was to look with him into an uncertain future. What was unravelling was the only way of being a man he knew. If I asked him about change and what kind of world he wanted he talked about 'real jobs'. He talked about ending the cycle of training for jobs that didn't exist; the training, Matt said, that is basically done for the benefit of 'the people in Canberra who can say "Look what we've done. There's 1 per cent less on the dole. They're all being retrained." And what are we being retrained for? To go back on the dole queue. It's bullshit.'

We need to make work. What these young men said they wanted was a job, a real job that didn't end after three months and that didn't pretend a family can live on little more than the dole. It's fairly straightforward, even if such simple claims lead to all sorts of huff and puff about self-reliance and claims that 'there are plenty of jobs out there'. It's easy to bluster about the crisis of unemployment in Australia, and pretend that the problems lie in the attitudes of the jobless.

Debra Gorman, then working at the Christian Brothers Youth Refuge in Bidwill, provided an effective alternative:

> Society has to be responsible for this. Bandaids aren't doing it. Real solutions, real answers, are expensive.

Real answers, real solutions. Investing in hope and effort. It would make for a very different world. It is a world that can be built, but only by beginning with what the people of Inala, Broadmeadows and Mount Druitt know, and trusting what they say. Joblessness is a major economic and social problem, a criminal waste of resources and talents. Reducing it and banishing it for good should be among our first economic priorities. Yet if the chances of that were slim then, they seem even slimmer now.

Chapter Six

HOPE

The people of Inala, Broadmeadows and Mount Druitt believed, by and large, that they were living in a good country, with riches to share. They believed that other people could only agree that what they suffered was unjust and would be moved to help them find solutions. For all their anger and sense of loss, they were willing to believe that things could be different, and that the world could be transformed. Their capacity for hope, in the midst of hope's apparent destruction, was inspiring.

At the same time, they underestimated the transformations they had achieved themselves and how much their hope rested on the solid foundation of those achievements. Accustomed to defending themselves against stigma and ignorance, their first impulse was defensive. Not without reason: most questions asked about their communities presumed that racism, ethnic conflict or mindless violence were the natural products of disadvantage. Of course, no one can or should deny the fact of tension or that poverty causes terrible conflicts. Yet to listen to the people of these suburbs also means recognising what they had built. Out of shared difficulties had come a vigorous tradition of women's activism. Amid the jostle of ethnic diversity emerged real collaboration. And from both came crucial insights about the most effective architecture for a just and tolerant society. It will seem a striking thing to say that the outlines of a better society might be discerned in Mount Druitt, Inala and Broadmeadows. Yes, these are worlds of rocks and hard places. But they say more about the best of our possibilities than the worst.

Sparks and flashes

There is a hidden history of creativity and imagination, of activism initiated by the residents of these suburbs and nourished by compassionate, careful outsiders who listened to them and, as far as possible, asked them to lead the way. Teachers, social workers, nuns and priests recognised the capacity that was already there, and celebrated the abilities and the imaginativeness of people who were otherwise so easily discarded. If you spend some time in any new place you will find remarkable what the people who live there take for granted. These are the sparks and flashes that I saw, that I wrote about in my notebook, or that I remember now as I think about what to write. They sometimes lay underneath the stories, footnotes to tales of heroes or villains that tell of capacity and achievement.

Take, for example, Broadmeadows High School, where the Year Tens cooked lunch for Prince Charles and Lady Diana in 1985. Impressive stuff for a 'Broady' school, as its then principal laughingly remembered, but it was just one of many victories. He and his staff increased enrolments and retention rates, and provided rooms for adult creative writing classes. They engineered the location of an Adult Migrant English centre on the school grounds and then built a childcare facility. On Saturdays, the Turkish community held a school in the morning and the Vietnamese community held one in the afternoon. He was told by a senior bureaucrat that this would never work because of 'ethnic tensions' in Broadmeadows; the Turkish and Vietnamese teachers, already working out how to combine some of their activities, found that hilarious.

Broadmeadows High won the Victorian Schools Community Award in 1984. The achievement the principal remembered most was the process of distributing the prize of $5,000; this was their money, he insisted, and they should decide how to spend it. So, in a series of democratic meetings, students, teachers and parents decided on the investments they would make. They revelled in the implied trust, and reshaped their school to an ideal they devised. As he said, this was '*their* school, not the Department's school. For better or for worse, it's their school, and if they make a muck of it and learn something in the process, then it can be un-mucked.'

Ownership and trust were a powerful combination in 1980s Broadmeadows, before all the local schools and other organisations succumbed to what local people called 'Kennett's revenge'. By the middle of the 1990s, Broadmeadows' activists seemed more depressed than those in Inala and Mount Druitt. They were, they said, 'keeping their heads down', waiting for the storm to pass. Of course, people hadn't stopped battling, if only, as Brenda told me, 'so bastards like Kennett won't win in the end'. They did their best to protect their precious victories, found ways to qualify for a little federal funding, or went back to raffles and lamington drives. The local women at the Women's Community House and the Dallas Neighbourhood House continued their multicultural groups, while the dozen or so ethnic communities linked to the neighbourhood house at Coolaroo West built a children's adventure playground, with each of the main language groups – Turkish, Hmong, Arabic and Spanish – blending migrant culture with new versions of 'home' in Broadmeadows.

In Mount Druitt, Bidwill Primary School is built like a fortress. Yet it was breaking down its walls, wheedling unemployed parents into running reading programs and organising excursions, trying to overcome their fear of places in which most of them knew only failure and punishment. A few streets away, in Bidwill Community Support, Anne Neilsen was focusing on the people who weren't yet involved in any activity. 'There are times I have sunk with them', she said, but she stayed, and made sure that programs such as the parenting group were led by the people who used them. They'd just run a family camp for sixty people in the Blue Mountains; few of the residents had ever been on any kind of holiday, and many had never been outside Bidwill. It cost the Uniting Church $2,000. It was a great success. But it would never have been funded under government guidelines: it was too unstructured, could not guarantee outcomes, and didn't train people to do anything. In fact, as Anne said, it would have looked suspiciously like spoiling the poor.

Over in Shalvey, the new workers at the community centre talked about the length of time it took to get people involved. They didn't see the amazing rapport they had with the local teenagers, who had gone from smashing windows to tending the garden, running their own pottery classes and making all the centre's leaflets. Mount Druitt was also home to Artswest and Garage Graphix, astutely managed community organisations that brought together craft workers, budding artists and graffiti-prone boys. At the Women's Activities and Self-Help House, the volunteers – mostly single parents – were excited about their work with Aboriginal girls, and their new links with Aboriginal agencies, including the Pittuma Aboriginal Arts,

Craft and Resource Centre. At the time of my visit, the Pittuma volunteers and workers were designing a training scheme for young people, who would soon form a 'junior council' for the local Koori community. 'With that kind of knowledge', locally-raised worker Miriam Frazer said, 'we might start putting things right'.

In Inala, I spent an afternoon at St Hugh's in Tamarind Street, where the young mothers group meets. Some of them were very isolated because they had been moved into Inala's emergency housing from all over Brisbane. There were playgroups and outings, and the workers helped the young women find part-time paid work. The funding came from a program directed at reducing child abuse. Beth Morel and Tom Van Dyke chuckled at that. An intervention team had come in a few years earlier; they 'were very well-meaning, but unfortunately they started off with "now, you've probably all had terrible lives, and you've all been in situations of domestic violence, and you've all experienced sexual abuse" and so on'. Beth and Tom's approach was a little different: 'We don't even call it "parenting classes", we call it a social group, and we use community arts activities and so on. As a strategy for reducing child abuse it's actually about reducing people's social isolation.' At the young mothers group, Alison Brown spoke matter-of-factly, smiling occasionally but maintaining her distance. She was a gifted artist, and she eventually showed me some of the beautiful objects she had painted, sewn and drawn. 'It's great to do this kind of stuff', she said, 'but I'm not an artist or anything'. Alison was more impressed by the courage of some other young mothers, who were involved in the Inala Community Theatre and rehearsing in the hall.

Near the shopping centre are the Community Health Centre and the Community of Inala Legal Service (COILS), initiated, supported and often staffed by local volunteers since the 1970s. You didn't need legal training to get involved at COILS, and a couple of the volunteers didn't read and write very well, but there was always work for anyone who wanted to help. In the shopping centre there was an office for a new Community Police Network dedicated to improving the relationships between the police and young people, who had been staring each other down for decades. The two officers who had been given the job of making it work, a policewoman and a former Brisbane Broncos rugby player, wanted to make a difference, first of all by listening to why the local kids didn't trust the police.

The Wandarrah Child-Care Cooperative was set up by local Aboriginal women in the 1970s. Exasperated by state government neglect, they went to Save the Children instead and got a block of land. Wilma Fuller was still there; she was trying to move into the background so the younger women could take over, but they wouldn't let go of her wisdom. The Aboriginal and Torres Strait Islander Cultural Centre lies at a junction of many of the song-lines for the people of coastal south-east Queensland. It is part school, part workshop for artists, singers and dancers, part advocacy group. The Inala Community House, down in the 'bird' streets, is a former church built and then converted by local people back in the 1960s. Building your own church was a common enough activity in Inala's early days: you couldn't get a minister until you had a church and there was no money for churches until the authorities were ready to give you a minister. Inala people were used to resolving Catch-22s. A few streets away, in a house rented by the Catholic Church, Sister Marguerite spent years building the first support group for women enduring domestic violence. It wasn't advertised and it wasn't named; it was just a group, a place to share the pain and a place to start bringing that pain to an end.

I want to celebrate all that was there, in the hope that never again will it be possible for someone to say that the people who live in Broadmeadows, Inala and Mount Druitt are hopeless and helpless. I want to follow the path set out by residents and those workers who know that people have forged remarkable creations out of what must have seemed like nothing. I want to join Pam McShane in arguing that here 'people rediscovered, in themselves and in their local communities, some of the strengths that they thought that maybe they'd lost, or left behind when they were relocated'. I want to show the hope.

Building multiculturalism

Pauline: Our problem isn't race. Or not just our race, you know what I mean? You can't understand this place if you don't understand that.

Beth: You've actually got all the different kids here, all the different nationalities. It's not like the idea of multiculturalism at a nice

> private school or something. It's actually here; the kids are here. The racial issues are much stronger here, of course, but on the other hand, they get much more opportunity to practise tolerance.

Multiculturalism is made real in Mount Druitt, Broadmeadows and Inala. That might seem a provocative statement. After all, working-class suburbs such as these are meant to be sites of ethnic conflict, 'Asian' gangs and simmering racism. For well over a decade, conservative commentators have been looking for the onset of 'ethnic wars' between 'isolated enclaves', while liberals have been waiting for ordinary Australians to unleash their xenophobia and intolerance. In fact, taking up the challenges and the opportunities created by their differences, the people of these suburbs have forged common ground and a place to talk.

If one way of defining a successful 'multicultural community' is the absence of conflict in an area of significant cultural diversity, Inala, Mount Druitt and Broadmeadows seem to pass the implied test.[1] Perhaps wary of my preconceptions about suburbs in which a third or more of the adults were born outside Australia, English-speaking workers frequently mentioned the 'surprising level of tolerance'.

Deb Monaghan, who had worked as a teacher in Broadmeadows since 1969, was used to friends from other parts of the city reacting with surprise when she said there were very few incidents of conflict or tension:

> People are quite amazed that you could say that.
>
> It might be that there is a group of Vietnamese kids or Turkish kids or Iraqi kids who actually follow a particular trend of music or dress, and that is then seen as a 'gang'. But they could live in the same neighbourhood, their parents could be friends, and they hang out together anyway.

Ethnic community worker Delia Cobb said: 'If there's conflict, it's not people down at Blacktown Station wrestling each other to the ground. But people tend to see that conflict in those terms, you know, race riots, Brixton. And everybody here is saying "What riot? Where's the riot?"' Pam McShane put it bluntly: 'I find that it's got nothing to do with gender or race'. Patrick Nolan agreed: 'Culture and religion have very little relevance, because you have a common denominator, which is the common struggle. You don't have the luxury, if you know what I mean.'

Because I speak only English, I was not able to explore these issues with people who only spoke other languages. Bilingual and trilingual workers certainly confirmed that shared problems, hopes and responsibilities connected people across divisions of language and culture. Chuong Vinh, of Inala's Vietnamese Association, remembered that 'the majority of us were using the Housing Commission, the public housing. And we are friends … They don't say, "You are a wog, get away", or something like that. Nothing ever happened.' Chuong was also angry about outsiders' determination to see every fight between local kids as racial:

> Every time the youth have that sort of contact, they say it's racial. I told the police, I told the worker in the Family Service Department, 'Don't ever say that it is racial'. The youth go there just to show that they are young, they want to fight. They never go there saying, 'I am a Vietnamese going to fight Aborigines'.
>
> I did ask some of them once whether they thought they were fighting for the Vietnamese people. They said 'No, no, we fight for our own group. We are not Vietnamese.' (*Laughs*) They're not representing us. I think there are a lot of people who want this to fail, who want it not to work. It's just the youth.

Turkish community worker Fusun Bakir argued, 'There is a unity, but also division, not in terms of what is needed in Broadmeadows, or what their needs are – their needs are pretty much the same and they're well aware of that – but in terms of the language barrier. That's the only thing that divides them.' She added: 'But you don't need one particular language, they just unite, they click together very quickly once they're aware of the issues as common issues'.

Pauline Moore, of Inala's Cultural Studies Centre, said that in her experience 'more often than not everyone got on because you're all in this situation together, you're all isolated together, your backgrounds, your struggles, all that sort of thing'. Her co-worker, Christine Thomas, agreed, and added, 'Look, it's difficult. On the one hand, their best friend is an Aboriginal person, but on the other hand, you know, they're saying "you have to be careful because you can't trust any Aboriginals". There's racism, but it's generalised stuff. It's difficult.'

One of the most careful investigations into local relationships in Broadmeadows surveyed a range of incidents of supposed ethnic violence in the middle of the 1980s. The author, Jim Houston, argued:

> Virtually all the above incidents were also described by other interviewees as not in fact primarily related to ethnic tensions at all … An alternative approach was to see such incidents as reflecting conflicts of class, high unemployment and the dearth of community resources to meet endemic social needs; the so-called incidents were said to be random ones, unrelated to patterns of inter-ethnic tension, still less the evidence of antipathies between old-established Anglo-Australian residents and NESB newcomers.

He concluded that this 'was a remarkable tribute to people's common sense, responsibility and hopefulness'.[2]

The evidence that these were and are successful multicultural communities extends beyond the mere absence of conflict. It lies in the frequent interactions that overcame potential feelings of distance, in conversations and friendships, and in the everyday work of neighbouring. Connections were forged at the local Catholic church, a childcare group, a queue at the community health clinic or a union meeting. Hard to see, but just as important, were the greetings across a front fence, the shared exasperations of mothers with risk-taking toddlers, the half-smiles exchanged with neighbours at the DSS office, or the joint deciphering of a new healthcare pamphlet.

More formal versions of multiculturalism were promoted by social workers, migrant advocates and community activists, but they needed, and found, fertile soil in the streets and estates of these suburbs. In Broadmeadows, Helen Croydon and Patricia Stephenson described their successful women's multicultural group:

> We actually did some research a couple of years ago, about how to go about accessing people from non-English-speaking backgrounds … [and] one of the things we came across very clearly was that we thought maybe these women would want to have a Turkish group or a Spanish group or whatever, but what they were saying was that they wanted Anglo women to be part of that because they saw Anglo women as being very liberated. They saw them as giving them some of those skills that they thought they needed in our society.
>
> And what we've noticed by them coming together is that the understanding has changed … They have actually been able to come and share with these women and exchange skills. I've been blown away by this, because I

> thought it would be: 'This is our space, and how dare they? We have so little now.' But, again, if you give women the opportunity they will start to break down those barriers. And, of course, that is then reflected in the community; kids start to talk to kids, and so it goes. It's a great way of making change.

At the Dallas Neighbourhood House, Barbara Cook and several volunteers, all English-speaking, wanted to involve the Turkish and Aboriginal women who had moved into the surrounding streets. What they found most effective was providing opportunities for women to talk to and learn from each other in settings that did not focus on particular problems. Children's play sessions, for instance, were transformed by the local mothers into discussion groups on difficult subjects like racism, domestic violence and drug-taking. The international cooking class had become a place for Turkish women to practise English, and for English-speaking women to learn Turkish words and ask questions about Turkish culture. 'It might have started off with us learning how to make kebabs', Geraldine laughed, 'but sometimes we hardly get to the stove we're so busy nattering'. At the recent anniversary celebration for the house, local Koori women had shared the skills of emu-egg carving, and the house had just received funding to run both a metal-working program for young Koori men and another childcare group, which the Koori women had pointedly declared multicultural because 'they wanted to be in a sharing and learning group'.

Kylie Jones and Liz Avenel described a similar experiment at the Emerton Health Centre in Mount Druitt:

> Kylie: Basically, this started as a Filipino women's group, and now it's a multicultural women's group, so it's moved from being specific. Their aim is to support people who are living in two cultures, so it's broadened itself out.
>
> Liz: I think originally it was the Asian women's group, then it became a Filipino women's group, but then they had people from Sri Lanka and a lot of other nationalities come in, and then 'Australians', you know, English-speakers. They have an Australian woman on the committee now as well ... All people just come in. It's wonderful.

Of course, cultural distance had caused some tensions between 'Australians' and 'newcomers'. English-speaking women sometimes rued a chance remark or a question that caused offence, and in some of the groups it had been hard to ensure that the banter about what 'they' did and didn't do remained good-natured. Yet these local residents, volunteers and community workers had mostly overcome the problem of respecting differences without making them the boundaries of their world.

Migrant community workers in these suburbs also wanted to emphasise that the struggle for recognition, respect and rights – in factories, schools, government institutions, welfare agencies, and so on – was not directed primarily at local attitudes. They emphasised instead the inadequacies of policy, especially clumsy consultation: 'The government's rationale for consultation is to get it done as quickly as possible and to just consult one or two leaders'. They derided the targeted programs, and the increasing insistence that the migrant worker's role was to provide services, not to make or challenge decisions. They talked about constant reminders 'that governments don't have enough money for this, don't have enough money for that, and that we shouldn't always be "putting our hands out".' And they described the problem of 'Balkanisation', which stemmed from a top-down insistence on competition between ethnically identified agencies, rather than the wishes of the groups themselves:

> We had a planning day and all the groups were present, and there was a respect, a recognition of the needs of each community, so they weren't saying, 'Hang on a minute, we need more childcare than you, and we've been here longer than you'. There is a sense of mutual respect. In a sense, it was like they all know about the struggles people have when they come here, and they recognise that, for instance, the Vietnamese might need more time now, so maybe we need more attention for them.

Aboriginal and Torres Strait Islander people consistently told me that while there was 'subtle' or 'generalised' racism in their neighbourhoods, it was not the most important problem. There were good strategies that had overcome it in the past and would overcome it in the future. The racism that most limited their lives wasn't invented by their neighbours, and they were of one voice about the 'real problems': poverty, unemployment, police targeting, especially of young men, feelings of uselessness drowned in grog or allayed by heroin, and people who were disconnected from their communities. I asked the women at the Murawina Centre in Mount Druitt if there was any common ground, or shared issues. 'Absolutely', they said. 'Oh yes, all the same'. They reminisced about the centre's founding:

Barbara: When this place was built, all the plans went through the council and that, and all the neighbours here were against it. Now you couldn't ask for better neighbours. They keep an eye on the place. It was simply because they didn't understand. Once they understand the culture it's fine.

Sandra: Yes, they came in and had a look around.

Barbara: They were amazed when they came in here.

Liz: Well, it would have been like, 'Oh God, we're going to have these black drunks all around us, laying in the gutters.' (*Laughs*)

Barbara: But I heard some kids come past here, when we first moved in here. They would have been about 10 years old, and they said, 'How come those kids can't go to an ordinary school?'. So I reckon what their parents had told them, you know, was why do those kids have to have their own school? But now, everybody's so positive. But we have to prove that.

Sandra: You're always proving it.

Liz: And the thing is, it's a mix. There are non-Koori kids here, and by having that, those kids are going to grow up understanding the culture and the meaning as well.

In all three suburbs, Aboriginal workers expressed a similar faith in their non-Aboriginal neighbours: a faith that proximity, information and openness created shared ground, a faith realised in a group of neighbours who regarded Murawina as 'ours' and made sure it wasn't broken into. As Sandra said, 'You're always proving it', and it would be better if the initial suspicions and prejudices weren't there. But they didn't stop the school being built and they had been overcome.

In Broadmeadows, Mount Druitt and Inala, people who spoke different languages and came from different backgrounds had the opportunity to practise real tolerance. They shared a place and similar problems. They also shared the trials occasioned by ignorant and patronising outsiders. Their pasts might have been very different but their present and their future could be made together, at least in part. At its best, theirs was not a form of tolerance in which one dominant group more or less grudgingly accepted the presence of a minority and then praised itself for its magnanimity. It was a form of tolerance in which a range of people saw their differences as less significant than their common cause.

The official rhetoric of Australian multiculturalism rarely acknowledges such undramatic achievements. Neither is there much sense that grumbles from places like these might stem in part from ordinary people's dislike of being told that they need to be educated about cultural differences, largely by people whose experience of the everyday difficulties and opportunities created by those differences is much less than their own. As anthropologist Ghassan Hage argued, in areas of significant population diversity, 'people are too busy mixing even to notice such a thing as "the mix"'; indeed, the 'problem' of racial mix or ethnic balance is most often produced 'by those who are not mixing'.[3] Like Hage, I don't want to idealise or oversimplify relationships in these suburbs. We must heed their complexities. What must be acknowledged, however, is that expressions of intolerance neither define these communities nor provide the main threads in the local story. The best way to describe this is to say that these suburbs manifest a practical tolerance that the people who built it find unremarkable.

In some of my conversations with people who were Australian-born, I heard statements such as, 'Well, I guess I'm a racist'. There was talk of conflicts and unfairness, or Aboriginal people and migrants receiving preferential treatment. Yet these same self-identified 'racists' invariably talked about relationships with neighbours, friends, and co-workers who were Aboriginal or Guatemalan or Turkish. Or they proudly described the complexities of their territory, telling me that there were seven different languages in the street. In comparison, expressions of intolerance were almost always abstract, and concerned people who were not known. Statements about 'the Aboriginals' were not meant to describe your neighbours, and they were always contradicted by concrete examples of commonality. I think we can distinguish this combination of concrete tolerance and abstract intolerance from another version of multiculturalism, in which abstract tolerance – such as temporarily enjoying someone else's culture and cuisine – exists alongside a very concrete intolerance.

In most conversations, avowals of prejudice were also challenged by other members of the group. Arguments that 'Aboriginals get everything they want' were questioned by someone pointing to the real struggle of a nearby Aboriginal family. A statement about 'Muslims keeping to themselves' was challenged by the story of a Muslim neighbour who had been very helpful to an old lady living on her own. Also, I always raised questions about statements of racial identification or prejudice. When I began doing these interviews I kept in mind the advice given me by Janet McCalman that it was unethical to ask people to share their views, say nothing at the time, and then excoriate in writing those with whom I disagreed. So with every self-styled racist there was a conversation. And invariably, the most important challenges came not from me but from the alternatives raised within the group or by the 'racists' themselves.

It is important to make sure you understand the problem that is being raised. Val Stephens and Lorraine Goodman of Inala were two people I very much liked and enjoyed spending time with. Val said something that, taken in isolation, seems a good example of intolerance:

> I've worked it out. There are roughly 900 Aboriginal and Torres Strait Islander people here. Now those 900 people have a neighbourhood centre, they have a pre-school, they have a cultural centre, they have a family education centre, they have the ATSI Legal Service, they have a house in Inala Avenue, and I'm not sure what it's used for, and they have another house in another street.
>
> Now, 900 people have had all that money spent on them. The other 15,000, we have to make do with virtually the same or less than those 900 people. That's why we're saying there's racism in Inala, but not the way it's generally seen.

On the face of it, this might be called racist: lumping together a group of diverse people in terms of their assumed race, describing them as privileged and implying that this is unmerited, and criticising the use of 'our' money on 'them'. I asked Val to tell me more about what she considered to be the problem and said that, in my opinion, the provision of money and services to Aboriginal and Torres Strait Islander people was long overdue, especially if they could define and use those resources in their own way. She responded:

> I'm not saying the Aboriginals don't need the services and the money. That's what I'm trying to get through: we don't want them to stop funding the Aboriginals, we want them to fund us to the same extent. I am not attacking the Aboriginals, I am attacking the government that is funding them.

At this point, Lorraine joined in, and remarked that Val knew many local Aboriginal people and had provided a foster home for six Aboriginal children during the 1970s and 1980s, one of whom had stayed with her until he was 18. Val continued to explain her point: she was pleased that local Aboriginal and Torres Strait Islander services were being funded; 'The more the merrier', she said. Her argument was not about stripping resources away from them; it was a rejection of the claim that resources had to be targeted at all. Her claim was for greater generosity, not denial. I asked whether in order to make the point as accurately as possible, it might be better to say 'us too' rather than 'why them?'. She and Lorraine agreed with that. Val laughed and said, 'Well, that's what I've been saying. You just have to listen more carefully.'

I don't think Val Stephens was being racist; at least not in any meaningful sense of that term. She was not making negative judgements against people simply because they were different, did not deny all commonality, or remain impervious to contrary arguments. By the same token, I don't think the great majority of the people I met in Inala, Broadmeadows and Mount Druitt needed an education in tolerance. Real tolerance was already there, in the conversations they'd been having before I arrived and the conversations they are having now.

Certainly, most of the people with whom I spoke shared a very strong and deeply held interpretation of the world as divided into a 'them' and an 'us'. For a few, a very few, that division was racial or ethnic. The most consistent identification of 'them', however, measured the gulfs of place and class. 'Us' was Broadmeadows, Inala or Mount Druitt. 'Them' was whatever place name or epithet conjured up the comfortable, the powerful and the rich. Indeed, one of the crucial divisions was that 'they' didn't live in a world that included real racial and cultural diversity; 'they' 'think we're all a bunch of racists and no-hopers' and 'treat us like we are worth nothing'. In all our practical efforts to understand and combat the prejudice directed at outsiders, and for all of the successes of those efforts, little is said about the disdain for those who are outsiders because they are poor.

These suburbs actually provide part of the answer to the question of how a multicultural society has developed. And I think most of the people with whom I spoke were likely to undervalue what they'd done. In the midst of persistent economic insecurity and rising unemployment, they had avoided serious conflict. Despite the arrival of more and more impoverished people they had built relationships and common causes and managed a degree of interaction few middle-class people could claim. There were rumblings and tremors, misunderstandings and unsympathetic words. A few people said stupid things. But if a multicultural Australia is anything more than a figment of policymakers' imaginations, it is because the people of places such as these have made it so. It is, I think, a remarkable achievement; one in which the people of some of our most impoverished places should take pride, one for which everyone else should be grateful. Most of all, it is another reason to trust in the capacities of people too often derided for faults that don't belong to them.

Women and the work of caring

In one of the lanes of Bidwill one murky July morning, two women returning from walking their children to school made a quick detour to check on 'their crazies' – two or three 'de-institutionalised' and homeless alcoholic men. This was a quiet day, they told me. Another day the man living down by the letterboxes might be too far gone. If he threatened some of the kids or attacked the demons he saw in people's faces they had to resort to the police. But they made sure when he returned that he had a blanket or knew that it might be warmer to sleep in the abandoned car at the other end of the lane.

After speaking to dozens of women living in impoverished neighbourhoods in the United States, sociologist Nancy Naples coined the term 'activist mothering' to describe the links they forged between taking care of children and taking care of their communities.[4] The women to whom I spoke used a similar vocabulary for talking about what they did. They also emphasised mothers' work on behalf of strangers and neighbours, and treasured the arts of mothering. There was a universal regard – among women and men – for the competence of mothers, and great pride was taken in being seen as a 'good mum'. Some of that pride could be deployed against 'bad' mothers, for there were sanctions as well as supports in these networks. Yet the bond of shared objectives was very strong, especially in neighbourhoods where motherhood was a common aspiration and many women were embedded in two or three generations of activist mothers. Shared pride also connected women across different life stages and personal situations: single parents, widows, and official or unofficial foster carers. Their regard for strong, capable mothers focused less on how you became a mother and more on what you did once you were one.

Women's caring work began but rarely remained close to home. They fronted the welfare agencies, the schools, and even the police if they had to. A good mother had to prevent unwelcome intrusions upon her home, find networks of support and contribute to those networks as best she could in order to ensure that she would be helped in turn. Poverty is far easier to manage with a bit of shared knowledge. Other mothers would know about the people who could be trusted, the methods that worked, agencies that asked stupid questions and agencies that didn't. 'I'd always ask Grace next-door where to go when I first came', said Marie in Inala. 'She knew where they would treat you right, you know, with a bit of respect.'

Through the coordinated efforts of neighbours, friends and relatives, women's work of care gradually extended to a cluster of houses that formed the neighbourhood, and sometimes beyond. Mothers came together in schools and playgroups, or in the community centres. They joined in, maybe attended a class, shared a problem over coffee. They did a little volunteering, and eventually took on some paid work. Bev answered phones at the neighbourhood house, helped with emergency relief, and eventually took over the food cooperative. Mary and Pam joined a childcare group, stayed on to help after their own children had gone to school, and then set up a new creche. Brenda was good with numbers and helped her neighbours comprehend letters from the DSS. She became a volunteer financial counsellor. 'It's not my real job', she said, 'because I'm a mum, really. But it feels good to help.' Play clubs, childcare and schools also brought together mothers from different backgrounds, including the Aboriginal women who traced their activism to strong networks of female kin, and the Vietnamese and Spanish-speaking women. Shared mothering is a powerful bond, and it is no exaggeration to suggest that mothers built the strongest foundations for multiculturalism.

In their personal histories, women described their movement into community work or activism in terms of 'giving back' what they felt they 'took out' as young mothers or at times of great need. Veteran Broadmeadows activist Joan Klug was widowed in 1961, with five children at home and another on the way. She went on to spend years in local counselling organisations helping other widows and single mothers: 'I felt that I had to build a better world for my children and for other children who were going to have the same problems'. Joy Round's father had been an alcoholic and she was devoting much of her time to helping other families in the same situation. 'I see them do things exactly the same as my family did when I was little, and people didn't know why we did it either', she said, 'but I know why'. Jean Drake, who lost her job when she was nearly 50, explained:

> I happened to notice, on the noticeboard in Social Security, 'Volunteers wanted to help the community'. I thought, well, I'd been a deserted wife, brought the kids up on my own but I always got help from the community, support from different areas. So I figured that I could give something back.

Caroline Blake, a member of a young single mothers group in Broadmeadows, said, 'I don't really need the group any more, but then other times I think the group needs me because there are new people coming in all the time. Now I guess I can be a role model, you know, give back what I got out of the group'.

Their activist mothering was strongly reciprocal. They lived in a world of implied as well as real obligations, of experiences gained that should be shared, which stretched out beyond the home and forward in time. New workers quickly learned to nourish these connections: 'It's women who have the energy to make a lot of these things happen … [and] it's groups of women who really get things going'. 'They're the ones who steer and struggle. Who go on.' As one minister put it, 'You belt your head against a brick wall to try and get the blokes to take a part, though they'll always go along with it'. In Inala, social worker Pam Wilson laughed about 'the army of unofficial social workers out there'. Two coordinators at the Broadmeadows office of the Department of Housing confirmed that women dominated tenant participation. I asked if the women ever offered explanations for that:

> Rosie: No, it's just part of the way it is.
>
> Monica: It's part of life, the sort of stuff that women do. It's funny when you do have men come to meetings sometimes, that the women actually do speak up and just cast them aside.
>
> Rosie: Yes, dismiss them.
>
> Monica: 'This is not your place', sort of thing.

Mark: It's maybe something men don't know much about?

Monica: Yes.

Rosie: And they're prepared to argue with them: just because there's a male present doesn't mean that they're going to change the way they've thought previously. It's just a quick dismissal, sometimes of whatever that person has got to say. Men are seen as having other areas of expertise, driving the buses and doing the rubbish, I guess. (*Laughs*)

Youth worker Matthew O'Neill was a new arrival in Broadmeadows, and was setting up a placement program for homeless teenagers. Senior bureaucrats told him he would be lucky to get caregivers 'up there', so he was amazed by the number of women raising children alone who wanted to take in one or two homeless teenagers: 'You think "God, you have enough on your plate", and there are these Trojans of women who are inspiring. They really are.'

These activist mothers never begrudged their caring work. If they occasionally rued the fact that the work was never done, and that men just didn't seem able to pitch in in the way they should, there was no fatalistic resignation to a life of continued hardship. Theirs was a commitment born of hope, and a statement about changing the world, not accepting your lot. Marianne Carr cut her activist teeth on sit-ins to demand a playground and a pedestrian crossing at her children's school and then moved into tenant participation and women's refuges. More than most, she had developed a political interpretation of what she and others had done: 'The thing about a working-class background is it gives you a great sense of responsibility, for everyone. You've got to do the right thing at all bloody times'. She was laughing when she said it, but her point was serious; 'care-taking', she said, was 'our feminism'.

Like Marianne, Broadmeadows community activist Bev had done women's studies courses at the TAFE college, reading books and finding new words to make sense of her situation. Her judgement was that 'maybe this is what we've made out of feminism, you know, what we've taken from feminism'. From their long experience of cooperation and tension with middle-class workers, Marianne and Bev insisted that the origins and meaning of their activism were different. Like the African-American and Latina activists interviewed by Nancy Naples, they focused on collective rather than individual gains, on working for others as well as for yourself and your children.[5] The needs of your own children might have been activism's beginning but it spread beyond that to other people's children and then to all the others who were suffering. It also extended forward in time to the mothers who would follow you into the street or the neighbourhood and who would be grateful that they didn't have to fight for the things mothers needed to do their job.

If anything, these activist mothers underestimated the significance of all that they had achieved. They tended to talk in terms of personal experience, about lessons learned from coping on low incomes that they had simply carried out into the world. Few, for instance, recognised how their talk of a common cause helped strengthen a political language about rights and social justice, or how that language was bringing people together across the potential barriers of class and cultural background. In Broadmeadows, Carol Hills responded to my question about the beginnings of her involvement:

> Well, I want the rights for these children, that's what I want, and they haven't got any rights so I'm going to keep going.
>
> I don't need to be doing this, because I've got lots I could be doing, but I just can't stop. It's like an obsession because it's wrong, what they're doing is wrong, and they're getting away with it and I don't want them to.

When I asked her to tell me more about 'them', she laughed a little and waved her hand in the direction of the central city; 'Them down there', she said, 'and the people who think like that and work in our schools or in the departments'. She continued:

> It's not right and it's not justice. And if its injustice then you fight. Fight with all you've got. Find the other people who want to fight with you. Doesn't matter who they are.

In the everyday work of mothers, and in the neighbourhood houses, women's centres and community organisations, women of different backgrounds and languages had shared their sense of injustice and discovered their common ground. Inclusiveness extended also to the welfare workers. Of course, many of them were also residents or had lived on low incomes in similar places; by bringing local women into activism, they were encouraging others to follow their own paths. But even with a professional salary they remained tied to the work of care. Other workers had come without much personal experience of impoverishment but with commitments to justice, derived in equal measure from feminism and their training in community-focused social work. They saw themselves as more the beneficiaries than the providers of education; in these suburbs, as Inala worker Eva said, 'we learned the meaning of *real* empowerment and *real* community development. We learned how *we* had to change.'

Certainly, professional women with little experience of the world they were entering had to negotiate strong traditions of suspicion towards people from the outside. Yet it seemed to me, listening to both residents and workers, that women from different class backgrounds met here on a relatively egalitarian ground. One ingredient was the willingness of workers to listen and to allow local people to speak for themselves. It meant starting from where they were, not where they should be, and allowing coalitions to emerge how and when they did. Yet it also showed the capacity of local activist mothers to acknowledge that these outsiders could contribute their own rather different wisdom to the work of care.

Activist mothers were also beginning to deal with a larger number of male workers. Religious men had always been present, and male welfare workers became more common in specific areas, such as youth work, during the 1980s. In 1994, the Shalvey Community Centre made a conscious decision to hire a male and a female community worker, partly to help foster men's involvement in programs. The centre was also working closely with a new male community support worker at the local high school. In the neighbouring estate, Bidwill Community Support had just hired a male worker to coordinate the children's playgroup.

Such was the work of women in Inala, Broadmeadows and Mount Druitt. It was hard, piled on top of the sometimes exhausting labour of caring for family members. It had a long history and reflected tenacious traditions of female responsibility and competence in working-class life. And it was dynamic. Since the 1970s local activists and the women who took jobs in agencies had expanded their care work into school committees, advocacy groups and tenant participation. They had emphasised collaboration and produced a sense of common cause across class and ethnic divisions. They had also welcomed men into the work of care.

These were precious achievements, and women's caring work remains one of the best practical examples of what flows from people talking together about shared injustices and ways of making them right. In more theoretical discussions about inclusive justice, perhaps the most difficult question is how to bridge differences between people without overwhelming them in expectations that there is a single universal solution.[6] Some answers might be found in the work of these women, in the ethic of solidarity they had achieved and in the talk about needs and justice that hadn't been spoken in just one language.

Women's caring work also helped create fundamental change in social welfare. They were in one sense recipients of change, making use of an emerging community development model that softened the hand of external direction. They also benefited from the social justice work of churches: in Inala, Catholic nuns were especially important, while the Christian Brothers and the Baptist and Uniting churches were active in Mount Druitt and Broadmeadows. Yet they were hardly the passive beneficiaries of innovation. Little of the effort to improve social welfare would have worked without networks of local women providing ideas and suggestions, as well as most of the energy needed to make it happen:

> In 1984, two social workers came out … and they called a public meeting, and they asked us what we thought Inala needed. Now that was the first time I can ever recall anyone ever asking a public tenant what Inala needed.
>
> So we said, right, we need something for homeless kids. We said we need a legal service, a free legal advice service, so we formed the Community of Inala Legal Service. We decided we needed a neighbourhood centre, somewhere where we could meet, so we started the Hub Neighbourhood Centre. We decided we needed a drama group, a theatre group. We now have the Inala Community Theatre. These were all initiatives that we came up with. The Food and Vegie Coop was another one.

The caring work of women also expanded as some of them moved up into housing and welfare bureaucracies. At times of political transition – with the election of Queensland's Goss Labor government in 1989, or in Victoria with the Cain Labor government in 1982 – workers with years of local experience reached positions where they could apply the lessons of their own activism and nourish the endeavours in which they were once immersed. Over time they developed some of the most constructive reforms in tenant participation, public housing management, and a range of welfare services. For example, activists brought into Queensland's Department of Housing during the early 1990s produced new initiatives – including the Housing Improvement Strategy in Inala – and a commitment to tackling and changing the Department's relationship with its tenants. It didn't all work out, but local people remembered this particular experience of being trusted and represented in a way that hadn't been true before.

For all of the most difficult challenges in social policy – dealing with the changes in men's lives that have accompanied widespread unemployment, for instance, or designing services to meet the particular needs of different cultural groups – the work of women in these suburbs provides ideas and examples. As unemployed men and single fathers began to filter into voluntary work and parenting groups, neighbourhood houses were developing new programs, hiring male workers and experimenting with activities to bolster men's contributions as carers and fathers. As agencies tried to tackle the isolation of some older residents, they also created new groups for people caring for incapacitated spouses and parents, and fostered multicultural clubs to ease the loneliness of older people whose languages were disappearing. As community houses responded to the changing cultural fabric of the surrounding areas they used language classes and job training to reach new groups and nourish neighbourhood networks.

If there is much to admire in the caring work of women, however, the hope it bore then and bears now can only be fulfilled if its claims and implications are heard in full. In the first place it is important to resist opportunistic expectations of continuing female self-sacrifice or the idea that people are best off looking after themselves, which invariably means poorer women, paid or unpaid, looking after everybody else. The caring work of women is not a cheap alternative to adequate social welfare. The ideal world of the activist mother demands significant public investment, and a way of spending it that protects and trusts her definition of problems and solutions. These women used terms such as a 'decent income' or 'real welfare', talked about dignity and respect, and were angry about cutbacks and short-sighted decisions. Their work has depended and will always depend upon the willingness of those who know little about hardship to contribute to the efforts of those who know it all too well.

In the middle of the 1990s the importance of their work was increasing. While full employment for men and the relative prosperity of the middle part of the twentieth century lessened working-class families' dependence upon women's survival skills, the caring work of women did not simply fade away, especially in poorly-serviced outer suburbs. In recent years, as some neighbourhoods became harder places in which to manage, their fate had once again come to rest largely on women's competence. As funding was cut for community agencies and relief, as unemployment and years of low income reduced the capacity of families to cope on their own, and as public housing estates brought together more and more impoverished people, there was an ever greater reliance on women's paid and unpaid work, and on neighbours and family. With increased economic vulnerability, women would end up doing most of the work involved in drawing their families back from the brink of disaster.

At the same time, this tradition of activist mothering seemed to its builders to be at something of a crossroads. Some feared it might wither away. Older women were worried about the willingness of younger women to carry on. Younger women, including some who had arrived just a year or two earlier, weren't sure if their contributions would be welcomed. More and more women needed to or wanted to work for wages, and some had paid work that did not mesh easily with their unpaid responsibilities. Activist mothers were also worried that unemployed men and younger men, at home and with nowhere else to go, would interfere with and even feel threatened by women's wider responsibilities.

To me, however, their anxieties seemed misplaced. It was clear that some women's involvement in the work of care had triggered a re-negotiation of their relationships. Many had nonetheless endured, while new relationships reflected changed expectations. Men talked about women as 'the rocks of this place', the 'strong ones' and 'the foundations', even if that respect wasn't always relayed so directly when the women were actually in the room. When there was no respect, when men tried to rule, the very extent of informal and formal support helped women move away from men who did them harm. A community of grandmothers, mothers, aunts, sisters and neighbours also made it more possible for younger women to mother on their own. There were different ways of being a woman, and the range of differences had undeniably increased since the 1970s. But that did not, by and large, mean that women wanted to give up their work of care any more than men wanted to give up working for wages. In the midst of increasing vulnerability, few wanted to take that kind of risk.

If the women who pioneered this public work in the 1970s and 1980s were a little nervous about its future, it was in part because they did not always recognise what they had achieved. In the organisations I visited there were more signs of tradition being transmitted rather than lost. The number of single mothers becoming involved in this work and the connections forged between women from different backgrounds was further testimony to the way common cause could transcend potential barriers of personal experience or generation.

Indeed, what I saw and heard about in these disadvantaged neighbourhoods was a structure of care, based largely upon the shared capacities and commitments of women, which belied any pessimism about disintegrating community. Those who built and sustained it worried that it was coming apart under the pressure. Looking from the outside, I was more impressed by its robustness. This doesn't mean insisting that women must and should take on the work of care by themselves, nor that the sacrifices made by activist mothers should be seen as inevitable and unchangeable. The younger women who were moving into the work of care will strike out on their own paths, and may be much less accepting of compromises and constraints, especially at home. Yet if one of the most important resources for the future is a greater regard for strangers, a rejection of anxious self-reliance in favour of shared responsibilities, there is much to be learned from the women of Inala, Broadmeadows and Mount Druitt. Theirs are lessons about the well-springs of hope, not despair.

Everyday justice

There are two damaging misconceptions about impoverished people. One is that they are flawed and must be improved in some way. The second more readily accepts poverty's structural causes and unfairness, but tends to regard poor people as ignorant, perhaps fatalistic, and easily distracted by prejudice and tradition. The idea that poor people must be rescued by their superiors dies hard.

Of course, it's not all or nothing. Neither I nor the people with whom I spoke would claim that every bit of local knowledge was accurate, or that every person was capable and responsible. Nor was everyone an activist. Some people were helpless and hopeless. Even some of the activists were weary and disillusioned. For many people, involvement in the community might be limited to a pottery class or a childcare group. And others were simply too miserable; defeated by their daily confrontation with poverty, they stayed at home and tried to cope alone. But the many who had participated and worked in neighbourhood houses, community centres, childcare cooperatives and schools had built a remarkable architecture of care, compassion and collaboration.

I want to go further yet. It seems to me that they had also developed a knowledge of social justice, a practical substance for what can often seem like vague and perhaps even unrealistic claims. They shared a vision of what it meant and how it might be achieved. When I asked them what they thought it was, they inverted their experience of injustice: social justice certainly began with money and resources but also included security, dignity, the freedom to enjoy one's capacities and the right to be protected from the results of one's incapacities. Further clues lay in the stories about activism, in the muted accounts of women's work and common cause.

To understand their version of social justice we don't need more studies of disadvantage. The problem is not that the people of Broadmeadows or Mount Druitt or Inala don't speak; the problem is that they don't get heard. Greater trust must be placed in their ideas and in their ability to improvise and find solutions. There needs to be room for surprises – even mistakes – and some acknowledgment that the most effective ways of achieving justice might not be obvious at the beginning or from the outside. As geographer David Harvey argues, intellectuals, no less than policy-makers, must accept responsibility for arbitrating between competing definitions of justice. But they must also accept responsibility for listening to ideas 'to which people do attach importance and which to them appear unproblematic'.[7] If we actually listen to the voices of people who suffer injustice, then our conception of justice might have to change.

Their ideas were often fundamentally different from the version of social justice promoted by the government at the time, before the words, and indeed the concept, virtually disappeared from political language. For one, they insisted that injustice is caused, and stems from political and moral choices that consistently disadvantage people like them. While the powerful (and the short-term winners) might prefer a more passive language, in which growing inequality and injustice are the inevitable outcomes of 'global' processes over which no one has any control, those who suffer the consequences understand that wealth and poverty are always produced together, in real places and by real people.

'We're poor because the people down there are rich. Simple as that', said Ann, while Barry suggested, 'If they didn't need so much and want so much and take so much, there'd be more to go around'. As such, they emphasised potential conflict and the need for political courage and persuasive skill. They knew that other Australians would have to agree to change the distribution of wealth, rewards and penalties. And because they had so often experienced the consequences of crisis-provoked policy – a flurry of social workers, investigators and missionaries eager to counsel and save the poor – they knew that the political arguments had to be about long-term change. In their form of justice, good services and better opportunities would be provided as a matter of right. Their claims would be trusted, in other words, not because they were urgent or extreme or threatened the interests of wealthier people, but because they were reasonable.

They also focused on collective achievements, the justice done to others, rather than on individual gains. People always referred to others worse off than themselves, placed the needs of the neighbourhood above their own, and defined justice largely as something they wanted to achieve for their own children and for the next generation. They spoke of justice for everyone, I think, because in a world where so much had gone wrong, only a problem shared could be promoted over others. As they looked around them, the people of these impoverished neighbourhoods judged justice by what happened to those who were least able and most despondent. They pictured a decent society as one in which their most vulnerable and even most insufferable neighbours could find a place. It was a defiantly simple proposition, one often absent from the definitions of justice being formed somewhere above their heads.

They also talked about how people were treated, not financial gain. A really fair world was not one in which they became the winners and everyone else the losers, nor was it one in which success was measured by what they could get at any cost. What mattered to them was acknowledgment of capacity and intelligence. Their justice was distributive and procedural, and intimately connected with dignity and self-determination.[8] Justice was about being respected, trusted and listened to because what you had to say was important. If social justice is a response to poverty, they argued, it must be a response to poverty's psychological and emotional wounds, not just its financial consequences: 'You can put up with the struggle, you know, just get by, if you get respect and if you're treated right', said Grace. Her neighbour Marie concurred: 'That's right. It's not being treated like an idiot, like you're a criminal.'

Even disruptive changes could be seen as just if they treated people fairly. To take one example, the redevelopment of dilapidated estates was being talked about in all three suburbs. We know such redevelopment can be painful: if it provides better housing and breaks up concentrations of disadvantage it can also break up the networks impoverished people have built around themselves. Criticism of redevelopment projects in Bidwill or Inala was partly based on the slim prospect of real improvement. But the most important issue was the workers' willingness to listen to people's stories and understand the depth of their connections to their home place. Nothing boiled the blood of Inala's inhabitants more than a story about one redevelopment worker's alleged amazement that 'people seem to like living here'.

Lorraine and Bill Goodman were renting a three-bedroom house from the Queensland Housing Department and were considering the suggestion that they move into a smaller unit. What angered Lorraine and Bill was not the idea that they should vacate a house in which they had lived for thirty years, but their difficulty in making the Department understand that even though they were getting old and didn't have much money they still had a jumble of treasures and photographs that were important to them and wouldn't fit into a one-bedroom flat. 'I mean, we'll move', Lorraine said, 'because a family should have this house, but we want them to understand. We want them to recognise that it's hard and that we need time.'

By the same token, people in Bidwill didn't reject redevelopment out of hand. They wanted to be heard. They also wanted, as Graeme said, 'someone to make and keep a promise'. In their version of social justice, powerful people should be held to account in the same way they were. It was a simple enough demand, but not one they'd seen satisfied too often. For powerful people there was always an excuse: 'unexpected budget problems', 'necessary compromises'. As Col argued,

> Try fronting up to the DSS counter and saying you've decided not to take a job because you'd lose all your income supplements and there'd be an unanticipated bloody shortfall. They'd be really understanding, wouldn't they.

A few minutes later, he returned to the issue:

> You see, the difference is we pay for our mistakes. They don't. We have to understand limitations and forgive them and be reasonable and make the best of it. They don't. That's not fair.

As Patrick Nolan suggested, 'People here always pay a very heavy price, and usually for the mistakes of others'.

If they wanted one thing to change, it was that they be treated as knowledgeable, that outsiders should expect to learn and to listen. As one worker in Broadmeadows put it, 'What they say is what they mean, and there isn't anything behind it. There isn't any other agenda. It's grounded in real things … [and] really what people are after is sensible stuff.' So much of what was said to me revealed better ways of tackling a range of problems. People focused on small, practical experiments, on changes that would make sense to anyone who really knew what poverty was. Indeed, what they suggested would be more effective – and probably more cost-efficient – than the project teams that come in every few years to re-invent the wheel.

Their versions of social justice in many ways echoed the conclusions of scholars exploring the meanings of justice in a twenty-first-century world. Like participants in other studies they gave priority to collective injustices, spoke about the significance of optimism and faith in change, and rejected processes in which they would win in favour of processes that they thought would be fair.[9] In line with the principles advanced by philosopher Brian Barry, they insisted on a version of justice 'that can be defended to oneself and others without appealing to personal advantage'.[10] In their work as neighbours and activists, they tackled the key political question of how to forge common ground between different people, based on a similarity of experience, without implying or insisting upon sameness.[11] And they knew from their experience and their activism that cultural or language differences between people did not preclude and could in fact nourish a 'politics of inclusion'.[12]

I don't want to portray their version of social justice as a kind of homespun wisdom that must not be debated or questioned. Disadvantaged people are not always right, though I venture that they are right more often than many people would allow. On the evidence of this and other studies they do not regard their views as immune from challenge. Some of their arguments were simplistic or contained contradictions, and some – such as the strong emphasis on self-sacrifice, particularly among women – need to be debated, not taken for granted. There is a difference between acknowledging something that works in a particular situation, at a particular time and within particular constraints, and idealising it as the best or only solution. Also, the very fact that these ideas are embedded in specific experiences and particular personal histories is both their strength and their potential weakness, especially in regard to their capacity to inform broader or more abstract principles.[13]

Yet in diverse, changing places such as these, people had already explored and to an extent overcome some of these limitations. They had built common cause among people who spoke different languages or came to these neighbourhoods along very different paths. They had built enduring collaborations with workers who did not grow up in their world or share their past. In their dealings with each other they had explained, debated, questioned, agreed and disagreed. And they had managed to listen and learn.

Even more than the ideas about social justice that emerged from these conversations, this inclusive deliberation might serve as their most important gift. Against all the expectations that working-class and disadvantaged people need to be taught about abstract principles – justice, tolerance, multiculturalism or mutual obligation, for instance – perhaps there is something that they can teach others. Like the people celebrated by Raymond Williams, we might acknowledge not just their 'infinite resilience' but their 'ingrained and indestructible ... embodiment of the possibilities of common life', which is perhaps even more impressive here, in the midst of possible defeat and potential division.[14]

The point is not merely to celebrate. Nor is it to romanticise them as some marginal or revolutionary 'other', and then crowd the space they have created with demands they don't recognise as their own. The point is to listen to what they are saying. It won't be easy, because it depends upon getting close enough to hear words that aren't about pain, suffering and heroic endurance but about hope and anger.[15] It demands an approach based on working with people, not on them. It is the difference between what activist Pam McShane called 'the model of discernment at a distance' and 'empowering them, trusting them'. It is the difference between telling them what to do and asking them what needs to be done, in the belief that they know best.

CONCLUSION

Dark

As I made my final trips to Broadmeadows, Inala and Mount Druitt, brave words were being spoken about their future. Words, like renovation and rehabilitation, which spoke of a conviction that these suburbs were damaged and deficient. It was a refrain strongest among strategic planners and development consultants who spoke in interviews of 'innovative place management', 'selling Mount Druitt', 'facilitating community synergies' or 'forging a competitive hub'. They wanted to work on 'image' and change the 'living environment' to attract 'high-calibre businessmen'.

The prominence of image was a telling signal of their perception of poverty. It demanded less change outside disadvantaged places and more within them. The problem wasn't inequality or injustice but the 'over-concentration' of poor people in particular places. Poverty could not be eradicated, only shifted from your patch into someone else's. While it was the nature of their task to start with what they had, I was surprised at how easily these strategists could explain away the harsh facts of entrenched unemployment and neglect. One told me that 'we're going through a major evolutionary change in this country, where we simply have to recognise that we're not going to be able to provide jobs for everybody'. Honest enough, perhaps, but rather unnerving given the dozen or so unemployed young men who were standing nearby.

At least they were talking about poverty. They were moved to do something about a problem they took seriously and thought should be solved. At the time it seemed important to criticise some of their plans on the grounds that they simply moved the problem around and didn't offer long-term solutions.[1] Several years later, well-meaning if sometimes clumsy interventions had given way to contempt and blame as Australian ways of writing and speaking about poverty began to mirror America's obsession with the pathologies of poor people.[2] The problem of what to do about poverty was becoming the problem of what to do with the poor.

All eyes turned to welfare fraud. In 1998 newspapers reported that 570,000 welfare cheats would be forced to return money, saving taxpayers tens of millions of dollars. In fact, 99.3 per cent of the overpayments were due to administrative errors or other reasonable causes; just 4,471 people, less than 1 per cent of the so-called cheats and an infinitesimal proportion of the total number of people receiving welfare payments in Australia, had made fraudulent claims. That fact was reported, but later and without a headline.[3] It is a common strategy: a misleading allegation, usually in the headline, with muted prevarication in the first article and whispered correction later, by which time the allegation has already become part of a common misconception about welfare as a burden and a problem.

In January 2002, Melbourne's *Herald Sun* featured another crackdown on 'four thousand fraudulent claims' on its front page, again with no acknowledgment of how tiny a fraction this represented of the people claiming benefits.[4] A month later, Minister for Family and Community Services Amanda Vanstone warned that the 'days are numbered' for welfare cheats. This time, the *Herald Sun* at least mentioned the fact that just 0.05 per cent – five people in every 10,000 – of welfare recipients were convicted of actual fraud.[5] According to the *Age*, the Department's official report on compliance did not even clearly indicate the extent to which overpayment stemmed from mistakes rather than fraud, nor the proportion of those mistakes that were made by Centrelink rather than the recipients.[6] It hardly seems accidental: the worst aspect of these stories about cheating is the eagerness with which powerful people encourage their spread. Some politicians and public policy-makers even created fictional stories to demonise welfare recipients; in the absence of sufficiently dramatic empirical evidence, fiction does just as well.

The most visionary thinkers of the late twentieth century warned us about the walls that would be built between the rich and the poor.[7] Closer to the ground, the people of Mount Druitt, Inala and Broadmeadows had their own prophecies. In 1995, unemployment was a major issue. The federal conservative parties were shaming Labor with a double-digit jobless rate, though John Hewson's desire to chisel the commitment to full employment from the wall of the Reserve Bank rather undermined his moral high ground. But the people living in the midst of mass unemployment were not confident. Some predicted that it wouldn't be a major issue in four or five years, that a federal election would be fought with neither the Liberals nor 'their' party making any mention of the jobless and that governments would regard the unemployment and underemployment of one million or more Australians as inevitable. Others said governments would devote most of their energy to driving people off the dole, cutting or privatising job programs, and bringing the official rates down by massaging the statistics. Still others said that once the official rates started to fall there was likely to be a renewed effort to demonise jobless people as 'bludgers'. For all the assumptions often made about their incapacity, they were adept at predicting the future.

In a way, Australians have become almost silent about poverty unless it is linked to something called 'the welfare problem'. As Graham Little observed, whenever equity is mentioned – and it isn't mentioned very often – someone will raise 'the politics of envy'.[8] Perhaps people have become self-centred, uninterested in those outside their circle of responsibility and affection. Moral issues have become the preserve of so-called lobby groups or people devoted to 'political correctness'. Australians have been urged to identify themselves in terms of their consumer desires and to seek and even enjoy the exclusion of others from privileges. Rights have become even more a matter of purchasing power. Without money you get the bare minimum, so long as you follow the rules and don't complain too much. With money you find your place in the hierarchy, up to and including gold class. A principle that might be unobjectionable when applied to theatre seats means something altogether different when it is applied to education or health care.

To even think about making arguments for transformation means confronting a powerful logic. Resources are limited, we are told. People will have to do more to look after themselves. It's better to privatise public services and give back taxes so most people can spend more of their income on private health, private education, private security and private transport. To reinforce those choices you need to create incentives, which are actually financial penalties for not using the private alternatives. There are some customers private companies don't want to serve, so educating, healing and supporting people who have no money is left to public services that no longer have funds from people who can pay to subsidise those who can't. In this view of the world, inequality is natural and unavoidable. The successful, the lucky and the strong have little reason to concern themselves with the unsuccessful, the unlucky and the weak. Such, it seems, are the hard realities of the early twenty-first century.

Light

And yet pessimism is somehow not the right mood. Astute commentators like Graham Little saw something else. Hugh Mackay captured it, too, in his national temperature-takings: emulation and competition also produce a good deal of fear, distrust and insecurity.[9] The world made by and for the winners isn't necessarily a world in which other people want to live, if it means they are always a little behind, always being urged to catch up, always anxious about competition because they know in any competition there are losers as well as winners. Of late, there has also been a growing recognition that fuelling aspirations for self-fulfilment may not be the only politics with a chance of electoral success; instead people might want to share and be sustained by a sense of hope, and even the joint responsibilities of building a better world.[10]

The contention that hearts have hardened towards needy others is also debatable. At the very least it merits careful investigation. Witness the complicated public response to the moving stories of the stolen Aboriginal generation. Or studies of people's views about taxation and public services, which show the majority of representative samples of Australian citizens think governments should raise taxes to provide better education, health care and training for unemployed people.[11] Or studies in social psychology that show most people intuitively act kindly towards others, even people they do not know, and place a high value of being seen as a 'just person'.[12]

If most people aren't talking about injustice, inequality or poverty at the beginning of the twenty-first century, I don't think the problem is their hard-hearted incapacity to be moved. It is more complicated. Views are inconsistent, jarring, even contradictory. If there is an absence, it is of sensible discussion. The major political parties seem convinced that we ordinary voters are resolutely selfish, so they have trapped each other in a lacklustre debate about self-interest, lower taxes and the need to police welfare beneficiaries. Too many commentators are caught in the same tangle of 'spin' and bullyboy rhetoric. The failures have occurred at the peak of power in Australia, particularly among people who have mistaken ordinary citizens' dislike of politics and rhetoric for a dislike of government and ideas.

I share philosopher Raimond Gaita's view that there is an underestimated constituency in Australia for talking about decency, justice and hope.[13] I believe we need good arguments and, like Inga Clendinnen and Janet McCalman, that historians have a particular responsibility to tell 'true stories' about the past and the present, stories that tell us where we have been and where we might be going, stories that recognise suffering but also invention and ideas about change.[14] It is possible to stress the obligations that are owed by all to all, including people we don't know but whose fortunes do in some way depend on us.[15] It is possible to argue that because very few of us are invulnerable – with hard times only ever a retrenchment, an accident or a bad decision away – protection from the consequences of our personal vulnerability is one of our most important gifts to each other.[16]

It's not as if we don't have good principles and practical proposals. Among the first, we might place the argument that the first priority of government is not to exacerbate inequalities but to reduce them by reinforcing common obligations. If ordinary people are to be held to account, then so must those who are rendered extra-ordinary by their wealth, their power, their luck or their talent. Further, real choice and real security, for the great majority of citizens, depend upon a productive mix of well-governed markets and well-managed governments, not trying to turn governments into businesses or businesses into legislators.[17]

If good government aspires to more than the efficient delivery of services to customers, it also challenges the pretence that in twenty-first-century societies we can look after ourselves. We all use services that were or are paid for by the public: roads, pipelines, bridges, schools, electricity grids and hospitals. We educate children by requiring that everyone, regardless of whether or not they are parents, contributes through the tax system. This is as it should be. Little that we choose or want to do is possible without other people sharing at least part of the cost. If forcing people to buy private alternatives rather than support shared ones is a peculiar kind of economic efficiency – and America's health system should be proof enough of that – it is also a peculiar vision of how to live together in one place.

All this will become more important, especially as growing inequalities between different classes are matched by those between different generations. Recent studies confirm fears that for the first time in more than a century each new generation is becoming poorer; wealth, along with the opportunities and security that it brings, will become concentrated among the elderly.[18] One or two generations, born between about 1920 and 1960, will do very well, but their children and grandchildren will have fewer assets and larger debts, often caused by the need to pay for education or for a range of other services that were once inessential, cheap or free. According to one recent study, more than a quarter of the people now in their twenties will endure significant disadvantage because of insecure employment, heavy debts and high living costs.[19]

There are responses. There is a developing international conversation about ways of building more cohesive societies and insisting that social justice and a demonstrably fairer distribution of resources and opportunities are two of their essential hallmarks.[20] We might take the longer view, evaluate each and every proposal 'for its likely contribution to social equality across two or more generations' and make the key factor its ability to 'benefit the greatest number of those who are most in need for the longest period of time'.[21] We might further explore the notion of 'social capital', both as a way of conceptualising the bonds that nourish individual and communal fortunes and as a generator of practical experiments in how to build trust, participation and a sense of connection among citizens.[22] We might think about paying for and receiving benefits in terms of a social contract, and in the belief that the good of the whole actually matters. In the same vein we might see our investment in the security and dignity of suffering others as a form of insurance for those times in which we will want to be treated just as kindly.[23]

Further still, we might remind ourselves that striving to live as equals does not mean creating conformity. We can also make different choices without producing less freedom for others. There are inequalities of ability and capacity we might decide to support – perhaps those of athletes, inventors, artists, philosophers or medical researchers – because of the pleasure and benefit we all derive from their achievements. Conversely, there are inequalities we might decide are unsupportable by the public because they do not enhance the common good, and inequalities that need to be repaired because they are produced by luck, inheritance and other forces outside of people's control.[24] And we might insist, too, that equity – social or generational – cannot come second to efficiency. As Amartya Sen puts it, if balancing equity and efficiency creates a dilemma that is because a dilemma 'is a battle between good things, each of which commands our attention'.[25]

The beginning of the twenty-first century is an opportune time for taking stock. As John Solas has demonstrated, the basic elements of a policy dedicated to reducing poverty and inequality are well established.[26] John Langmore and John Quiggin, for instance, show the importance of full employment.[27] To the argument that governments should not create jobs we might respond that they are creating many highly paid jobs for consultants, advertisers, lawyers and public relations experts. In a way, the servants of the political party have replaced the servants of the public. In the area of urban planning, Brendan Gleeson and Nicholas Low provide another blueprint for ethically-driven policies 'founded on a particular vision of freedom, justice and democracy' that is 'framed by public deliberation'.[28]

In my view, one of the most urgent requirements is a comprehensive study of wealth. We need to understand much better the ways in which inequality and poverty are produced and reproduced, and whether alternative arrangements in areas such as taxation, welfare and employment policy would generate a more equitable distribution of wealth. We also need a better understanding of public attitudes to inequality and poverty, following the start made by the Brotherhood of St Lawrence.[29] All of this could inform a wide-ranging debate about acceptable and unacceptable inequalities. We might focus less on the dimension of the problems – for instance, whether 5 per cent or 10 per cent of Australians are living in relative poverty – and more on the processes that create the problems.

A Social and Generational Justice Commission could lead that debate and begin applying shared decisions. If it is important to oversee the nation's competitiveness through a Competition and Consumer Commission, it is just as important to oversee its fairness, to assess whether different choices are likely to increase or reduce existing inequalities, and to rule out those policies or decisions that generate unjustifiable differences between citizens. To take one example, such a commission might have decided that the decision to give a 'GST bonus' to aged pensioners but not people on disability, sole parent or unemployment payments, was unjust and divisive, and that the bonus should have been paid to all or none. Or it might rule that a company accepting any form of funding or benefit from the public cannot offend principles of equity and long-term efficiency by offering its chief executives multi-million dollar bonuses for doing what they are already paid to do.

Perhaps the most important decision is to reject the proposition that the future is somehow fixed. The triumphant force in Australian political culture over the last twenty years has not been economic rationalism but a pessimistic 'inevitabilism', or what Albert O. Hirschman described as the 'futility thesis'.[30] Focusing on the hard realities of inescapable forces – which are more often than not half-truths based upon narrow assumptions – has tragically narrowed our field of vision. In a world in which the fundamentals can't be questioned, let alone changed, people reasonably strive to make the best of bad situations. They protect themselves and those close to them from the limits of what can be achieved. Talented people spend their time looking for loopholes in systems that won't be budged or ways of 'spinning' supposed facts that can't be challenged. You look after your own, and the devil take the rest.

The contribution I strive to make to all of these discussions is not one of technical design or theoretical elaboration. It is to listen to people who know injustice and to insist on seeing things from their point of view. It is to know that their anger is directed at real injustices, that their sense of loss stems largely from the tragedy of unemployment and the insecure future of their children, and that their hopes rest on real capacities and achievements. Doing them justice, in these terms, depends upon listening; it begins not from telling people what they should do, but from listening to them and then asking, 'What do you think should be done?'. Justice also means asking them what they can do and are already doing.[31]

Impoverished people don't need to be taught and they don't need to be told. They need to be trusted, respected and heard. They want to begin the conversation about poverty and injustice rather than always coming in at its end.

As a historian, my other contribution is to take their lead and insist on hope and change. History is never concerned only with the past. It is always about what might be. It explains the choices and decisions that have made the world we know, assesses why those choices and not others were made, and explores different paths into the future. History is also a powerful tool against continuing injustice. A large number of Australians can look back to a time when they or people like them were assumed to be inevitably inferior, incapable of being equal, and unfitted for such privileges as voting, earning equal pay or entering this country. The victories for equality and for inclusion in human history have been won because people refused to accept what was considered inevitable.

Those victories have also come because those who were excluded have been heard. The discarded and the disdained have created change, in part, because people who weren't either of those things have accepted the truth of what they said. We can look back into the past and find empathy, imaginative compassion and a belief in the possibility and necessity of change. We can find a regard for others and a desire to do justice. It is a good thing we can. Imagine a world in which we still applied nineteenth-century rules about who was unavoidably inferior, or about what was unimaginable, unnatural and unthinkable. Imagine if all of the things the people of the past were told could never happen never did, and if all the changes they were told would undermine the economy and create chaos never came to pass.

People's power to make choices and to refuse the logic of inevitable futures is history's richest lesson. The refusal to accept one way forward is in many ways the greatest contribution the people of the past have made to our own lives. They took up some of the possibilities embedded in the world as they found it and so can we. And as we did to them, the people of the future – a future that without action looks likely to see more inequality, more insecurity and more despair – will hold us to account for the choices we make and don't make now.

* * * *

How might the world look from Broadmeadows, Inala and Mount Druitt now? There has been an economic recovery. Official statistics show unemployment rates of 6 per cent for Australia as a whole. In 2001, after all the experiments in employment policy, the unemployment rate had also fallen in Inala, Mount Druitt and Broadmeadows – to 11 per cent in Inala, 10 per cent in Mount Druitt and 8 per cent in Broadmeadows. Also, the number of men and women with jobs had risen slightly since 1996. In between lay the men and women who weren't looking for work any more: one-third of the families in these suburbs had no earners at all, and the men not working still outnumbered those working in Inala and Mount Druitt.[32]

What little comfort might be taken from falling unemployment rates is further reduced when the problem of under-reporting and the manipulation of statistics are taken into account. Most recently, the Australian Bureau of Statistics has estimated that the 600,000 Australians classified as 'unemployed' in 2001 did not include another 800,000 or so who were also jobless but not counted in the official unemployment figures, or the 700,000 part-time workers who wanted more work than they had.[33] Perhaps these are just inaccurate snapshots. Perhaps hundreds of thousands of people are earning on the sly. Or perhaps there is a real and endemic problem of work in this society.

I don't doubt that the world I visited seven or eight years ago is in some ways the same – for good and bad – and in some ways very different. The places from which people have arrived will be even more diverse. There will be new ventures in the neighbourhood houses and community centres. In Inala there has been substantial redevelopment and housing renewal. Other experiments, imposed from the outside, have hardened the welfare system upon which many will still depend. Caring observers have tried to reveal the basic nastiness of the harsher compliance rules and the savage penalties for mistakes. They have told us about the presumption of guilt before innocence and about investigations that would unseat governments if they were carried out on taxpayers.

Despite genuine desires to improve the welfare system, and whatever the potentially helpful recommendations of reforming committees, few have bothered to ask the poor for their ideas. The debate about 'work for the dole' is a good example. The people to whom I spoke in the mid-1990s were full of thoughts about how to design a scheme that gave unemployed teenagers and men something to do and a place to go. Their stipulation was that any such scheme should be tied to the provision of real, lasting jobs. For the conservative parties, the idea seemed driven as much by polling as by principles. But if the conservatives introduced it, Labor had to oppose it, as did some welfare advocates. A debate we might have had about the shortage of real jobs became a debate about 'job snobs' and welfare dependency. So now we have a scheme around which conservatives have built an unnecessary and offensive rhetoric of obligation, as if people who don't work make no contribution to their families, neighbourhoods and communities.

Just before Christmas 2002, the federal government released its report on welfare reform. Some of the changes seemed sensible, such as removing the distinctions between different kinds of payments and tackling the so-called 'poverty traps' in which working for a wage or receiving a raise cancels out a range of benefits. However, it is still a system in which the first impulse is to uncover the ineligible, rather than support the eligible. And it is still a system designed largely by and for people who don't need welfare assistance rather than those who do. Ministers Tony Abbott and Amanda Vanstone were careful to remind the electorate that the main task was to ensure that work was always more attractive than welfare and once again lectured the unemployed and the poor on the importance of effort. I fear we are moving closer to the American enthusiasm for 'welfare repeal' and 'ending welfare'. As we do, we might also move closer to the American recognition, hard learned over twenty years, that poverty can't be blamed on dependency, that forcing people into low-income jobs has worsened problems such as homelessness and ill-health, and that similar welfare reforms in that country have widened rather than decreased social divisions.[34]

On the same day it was announced that the federal government's tentative proposal to remove the tax advantages of trusts had been shelved. An independent report in 1999 discovered that tax avoidance through trusts was costing the government at least $700,000,000 a year in lost revenue. But the Board of Taxation thought experiments would be too expensive and did not see any justification for sweeping changes.[35] According to the *Age*, the Board of Taxation includes people who themselves benefit from the use of trusts. As far as I can tell, the Reference Group on Welfare

Reform contained no one who actually needed welfare payments in order to live.[36] While trusts are estimated to cost us $700,000,000 a year, actual welfare fraud, even on the basis of the most enthusiastic assumptions, might cost us $15,000,000 a year. The contrast could not be more stark.

There is a crisis that surrounds our most disadvantaged neighbourhoods, but it's not a crisis of dependency or racial tensions or even hope. And it doesn't actually happen in Inala, Broadmeadows or Mount Druitt. It's a crisis of compassion, among those with much for those with very little. It's a crisis of belief, based on arguments about poverty and undeserving people that are just as cruel and untrue now as they were sixty or 100 years ago. It's a crisis of obligation, from the lucky to the unlucky, the old to the young, the insider to the outsider, those rich in confidence and chances to those who despair of either. It's a crisis of empathy. It might not seem that these are our neighbours, our sisters, our parents, our daughters and sons, our nieces or nephews, but they are, given different decisions, harder luck and fewer resources.

Inequality is not just an Australian drama but a global one. And the anger it creates will get worse each time someone poor watches television or reads newspaper advertisements for executive homes and corporate retreats or hears someone powerful tell them to wait their turn. In the old century of mass communication, and in the new century of global immediacy, the impoverished will know if the privileged don't care. The lies and the contradictions will keep hitting them in the face and it will be increasingly impossible to forget the images of what their lives are meant to be. As the keenest observers of feelings in these three suburbs realised, people were becoming more aware of their losses. They were more aware of what they didn't have, more aware that the problem was other people's unwillingness to be fair.

You can pretend that it's all envy, and you can say that we're all equal and we all get what we deserve. Or you could listen to their prophecy and the challenge poor people don't always dare to proclaim on their own. That they are people. That they are citizens. That they have rights. That they don't have to deserve anything and keep showing how grateful they are. That they shouldn't have to be heroes or victims because, in a decent society, that isn't what entitles them to justice. Most of all, that you can't do justice if you don't listen to the people who know injustice. It's time for them to be heard.

NOTES

Introduction

1 Janet McCalman, *Struggletown: Public and Private Life in Richmond, 1900–1965*, Melbourne, 1984; Richard Sennett and Jonathan Cobb, *The Hidden Injuries of Class*, New York, 1972; Carol Stack, *All Our Kin: Strategies for Survival in a Black Community*, New York, 1974. I have in mind here, too, the rich Australian writing about poverty in which the voices of the poor play a central role, such as Graeme Brewer (ed.), *On the Bread Line: Oral Records of Poverty*, Melbourne, 1972; Lois Bryson and Faith Thompson, *An Australian Newtown: Life and Leadership in a Working-Class Suburb*, Melbourne, 1972; and Jenny Trethewey, *Aussie Battlers: Families and Children in Poverty*, Melbourne, 1989.
2 Lois Bryson and Ian Winter, *Social Change, Suburban Lives: An Australian Newtown 1960s to 1990s*, Sydney, 1999, pp. 68–70.
3 Elizabeth Tonkin, *Narrating Our Pasts: The Social Construction of Oral History*, Cambridge, 1992, p. 67.
4 I draw here and in the subsequent discussion of oral history on Bain Attwood, 'Oral Narratives, Autobiography, and History', in Bain Attwood, et al., *A Life Together, a Life Apart: A History of Relations between Europeans and Aborigines*, Melbourne, 1994; Paula Hamilton, 'The Knife Edge: Debates about Memory and History', in Kate Darian-Smith and Paula Hamilton (eds), *Memory and History in Twentieth-Century Australia*, Melbourne, 1994; John Murphy, 'The Voice of Memory: History, Autobiography and Oral Memory', *Historical Studies*, 22, 1986, pp. 157–75; Alessandro Portelli, 'The Peculiarities of Oral History', *History Workshop Journal*, 12, 1981, pp. 96–107; Raphael Samuel, *Theatres of Memory*, London, 1994, pp. 3–17.
5 Jerome Bruner, 'The Narrative Construction of Reality', *Critical Inquiry*, 18, 1991, pp. 1–18.
6 Tonkin, *Narrating Our Pasts*, p. 12.
7 I derive these points largely from the work of British historian Carolyn Steedman, especially *Landscape for a Good Woman*, London, 1986.
8 Tonkin, *Narrating Our Pasts*, p. 134.
9 A particularly impressive example of how to read and understand silences is Ruth Wajnryb, *The Silence: How Tragedy Shapes Talk*, Sydney, 2001.

Chapter One: Describing Disadvantage

1 *Sydney Morning Herald*, 8 February 1973; *Australian*, 30 June 1972; *Age*, 16 August 1973; *Australian*, 30 December 1991.

2 See, for instance, 'Life in a Fast-Growing Bronx', *Sydney Morning Herald*, 19 October 1985.
3 'The Broady Boys', *Herald*, 1 March 1977.
4 'Inala: The Model All Dressed Up, But Going Nowhere', *Courier Mail*, 4 November 1966.
5 'Blacks Riot After Arrest at Inala', *Courier Mail*, 3 November 1990.
6 *Australian*, 30 December 1991.
7 *Daily Telegraph*, 15 October 1981; *Sun*, 15 October 1981.
8 *Sun*, 16 October 1981.
9 'Teenage Riots: A Symptom of Our Housing Disease', *Sydney Morning Herald*, 28 October 1981.
10 'Boredom Blamed for Riot', *Daily News*, 9 January 1984. See also Diane Powell, *Out West: Perceptions of Sydney's Western Suburbs*, Sydney, 1993, pp. 100–4. The continuing importance of such stories is also described in Robyn Dowling and Kathleen Mee, 'Tales of the City: Western Sydney at the End of the Millennium', in John Connell (ed.), *Sydney: The Emergence of a World City*, Melbourne, 2000.
11 *Weekend Australian*, 5–6 September 1998.
12 'Banksia Battlers', *Age*, Saturday Extra, 6 July 1991.
13 'A Land Like No Other', *Age*, 25 January 1995.
14 Martin Mowbray, 'Social Unrest Sparks the Welfare Response: Mount Druitt 1981', *Australian Quarterly*, 57, 1985, pp. 85–94.
15 Tony Birch, 'The Battle for Spatial Control in Fitzroy', in Sarah Ferber, Chris Healy and Chris McAuliffe (eds), *Beasts of Suburbia: Reinterpreting Cultures in Australian Suburbs*, Melbourne, 1994.
16 Peter Putnis, 'Popular Discourses and Images of Poverty and Welfare in the News Media', in Ruth Fincher and Peter Saunders (eds), *Creating Unequal Futures? Rethinking Poverty, Inequality and Disadvantage*, Sydney, 2001.
17 *Herald Sun*, 7 May 1992 and 8 May 1992; *Weekend Australian*, 2 May 1992.
18 *Sydney Morning Herald*, 17 July 1993.
19 *Courier Mail*, 14 June 1995 and 17 June 1995.
20 Deborah Hope, 'Poverty Doesn't Spell Underclass', *Australian Magazine*, 3–4 June 1995, pp. 12–23.
21 *Time*, 28 September 1998.
22 Ruth Fincher and John Nieuwenhuysen (eds), *Australian Poverty: Then and Now*, Melbourne, 1998; Fincher and Saunders (eds), *Creating Unequal Futures?*
23 See, in particular, Peter Saunders, *Ends and Means in Welfare*, Melbourne, 2002.
24 A particularly useful description of this tradition is provided by Graeme Davison, *The Compassionate Eye: Research and Reform*, Seventh F. Oswald Barnett Oration, Melbourne, 2000.
25 Peter Saunders, *Poverty, Choice and Legitimacy*, Social Policy Research Centre Discussion Paper No. 76, 1997, p. 1. See also Peter Travers and Sue Richardson, *Living Decently: Material Well-Being in Australia*, Melbourne, 1993, pp. 157–99.
26 Anthony King, *The Changing Face of Australian Poverty: A Comparison of 1996 Estimates and the 1972–73 Findings from the Commission of Inquiry*, National Centre for Social and Economic Modelling Discussion Paper No. 23, 1997.
27 Peter Saunders, *The Role, Value and Limitations of Poverty Research*, Social Policy Research Centre Discussion Paper No. 53, 1994.

28 Travers and Richardson, *Living Decently*, p. 197.

29 Peter Saunders and George Matheson, *Perceptions of Poverty, Income Adequacy and Living Standards in Australia*, Social Policy Research Centre Report No. 99, 1992; Janet Taylor and Michael Challen, 'Voices of Poverty', in Fincher and Nieuwenhuysen (eds), *Australian Poverty*; Peter Saunders, 'Defining Poverty and Identifying the Poor: Reflections on the Australian Experience', in Jonathan Bradshaw and Roy Sainsbury (eds), *Experiencing Poverty*, Aldershot, 2000.

30 A. Harding, R. Lloyd and H. Greenwell, *Financial Disadvantage in Australia, 1990 to 2000: The Persistence of Poverty in a Decade of Growth*, Sydney, 2001, p. 4.

31 Kayoko Tsumori, Peter Saunders and Helen Hughes, *Poor Arguments: A Response to the Smith Family Report on Poverty in Australia*, Centre for Independent Studies Issue Analysis No. 21, 2002.

32 Sanford F. Schram, *Words of Welfare: The Poverty of Social Science and the Social Science of Poverty*, Minneapolis, 1995, p. 5. One Australian exponent of the claim that poor people's poor behaviour helps explain their poverty is Lucy Sullivan in *Behavioural Poverty*, Centre for Independent Studies Policy Monograph No. 45, 2001.

33 Putnis, 'Popular Discourses', pp. 89–92.

34 Alice O'Connor, *Poverty Knowledge: Social Science, Social Policy and the Poor in Twentieth-Century US History*, Princeton, 2001, p. 7.

35 Bronwyn Long (ed.), *The State Budget 1982 and Community Services in Western Sydney*, Western Sydney Regional Information and Research Service Discussion Paper No. 7, 1982, p. 3.

36 Sydney City Mission, *Poverty in Mount Druitt: A Grim Reality*, Sydney, 1981, pp. 1–2, 5 & 10.

Chapter Two: Heroes

1 James Scott, *Weapons of the Weak: Everyday Forms of Peasant Resistance*, New Haven, 1985, p. 37.

2 ibid., p. 23.

3 Elizabeth Janeway, *Powers of the Weak*, New York, 1980, p. 14.

4 Figures taken from Housing Commission of Victoria *Annual Reports*, 1952–67.

5 Figures taken from New South Wales Housing Commission, *Annual Reports*, 1963–75 and an untitled memorandum, 30 April 1976, outlining the Mount Druitt building program, held in the Local History Collection, Blacktown City Library.

6 Figures taken from Queensland Housing Commission, *Annual Reports*, 1950–61 and Queensland Housing Commission, 'Inala: History and Development', 17 February 1966.

7 Mark Peel, *Good Times, Hard Times: The Past and the Future in Elizabeth*, Melbourne, 1995, pp. 37–56.

8 New South Wales Housing Commission, *Annual Report 1965–6*, p. 19.

9 Letter from Mr Stephens, Minister for Housing, to J. B. Southee, MLA, 16 June 1967, and record of the meeting between the Minister and a Blacktown Council deputation, 2 March 1967, both in State Records, NSW: NRS 16338; Housing Commission, Secretariat, Correspondence files, 1966–76; file G. 72/1242, Mt Druitt, Plumpton, Rooty Hill Housing Areas 103–102 Site 3500 [10/25396].

10 Queensland Housing Commission, *Annual Report 1955*, pp. 8–9; Queensland Housing Commission, 'Inala: History and Development', p. 2.
11 Housing Commission of Victoria, *Annual Report 1953–4*, p. 11.
12 Broadmeadows Welfare Advisory Committee, 'Disadvantaged Groups in Broadmeadows', n.d. [1980?], p. 8, in Broadmeadows Welfare Advisory Committee Records, State Library of Victoria, PA 92/100 [hereafter BWAC Records], Box 5, File 15.
13 Letter from Vance Dickie, Minister of Housing, 26 November 1975, in BWAC Records, Box 3, File 10.
14 Letter from Vance Dickie, Minister of Housing, 23 October 1974, in BWAC Records, Box 3, File 10.
15 'A Position Paper; CARE and Emergency Relief', 31 July 1982, in BWAC Records, Box 3, File 8.
16 MSJ Keys Young, *Regional Community Development Program: West Sydney 2000*, vol. 1, Sydney, 1985, p. 2.
17 Jack Docherty, 'Housing Reform, the Newman Perspective: An Interview with Senator Jocelyn Newman', *National Housing Action*, 11 (4), 1996, pp. 5–15. On the broader history of public housing, see especially David Hayward, 'The Reluctant Landlords? A History of Public Housing in Australia', *Urban Policy and Research*, 14, 1996, pp. 5–36 and Chris Paris, *Housing Australia*, Melbourne, 1993.
18 *Sun*, 22 July 1976, in BWAC Records, Box 3, File 10.
19 As far as I can tell from the archival record, much of the actual credit for the sewerage, if not the houses, should go to the local state Labor member in the 1970s, Tony Johnson, who seems to have devoted much energy to overcoming this particular deficiency.
20 Beatrix Campbell, *Wigan Pier Revisited: Poverty and Politics in the Eighties*, London, 1984.

Chapter Three: Suffering

1 Kevin McDonald, *Struggles for Subjectivity: Identity, Action and Youth Experience*, Melbourne, 1999, pp. 114, 120.
2 Amartya Sen, *Inequality Reexamined*, Oxford, 1992, p. 116.
3 Nancy Fraser, *Unruly Practices: Power, Discourse and Gender in Contemporary Social Theory*, Cambridge, 1989, p. 178.

Chapter Four: Anger

1 For example, 'A Win for the Forgotten People', *Australian*, 16 June 1998 and 'How Hanson Became a Hero of the Poor', *Age*, 26 October 1998. This expectation also characterised most of the chapters in Bligh Grant (ed.), *Pauline Hanson: One Nation and Australian Politics*, Armidale, 1997. There is a comprehensive discussions of understandings of Hansonism in Andrew Markus, *Race: John Howard and the Remaking of Australia*, Sydney, 2001, pp. 143–95 and Michael Leach, Geoffrey Stokes and Ian Ward (eds), *The Rise and Fall of One Nation*, Brisbane, 2000.
2 Mudrooroo, 'The Perils of Pauline: Consensus and Dissent in Australian Politics', *Overland*, 148, 1997, pp. 3–7.

3 Booth statistics for the seat of Oxley in 1998 were calculated from Australian Electoral Commission, *Election Statistics: 1993, 1996, 1998*, Canberra, 1999. Results for 2001 were calculated from the AEC website: http://www.aec.gov.au/_content/when/past/2001/results/index.html.

4 Booth statistics for Chifley in 1998 and 2001 were calculated from ibid. Booth statistics for the seats of Mount Druitt, Blacktown and Londonderry were calculated from State Electoral Office of New South Wales, 'Election 1999 Results', at http://www.seo.nsw.gov.au/results/SGE99/laresults.htm.

5 Murray Goot and Ian Watson, 'One Nation's Electoral Support: Where Does It Come From, What Makes It Different and How Does It Fit?', *Australian Journal of Politics and History*, 47, 2001, pp. 159–91. See also Markus, *Race*, pp. 230–55 and Rex Davis and Robert Stimson, 'Disillusionment and Disenchantment at the Fringe: Explaining the Geography of the One Nation Party Vote at the Queensland Election', *People and Place*, 6, 1998, pp. 69–82.

6 Helen Irving, 'The Virtuous Citizen', *Arena Magazine*, 15, 1995, p. 19.

7 Tom R. Tyler, Robert J. Boeckmann, Heather J. Smith and Yuen J. Ho, *Social Justice in a Diverse Society*, Boulder, 1997, p. 225.

8 O'Connor, *Poverty Knowledge*, p. 244.

9 Robert D. Putnam, *Bowling Alone: The Collapse and Revival of American Community*, New York, 2000.

10 One of the most successful, the Elizabeth-Munno Para Social Justice Project in South Australia, is described in my book, *Good Times, Hard Times*, pp. 227–33. See also Donna Ferretti and Trish O'Donovan, 'The Elizabeth/Munno Para Social Justice Project: Integrating Social and Physical Planning in Adelaide', *Australian Planner*, 31, 1993, pp. 70–4.

Chapter Five: Loss

1 I draw in this and subsequent paragraphs on the following studies: Bryson and Winter, *Social Change, Suburban Lives*, pp. 71–104; Clive Forster, *Australian Cities: Continuity and Change*, 2nd edn, Melbourne, 1999; Robert H. Fagan and Michael Webber, *Global Restructuring: The Australian Experience*, 2nd edn, Melbourne, 1999, pp. 73–122; Jeff Borland, Bob Gregory and Peter Sheehan, 'Inequality and Economic Change', in Jeff Borland, Bob Gregory and Peter Sheehan (eds), *Work Rich, Work Poor: Inequality and Economic Change in Australia*, Melbourne, 2001; Bob Gregory and Peter Sheehan, 'Poverty and the Collapse of Full Employment', in Fincher and Nieuwenhuysen (eds), *Australian Poverty*; Martin Watts, 'The Dimensions and Costs of Unemployment in Australia', in Stephen Bell (ed.), *The Unemployment Crisis in Australia: Which Way Out?*, Melbourne, 2000.

2 Figures for 1971 calculated from Bureau of Census and Statistics, *1971 Census of Population and Housing, Characteristics of the Population and Dwellings, Local Government Areas*, Canberra, 1972; figures for 1976 calculated from Bureau of Census and Statistics, *1976 Census of Population and Housing, Characteristics of the Population and Dwellings, Local Government Areas*, Canberra, 1977; 1991 figures for Blacktown, Inala and Broadmeadows were calculated by Glenys Harding and the author from the Basic Community Profiles produced by the

Australian Bureau of Statistics; and 1996 figures for Blacktown, Inala and Broadmeadows were calculated by Virginia Rapson from CDATA96. Mount Druitt presented a problem because it is part of the much larger City of Blacktown. Accordingly, labour force and population data were also studied for approximately sixty census collection districts that made up Mount Druitt in 1991 and 1996. Finally, as Broadmeadows is also a large city, I also used census collection district data to examine local patterns of employment.

3 R. G. Gregory and B. Hunter, *The Macro Economy and the Growth of Ghettos and Urban Poverty in Australia*, Australian National University Centre for Economic Policy Research Discussion Paper No. 325, 1995, p. 11.

4 ibid., pp. 1–2.

5 My understanding of the ways in which stories about unemployment draw on and in turn shape life stories is based in part on Douglas Ezzy, *Narrating Unemployment*, Aldershot, 2001.

6 For detailed studies of this phenomenon, see Tony Eardley, *Working But Poor? Low Pay and Poverty in Australia*, Social Policy Research Centre Discussion Paper No. 91, 1998; John Buchanan and Ian Watson, 'The Living Wage and the Working Poor', in Michael Bittman (ed.), *Poverty in Australia: Dimensions and Policies*, Social Policy Research Centre Reports and Proceedings No. 135, 1997; and Yvonne Dunlop, 'Low-Paid Employment in the Australian Labour Market, 1995–97', in Borland, Gregory and Sheehan (eds), *Work Rich, Work Poor*.

7 Campbell, *Wigan Pier Revisited*, p. 190.

8 Trethewey, *Aussie Battlers*, pp. 58–79.

9 The most comprehensive studies have been carried out in Britain: Bill Jordan, Simon James, Helen Kay and Marcus Redley, *Trapped in Poverty? Labour Market Decisions in Low-Income Households*, London, 1992, pp. 84–132 and 175–80; Lydia Morris, *The Workings of the Household*, Cambridge, 1990, pp. 23–59.

10 McDonald, *Struggles for Subjectivity*, p. 3.

11 Carolyn Steedman, *Past Tenses: Essays on Writing, Autobiography and History*, London, 1992, pp. 37–8.

12 R. W. Connell, *Masculinities*, Sydney, 1995.

13 McDonald, *Struggles for Subjectivity*, pp. 67–93.

Chapter Six: Hope

1 This is, of course, neither the only nor the best definition, though it is the definition implied by most commentators and, I think, the definition routinely endorsed in public opinion polls and surveys. Other definitions are explored below. For a particularly important discussion of multiculturalism, and tolerance, see Ghassan Hage, *White Nation: Fantasies of White Supremacy in a Multicultural Society*, Sydney, 1998, pp. 78–104.

2 Jim Houston, 'Draft Report of the Preliminary Findings of the Broadmeadows Local Area Feasibility Study', Melbourne, 1986, pp. 45–6. I am grateful to Larry Stillman for pointing me to this report.

3 Hage, *White Nation*, p. 234.

4 Nancy Naples, *Grassroots Warriors: Activist Mothering, Community Work, and the War on Poverty*, New York, 1998, p. 11.
5 ibid., pp. 131–53.
6 See especially Iris Marion Young, *Justice and the Politics of Difference*, Princeton, 1990; Iris Marion Young, *Intersecting Voices: Dilemmas of Gender, Political Philosophy and Policy*, Princeton, 1997, pp. 60–74; David Harvey, *Justice, Nature and the Geography of Difference*, Oxford, 1996, pp. 341–65.
7 David Harvey, 'Social Justice, Postmodernism and the City', *International Journal of Urban and Regional Research*, 16, 1992, pp. 588–601.
8 On these issues, see especially Young, *Justice and the Politics of Difference* and Raymond Plant, 'Citizenship, Rights and Welfare', in Anna Coote (ed.), *The Welfare of Citizens: Developing New Social Rights*, London, 1992.
9 Tyler et al., *Social Justice in a Diverse Society*, p. 78.
10 Brian Barry, *A Treatise on Social Justice, Volume One: Theories of Justice*, Berkeley, 1989, p. 361.
11 Harvey, Justice, *Nature and the Geography of Difference*, pp. 358–65.
12 Young, *Justice and the Politics of Difference*, p. 119.
13 I am particularly indebted here to Harvey, *Justice, Nature and the Geography of Difference*, pp. 19–45, and Derek Gregory, 'Interventions in the Historical Geography of Modernity: Social Theory, Spatiality and the Politics of Representation', in James Duncan and David Ley (eds), *Place/Culture/Representation*, London, 1993.
14 Raymond Williams, *Resources of Hope*, London 1989, p. 322.
15 bell hooks, 'Choosing the Margin as a Space of Radical Openness', in *Yearning: Race, Gender and Cultural Politics*, Boston, 1990, pp. 145–53.

Conclusion

1 Mark Peel, 'The Urban Debate: From "Los Angeles" to the "Urban Village"', in Patrick Troy (ed.), *Australian Cities: Issues, Strategies and Policies for Urban Australia in the 1990s*, Melbourne, 1995, pp. 39–64.
2 O'Connor, *Poverty Knowledge*, p. 243. See also Herbert Gans, *The War Against the Poor: The Underclass and Anti-Poverty Policy*, New York, 1995.
3 Putnis, 'Popular Discourses', p. 87.
4 *Herald Sun*, 16 January 2002.
5 *Herald Sun*, 12 February 2002.
6 *Age*, 12 February 2002.
7 The most important work was Mike Davis, *City of Quartz: Excavating the Future in Los Angeles*, London, 1990; see also Harvey, *Justice, Nature and the Geography of Difference*, pp. 403–16.
8 Graham Little, *The Public Emotions: From Mourning to Hope*, Sydney, 1999, pp. 38–40.
9 ibid., pp. 65–94; Hugh Mackay, *Reinventing Australia: The Mind and Mood of Australia in the '90s*, Sydney, 1995.
10 Ghassan Hage, 'The Shrinking Society: Ethics and Hope in the Era of Global Capitalism', Sydney, 2002, at http://evatt.labor.net.au/publications/papers/5.html.

11 Eileen Baldry and Tony Vinson, 'The Current Obsession with Reducing Taxes', *Just Policy*, 13, 1998, pp. 3–9.
12 Tyler et al., *Social Justice in a Diverse Society*, pp. 135–93.
13 Raymond Gaita, *A Common Humanity*, Melbourne, 1999.
14 Inga Clendinnen, *True Stories*, Sydney, 1999; Janet McCalman, *The Learning of History and Learning How to Live*, University of Melbourne History Department Occasional Paper No. 14, 2001.
15 Robert E. Goodin, *Protecting the Vulnerable: A Reanalysis of our Social Responsibilities*, Chicago, 1985.
16 Kevin McDonald, 'Leeching the Meanings of Human Experience', *Arena Magazine*, 17, 1995, pp. 44–8.
17 See especially Hugh Stretton and Lionel Orchard, *Public Goods, Public Enterprise, Public Choice: Theoretical Foundations of the Contemporary Attack on Government*, New York, 1994, and Sharon Zukin, *Landscapes of Power: From Detroit to Disney World*, Berkeley, 1991, pp. 253–75.
18 Simon Kelly, 'Simulating Future Trends in Wealth Inequality', paper presented at the 2002 Australian Conference of Economists, Adelaide, 3 October 2002, at http://www.natsem.canberra.edu.au/pubs/cp02/2002_010/cp2002_010.pdf.
19 'Precarious Work, Uncertain Futures: The Labour Market Experiences of 25- to 34-Year-Olds', Brotherhood of St Lawrence at http://www.ceda.com.au/Research/ResearchNews/SocialSettlement/Precious.pdf. The best exploration of these issues is David Thomson, *Selfish Generations? How Welfare States Grow Old*, 2nd edn, Cambridge, 1996.
20 See, for instance, Bent Greve (ed.), *What Constitutes a Good Society?*, Basingstoke, 2000.
21 Humphrey McQueen, *Temper Democratic: How Exceptional is Australia?*, Adelaide, 1998, p. 60.
22 For a comprehensive examination of 'social capital' in an Australian context, see Ian Winter (ed.), *Social Capital and Public Policy in Australia*, Melbourne, 2000.
23 Will Hutton, *The World We're In*, London, 2002.
24 Ronald Dworkin, 'Do Liberty and Equality Conflict?', in Paul Barker (ed.), *Living as Equals*, Oxford, 1996.
25 Amartya Sen, 'Social Commitment and Democracy', in Barker (ed.), *Living as Equals*, p. 16.
26 John Solas, 'The War on Poverty in Australia', *Just Policy*, 27, 2002, pp. 11–18.
27 John Langmore and John Quiggin, *Work For All: Full Employment in the Nineties*, Melbourne, 1994; see also Jocelyn Pixley, *Citizenship and Employment: Investigating Post-Industrial Options*, Melbourne, 1993, and Stephen Bell, 'Unemployment, Inequality and the Politics of Redistribution', in Bell (ed.), *The Unemployment Crisis*.
28 Brendan Gleeson and Nicholas Low, *Australian Urban Planning: New Challenges, New Agendas*, Sydney, 2000, p. 204.
29 See Jeanette Johnson's reports: *The Invisible Australians: Community Understandings of Poverty*, Melbourne, 2000 and *Poverty in Australia: Developing Community Dialogue*, Melbourne, 2002.
30 Albert O. Hirschman, 'Two Hundred Years of Reactionary Rhetoric: The Futility Thesis', in Barker (ed.), *Living as Equals*, p. 64. On the importance of resisting the

argument of 'limited resources', in this case in disease prevention, see also Paul Farmer, *Infections and Inequalities: The New Plagues*, Berkeley, 1999.

31 A particularly important argument along these lines in advanced by Judith Bessant, 'The Politics of Official Talk about Welfare Reform in Australia', *Just Policy*, 28, 2002, pp. 12–22. While I disagree with some of his assumptions and conclusions, this is also a major aspect of the ideas advanced by Mark Latham, for instance in *Reviving Labor's Agenda: A Program for Local Reform*, Sydney, 1990, and in Peter Botsman and Mark Latham (eds), *The Enabling State: People Before Bureaucracy*, Sydney, 2001.

32 Analyses of 1999 Centrelink Data on 'breadwinner families' and on the 2001 Census, using CDATA2001, were carried out by Virginia Rapson, of Monash University's Centre for Urban and Population Research.

33 *Age*, 22 March 2003.

34 O'Connor, *Poverty Knowledge*, pp. 283–95; Barbara Ehrenreich, *Nickel and Dimed: On (Not) Getting By in America*, New York, 2001; Holly Sklar, *Chaos or Community?*, Boston, 1995.

35 *Age*, 13 December 2002.

36 Bessant, 'The Politics of Official Talk'.

BIBLIOGRAPHY

Archival documents

New South Wales Department of Housing Library

Research and Information Group, Housing Commission of New South Wales, 'New Tenants in Bidwill, Mt. Druitt', 26 August 1976.

Queensland Department of Housing, Local Government and Planning Library

Queensland Department of Housing and Local Government, 'New Trends in Public Housing', 6 February 1990.

Queensland Housing Commission, 'Inala: History and Development', 17 February 1966.

State Library of Victoria, Latrobe Library

Broadmeadows Welfare Advisory Committee, Records, PA 92/100.

State Records Authority of New South Wales

New South Wales Housing Commission, Secretariat, Correspondence files, 1966–76, NRS 16338: 10/25386–431.

Official publications

Australian Bureau of Statistics, CDATA 1996.

Australian Bureau of Statistics, CDATA 2001.

Australian Electoral Commission, *Election Statistics: 1993, 1996, 1998*, Canberra, 1999.

Australian Electoral Commission, 'Results of the 2001 Federal Election', at http://www.aec.gov.au/_content/when/past/2001/results/index.html.

Blacktown City Council, *Blacktown: The City on the Move*, Sydney, 1984.

Broadmeadows Development Committee, *Into the Future: Broadmeadows Community Strategy Plan*, Melbourne, 1984.

Bureau of Census and Statistics, *1971 Census of Population and Housing, Characteristics of the Population and Dwellings, Local Government Areas*, Canberra, 1972.

Bureau of Census and Statistics, *1976 Census of Population and Housing, Characteristics of the Population and Dwellings, Local Government Areas*, Canberra, 1977.

Commonwealth of Australia, Department of Urban and Regional Development, *Sydney Western Region: An Initial Discussion Report*, Canberra, 1974.

Housing Commision of Victoria, *Annual Reports*, 1952–67.

New South Wales Housing Commission, *Annual Reports*, 1963–85.
Queensland Department of Housing and Local Government, *Annual Report*, 1990–91.
Queensland Department of Housing, Local Government and Planning, *Annual Reports*, 1992–94.
Queensland Housing Commission, *Annual Reports*, 1950–89.
State Electoral Office of New South Wales, 'Election 1999 Results', at http://www.seo.nsw.gov.au/results/SGE99/laresults.htm.

Unpublished materials and reports

Broadmeadows Youth Unemployment Resource Centre, 'Jobless Youth, A Crisis of the 1970s: A Broadmeadows Experience', n. d. [1979].
Gardiner, Warren, 'The Wran Government's Urban Development Program and Western Sydney', Blacktown City Community Services Network, 1984.
Gibb, Greg, 'Social Justice in Western Suburbs', unpublished paper, New South Wales Planning and Environment Commission n. d. [1977].
Houston, Jim, 'Draft Report of the Preliminary Findings of the Broadmeadows Local Area Feasibility Study', Australian Institute of Multicultural Affairs, 1986.
McDonald, Louise, 'Information Kit, and a History of CUF', Coalition for the Urban Fringe, 1993.
Martin Lack & Associates, 'The Attitudes of Business Towards Employing Inala/Darra Residents', South West Economic Development Network, 1994.
North Western Suburbs Regional Consultative Council, 'Transiting Where? A Report on Youth Issues and Needs in Brunswick, Coburg, Broadmeadows, Bulla and Gisborne', 1982.
Pinchen, Suzy, 'A History of Broadmeadows', Broadmeadows Community Health Services, 1988.
Riley, G., 'Some More History of Our Inala and Suburbs', n. d. [1993].
South Community Development Team, 'Inala Community Mapping', n. d. [1994].
Stillman, Larry, 'Community Relations as Community Development: A Project Perspective', 1993.

Newspapers and magazines

Age
Australian
Courier Mail
Daily News
Daily Telegraph
Herald
Herald Sun
Sun
Sydney Morning Herald
Time
Weekend Australian

Books and articles

Allatt, Patricia and Yeandle, Susan, *Youth Unemployment and the Family: Voices of Disordered Times*, London, 1992.

Attwood, Bain, 'Oral Narratives, Autobiography, and History', in Bain Attwood, et al., *A Life Together, a Life Apart: A History of Relations between Europeans and Aborigines*, Melbourne, 1994.

Bagguley, Paul, Mark-Lawson, Jane, Shapiro, Dan, Urry, John, Walby, Sylvia and Warde, Alan, *Restructuring: Place, Class and Gender*, London, 1990.

Baldry, Eileen and Vinson, Tony, 'The Current Obsession with Reducing Taxes', *Just Policy*, 13, 1998, pp. 3–9.

Barry, Brian, *A Treatise on Social Justice, Volume One: Theories of Justice*, Berkeley, 1989.

Bauman, Richard, *Story, Performance and Event: Contextual Studies of Oral Narrative*, Cambridge, 1986.

Bell, Stephen, 'Unemployment, Inequality and the Politics of Redistribution', in Stephen Bell (ed.), *The Unemployment Crisis in Australia: Which Way Out?*, Melbourne, 2000.

Bertaux-Wiame, Isabelle, 'The Life History Approach to the Study of Internal Migration', in Daniel Bertaux, *Biography and Society: The Life History Approach in the Social Sciences*, Beverly Hills, 1981.

Bessant, Judith, 'The Politics of Official Talk about Welfare Reform in Australia', *Just Policy*, 28, 2002, pp. 12–22.

Birch, Tony, 'The Battle for Spatial Control in Fitzroy', in Sarah Ferber, Chris Healy and Chris McAuliffe (eds), *Beasts of Suburbia: Reinterpreting Cultures in Australian Suburbs*, Melbourne, 1994.

Bookman, Ann and Morgan, Sandra (eds), *Women and the Politics of Empowerment*, Philadelphia, 1988.

Borland, Jeff, Gregory, Bob and Sheehan, Peter, 'Inequality and Economic Change', in Jeff Borland, Bob Gregory and Peter Sheehan (eds), *Work Rich, Work Poor: Inequality and Economic Change in Australia*, Melbourne, 2001.

Botsman, Peter and Latham, Mark (eds), *The Enabling State: People Before Bureaucracy*, Sydney, 2001.

Brewer, Graeme (ed.), *On the Bread Line: Oral Records of Poverty*, Melbourne, 1980.

Bruner, Jerome, 'The Narrative Construction of Reality', *Critical Inquiry*, 18, 1991, pp. 1–18.

Bryson, Lois and Thompson, Faith, *An Australian Newtown: Life and Leadership in a Working-Class Suburb*, Melbourne, 1972.

Bryson, Lois and Winter, Ian, *Social Change, Suburban Lives: An Australian Newtown 1960s to 1990s*, Sydney, 1999.

Buchanan, John and Watson, Ian, 'The Living Wage and the Working Poor', in Michael Bittman (ed.), *Poverty in Australia: Dimensions and Policies*, Social Policy Research Centre Reports and Proceedings No. 135, 1997.

Campbell, Beatrix, *Wigan Pier Revisited: Poverty and Politics in the Eighties*, London, 1984

Clendinnen, Inga, *True Stories*, Sydney, 1999.

Connell, R. W., *Masculinities*, Sydney, 1995.

Cooke, Philip, *Back to the Future*, London, 1990.

Dalley, Gillian, *Ideologies of Caring: Rethinking Community and Collectivism*, Basingstoke, 1988.

Davis, Mike, *City of Quartz: Excavating the Future in Los Angeles*, London, 1990.

Davis, Rex and Stimson, Robert, 'Disillusionment and Disenchantment at the Fringe: Explaining the Geography of the One Nation Party Vote at the Queensland Election', *People and Place*, 6, 1998, pp. 69–82.

Davison, Graeme, *The Compassionate Eye: Research and Reform*, Seventh F. Oswald Barnett Oration, Melbourne, 2000.

Debouzy, Marianne, 'In Search of Working-Class Memory', *History and Anthropology*, 2, 1986, pp. 261–82.

Docherty, Jack, 'Housing Reform, the Newman Perspective: An interview with Senator Jocelyn Newman', *National Housing Action*, 11 (4), 1996, pp. 5–15.

Dowling, Robyn and Mee, Kathleen, 'Tales of the City: Western Sydney at the End of the Millennium', in John Connell (ed.), *Sydney: The Emergence of a World City*, Melbourne, 2000.

Dunlop, Yvonne, 'Low-Paid Employment in the Australian Labour Market, 1995–97', in Jeff Borland, Bob Gregory and Peter Sheehan (eds), *Work Rich, Work Poor: Inequality and Economic Change in Australia*, Melbourne, 2001.

Dunn, Kevin, 'Rethinking Ethnic Concentrations: The Case of Cabramatta', *Urban Studies*, 35, 1998, pp. 503–27.

Dworkin, Ronald, 'Do Liberty and Equality Conflict?', in Paul Barker (ed.), *Living as Equals*, Oxford, 1996.

Eardley, Tony, *Working But Poor? Low Pay and Poverty in Australia*, Social Policy Research Centre Discussion Paper No. 91, 1998.

Edwards, Anne and Magarey, Susan (eds), *Women in a Restructuring Australia: Work and Welfare*, Sydney, 1995.

Ehrenreich, Barbara, *Nickel and Dimed: On (Not) Getting By in America*, New York, 2001.

Ezzy, Douglas, *Narrating Unemployment*, Aldershot, 2001.

Fagan, Robert H. and Webber, Michael, *Global Restructuring: The Australian Experience*, 2nd edn, Melbourne, 1999.

Farmer, Paul, *Infections and Inequalities: The New Plagues*, Berkeley, 1999.

Ferretti, Donna and O'Donovan, Trish,'The Elizabeth/Munno Para Social Justice Project: Integrating Social and Physical Planning in Adelaide', *Australian Planner*, 31, 1993, pp. 70–4.

Fincher, Ruth and Nieuwenhuysen, John (eds), *Australian Poverty: Then and Now*, Melbourne, 1998.

Fincher, Ruth and Saunders, Peter (eds), *Creating Unequal Futures? Rethinking Poverty, Inequality and Disadvantage*, Sydney, 2001.

Forster, Clive, *Australian Cities: Continuity and Change*, 2nd edn, Melbourne, 1999.

Fraser, Nancy, *Unruly Practices: Power, Discourse and Gender in Contemporary Social Theory*, Cambridge, 1989.

Gaita, Raimond, *A Common Humanity*, Melbourne, 1999.

Gallie, Duncan, Marsh, Catherine and Vogler, Carolyn (eds), *Social Change and the Experience of Unemployment*, Oxford, 1994.

Gans, Herbert, *The War Against the Poor: The Underclass and Anti-Poverty Policy*, New York, 1995.

Gleeson, Brendan and Low, Nicholas, *Australian Urban Planning: New Challenges, New Agendas*, Sydney, 2000.

Goodin, Robert E., *Protecting the Vulnerable: A Reanalysis of our Social Responsibilities*, Chicago, 1985.

Goot, Murray and Watson, Ian, 'One Nation's Electoral Support: Where Does It Come From, What Makes It Different and How Does It Fit?', *Australian Journal of Politics and History*, 47, 2001, pp. 159–91.

Grace, Helen, Hage, Ghassan, Johnson, Lesley, Langsworth, Julie and Symonds, Michael, *Home/World: Space, Community and Marginality in Sydney's West*, Sydney, 1997.

Grant, Bligh (ed.), *Pauline Hanson: One Nation and Australian Politics*, Armidale, 1997.

Gregory, Bob and Sheehan, Peter, 'Poverty and the Collapse of Full Employment', in Ruth Fincher and John Nieuwenhuysen (eds), *Australian Poverty: Then and Now*, Melbourne, 1998.

Gregory, Derek, 'Interventions in the Historical Geography of Modernity: Social Theory, Spatiality and the Politics of Representation', in James Duncan and David Ley (eds), *Place/Culture/Representation*, London, 1993.

Gregory, R. G. and Hunter, B., *The Macro Economy and the Growth of Ghettos and Urban Poverty in Australia*, Australian National University Centre for Economic Policy Research Discussion Paper No. 325, 1995.

Greve, Bent (ed.), *What Constitutes a Good Society?*, Basingstoke, 2000.

Hage, Ghassan, 'The Shrinking Society: Ethics and Hope in the Era of Global Capitalism', Sydney, 2002, at http://evatt.labor.net.au/publications/papers/5.html.

Hage, Ghassan, *White Nation: Fantasies of White Supremacy in a Multicultural Society*, Sydney, 1998.

Hamilton, Paula, 'The Knife Edge: Debates about Memory and History', in Kate Darian-Smith and Paula Hamilton (eds), *Memory and History in Twentieth-Century Australia*, Melbourne, 1994.

Hamilton-Smith, E. and Balmer, C., *Broadmeadows: A Growing City, Volume 1*, Melbourne, 1972.

Hanna, Bronwyn, 'Green Valley: Sameness and Difference in Suburbia', *West*, 3, 1991, pp. 6–13.

Harding, A, Lloyd, R and Greenwell, H, *Financial Disadvantage in Australia, 1990 to 2000: The Persistence of Poverty in a Decade of Growth*, Sydney, 2001.

Harvey, David, *Justice, Nature and the Geography of Difference*, Oxford, 1996.

Harvey, David, 'Social Justice, Postmodernism and the City', *International Journal of Urban and Regional Research*, 16, 1992, pp. 588–601.

Hayward, David, 'The Reluctant Landlords? A History of Public Housing in Australia', *Urban Policy and Research*, 14, 1996, pp. 5–36.

Hirschman, Albert O., 'Two Hundred Years of Reactionary Rhetoric: The Futility Thesis', in Paul Barker (ed.), *Living as Equals*, Oxford, 1996.

Hodge, Stephen, 'Disadvantage and "Otherness" in Western Sydney', *Australian Geographical Studies*, 34, 1996, pp. 32–44.

Hollingworth, Peter, *Australians in Poverty*, 4th edn, Melbourne, 1985.

hooks, bell, *Yearning: Race, Gender and Cultural Politics*, Boston, 1990.

Hutton, Will, *The World We're In*, London, 2002.

Irving, Helen, 'The Virtuous Citizen', *Arena Magazine*, 15, 1995, p. 19.

Janeway, Elizabeth, *Powers of the Weak*, New York, 1980.

Johnson, Jeanette, *Poverty in Australia: Developing Community Dialogue*, Melbourne, 2002.

Johnson, Jeanette, *The Invisible Australians: Community Understandings of Poverty*, Melbourne, 2000.

Jones, Andrew and Smyth, Paul, 'Social Exclusion: A New Framework for Social Policy Analysis?', *Just Policy*, 17, 1999, pp. 11–20.

Jordan, Bill, James, Simon, Kay, Helen and Redley, Marcus, *Trapped in Poverty? Labour Market Decisions in Low-Income Households*, London, 1992.

Katz, Michael B., *Improving Poor People: The Welfare State, the 'Underclass' and Urban Schools as History*, Princeton, 1995.

Kelly, Simon, 'Simulating Future Trends in Wealth Inequality', paper presented at the 2002 Australian Conference of Economists, Adelaide, 3 October 2002, at http://www.natsem.canberra.edu.au/pubs/cp02/2002_010/cp2002_010.pdf.

King, Anthony, 'Income Poverty Since the Early 1970s', in Ruth Fincher and John Nieuwenhuysen (eds), *Australian Poverty: Then and Now*, Melbourne, 1998.

King, Anthony, *The Changing Face of Australian Poverty: A Comparison of 1996 Estimates and the 1972–73 Findings from the Commission of Inquiry*, National Centre for Social and Economic Modelling Discussion Paper No. 23, 1997.

Lane, Mary, Newman, P. and Moran, A., *The Needs of North Mount Druitt: A Submission to the Chairman, Housing Commission of New South Wales*, Sydney, 1976.

Langmore, John and Quiggin, John, *Work For All: Full Employment in the Nineties*, Melbourne, 1994.

Latham, Mark, *Reviving Labor's Agenda: A Program for Local Reform*, Sydney, 1990.

Leach, Michael, Stokes, Geoffrey and Ward, Ian (eds), *The Rise and Fall of One Nation*, Brisbane, 2000.

Lerner, Michael, *Surplus Powerlessness*, London, 1991.

Little, Graham, *The Public Emotions: From Mourning to Hope*, Sydney, 1999.

Long, Bronwyn (ed.), *The State Budget 1982 and Community Services in Western Sydney*, Western Sydney Regional Information and Research Service Discussion Paper No. 7, 1982.

Mackay, Hugh, *Reinventing Australia: The Mind and Mood of Australia in the '90s*, Sydney, 1995.

Markus, Andrew, *Race: John Howard and the Remaking of Australia*, Sydney, 2001.

McCalman, Janet, *The Learning of History and Learning How to Live*, University of Melbourne History Department Occasional Paper No. 14, 2001.

McCalman, Janet, *Journeyings: The Biography of a Middle-Class Generation, 1920–1990*, Melbourne, 1993.

McCalman, Janet, *Struggletown: Public and Private Life in Richmond, 1900–1965*, Melbourne, 1984.

McDonald, Kevin, *Struggles for Subjectivity: Identity, Action and Youth Experience*, Melbourne, 1999.

McDonald, Kevin, 'Leeching the Meanings of Human Experience', *Arena Magazine*, 17, 1995, pp. 44–8.

McGregor, Craig, *Class in Australia*, Melbourne, 1997.

McQueen, Humphrey, *Temper Democratic: How Exceptional is Australia?*, Adelaide, 1998.

Mee, Kathleen, 'Dressing Up the Suburbs', in Katherine Gibson and Sophie Watson (eds), *Metropolis Now*, Sydney, 1994.

Morris, Lydia, *Dangerous Classes: The Underclass and Social Citizenship*, London, 1994.

Morris, Lydia, *The Workings of the Household*, Cambridge, 1990.

Mowbray, Martin, 'Social Unrest Sparks the Welfare Response: Mount Druitt 1981', *Australian Quarterly*, 57, 1985, pp. 85–94.

MSJ Keys Young, *Regional Community Development Program: West Sydney 2000*, vol. 1, Sydney, 1985.

Mudrooroo, 'The Perils of Pauline: Consensus and Dissent in Australian Politics', *Overland*, 148, 1997, pp. 3–7.

Murphy, John, 'The Voice of Memory: History, Autobiography and Oral Memory', *Historical Studies*, 22, 1986, pp. 157–75.

Murphy, Peter and Watson, Sophie, *Surface City: Sydney at the Millennium*, Sydney, 1997.

Naples, Nancy, *Grassroots Warriors: Activist Mothering, Community Work, and the War on Poverty*, New York, 1998.

Neisser, Ulric and Fivush, Robyn (eds), *The Remembering Self: Construction and Accuracy in the Self-Narrative*, Cambridge, 1994.

O'Connor, Alice, *Poverty Knowledge: Social Science, Social Policy and the Poor in Twentieth-Century U.S. History*, Princeton, 2001.

Oppenheim, C. (ed.), *An Inclusive Society: Strategies for Tackling Poverty*, London, 1998.

Paris, Chris, *Housing Australia*, Melbourne, 1993.

Peel, Mark, 'Trusting Disadvantaged Citizens', in Valerie Braithwaite and Margaret Levi (eds), *Trust and Democratic Governance*, New York, 1998.

Peel, Mark, *Good Times, Hard Times: The Past and the Future in Elizabeth*, Melbourne, 1995.

Peel, Mark, 'The Urban Debate: From "Los Angeles" to the "Urban Village"', in Patrick Troy (ed.), *Australian Cities: Issues, Strategies and Policies for Urban Australia in the 1990s*, Melbourne, 1995.

Pixley, Jocelyn, *Citizenship and Employment: Investigating Post-Industrial Options*, Melbourne, 1993.

Plant, Raymond, 'Citizenship, Rights and Welfare', in Anna Coote (ed.), *The Welfare of Citizens: Developing New Social Rights*, London, 1992.

Portelli, Alessandro, 'Uchronic Dreams: Working-Class Memory and Possible Worlds', in Raphael Samuel and Paul Thompson (eds), *The Myths We Live By*, London, 1990.

Portelli, Alessandro, 'The Peculiarities of Oral History', *History Workshop Journal*, 12, 1981, pp. 96–107.

Powell, Diane, *Out West: Perceptions of Sydney's Western Suburbs*, Sydney, 1993.

'Precarious Work, Uncertain Futures: The Labour Market Experiences of 25- to 34-Year-Olds', Brotherhood of St Lawrence at http://www.ceda.com.au/Research/ResearchNews/SocialSettlement/Precious.pdf.

Putnam, Robert D., *Bowling Alone: The Collapse and Revival of American Community*, New York, 2000.

Putnis, Peter, 'Popular Discourses and Images of Poverty and Welfare in the News Media', in Ruth Fincher and Peter Saunders (eds), *Creating Unequal Futures? Rethinking Poverty, Inequality and Disadvantage*, Sydney, 2001.

Richardson, Sue (ed.), *Reshaping the Labour Market: Regulation, Efficiency and Equality in Australia*, Melbourne, 1999.

Riley, G. J., *History of Our Inala and Suburbs*, Brisbane, 1988.

Roberts, Elizabeth, *Women and Families: An Oral History*, Oxford, 1995.

Salvaris, Mike, 'Privatization, Citizenship and the Public Interest', *Just Policy*, 4, 1995, pp. 37–43.

Samuel, Raphael, *Theatres of Memory*, London, 1994.

Saunders, Peter, *Ends and Means in Welfare*, Melbourne, 2002.

Saunders, Peter, 'Defining Poverty and Identifying the Poor: Reflections on the Australian Experience', in Jonathan Bradshaw and Roy Sainsbury (eds), *Experiencing Poverty*, Aldershot, 2000.

Saunders, Peter, *Poverty, Choice and Legitimacy*, Social Policy Research Centre Discussion Paper No. 76, 1997.

Saunders, Peter, *The Role, Value and Limitations of Poverty Research*, Social Policy Research Centre Discussion Paper No. 53, 1994.

Saunders, Peter and Matheson, George, *Perceptions of Poverty, Income Adequacy and Living Standards in Australia*, Social Policy Research Centre Reports and Proceedings No. 99, 1992.

Schein, Virginia E., *Working from the Margins: Voices of Mothers in Poverty*, Ithaca, 1995.

Schram, Sanford F., *Words of Welfare: The Poverty of Social Science and the Social Science of Poverty*, Minneapolis, 1995.

Scott, James, *Weapons of the Weak: Everyday Forms of Peasant Resistance*, New Haven, 1985.

Sen, Amartya, 'Social Commitment and Democracy', in Paul Barker (ed.), *Living as Equals*, Oxford, 1996.

Sen, Amartya, *Inequality Reexamined*, Oxford, 1992.

Sennett, Richard and Cobb, Jonathan, *The Hidden Injuries of Class*, New York, 1972.

Sklar, Holly, *Chaos or Community?*, Boston, 1995.

Smith, David M., 'Back to the Good Life: Towards an Enlarged Conception of Social Justice', *Environment and Planning D*, 15, 1997, pp. 19–35.

Smyth, Paul and Cass, Bettina (eds), *Contesting the Australian Way: Government, Civil Society and Market Forces*, Sydney, 1998.

Solas, John, 'The War on Poverty in Australia', *Just Policy*, 27, 2002, pp. 11–18.

Spearritt, Peter and De Marco, Christine, *Planning Sydney's Future*, Sydney, 1988.

Spelman, Elizabeth, *Fruits of Sorrow: Framing our Attention to Suffering*, Boston, 1997.

Stack, Carol, *All Our Kin: Strategies for Survival in a Black Community*, New York, 1974.

Steedman, Carolyn, *Past Tenses: Essays on Writing, Autobiography and History*, London, 1992.

Steedman, Carolyn, *Landscape for a Good Woman: A Story of Two Lives*, London, 1986.

Stilwell, Frank, 'Unemployment: Economic Myths and Positive Alternatives', *Just Policy*, 7, 1996, pp. 35–42.

Stretton, Hugh, *Poor Laws of 1834 and 1996*, Fifteenth Sambell Memorial Oration, Melbourne, 1996.

Stretton, Hugh, *Ideas for Australian Cities*, 3rd edn, Sydney, 1989.

Stretton, Hugh and Orchard, Lionel, *Public Goods, Public Enterprise, Public Choice: Theoretical Foundations of the Contemporary Attack on Government*, New York, 1994.

Sullivan, Lucy, *Behavioural Poverty*, Centre for Independent Studies Policy Monograph No. 45, 2001.

Sydney City Mission, *Poverty in Mount Druitt: A Grim Reality*, Sydney, 1981.

Taylor, Janet and Challen, Michael, 'Voices of Poverty', in Ruth Fincher and John Nieuwenhuysen (eds), *Australian Poverty: Then and Now*, Melbourne, 1998.

Theophanous, Andrew C., *Understanding Social Justice: An Australian Perspective*, 2nd edn, Melbourne, 1994.

Thompson, Paul, *The Voice of the Past: Oral History*, 2nd edn, Oxford, 1988.

Thomson, David, *Selfish Generations? How Welfare States Grow Old*, 2nd edn, Cambridge, 1996.

Tonkin, Elizabeth, *Narrating our Pasts: The Social Construction of Oral History*, Cambridge, 1992.

Travers, Peter, and Richardson, Sue, 'The Elusive Quest for "Those Most in Need"', *Australian Journal of Social Issues*, 30, 1995, pp. 335–49.

Travers, Peter and Richardson, Sue, *Living Decently: Material Well-Being in Australia*, Melbourne, 1993.

Trethewey, Jenny, *Aussie Battlers: Families and Children in Poverty*, Melbourne, 1989.

Tsumori, Kayoko, Saunders, Peter and Hughes, Helen, *Poor Arguments: A Response to the Smith Family Report on Poverty in Australia*, Centre for Independent Studies Issue Analysis No. 21, 2002.

Tyler, Tom R., Boeckmann, Robert J., Smith, Heather J. and Ho, Yuen J., *Social Justice in a Diverse Society*, Boulder, 1997.

Wajnryb, Ruth, *The Silence: How Tragedy Shapes Talk*, Sydney, 2001.

Watson, Ian, 'Class Memory: An Alternative Approach to Class Identity', *Labour History*, 67, 1994, pp. 23–41.

Watts, Martin, 'The Dimensions and Costs of Unemployment in Australia', in Stephen Bell (ed.), *The Unemployment Crisis in Australia: Which Way Out?*, Melbourne, 2000.

Watts, Rob, 'Australia's Welfare Policy and Latham's Third Way: A Critical Commentary', *Just Policy*, 17, 1999, pp. 21–31.

Weatherley, Richard, 'Doing the Right Thing: How Social Security Clients View Compliance', *Australian and New Zealand Journal of Sociology*, 29, 1993, pp. 21–39.

Williams, Raymond, *Resources of Hope*, London, 1989.

Wilson, William Julius, *When Work Disappears: The World of the New Urban Poor*, New York, 1997.

Wilson, William Julius, *The Truly Disadvantaged: The Inner City, the Underclass, and Public Policy*, Chicago, 1987.

Winter, Ian (ed.), *Social Capital and Public Policy in Australia*, Melbourne, 2000.

Young, Iris Marion, *Intersecting Voices: Dilemmas of Gender, Political Philosophy and Policy*, Princeton, 1997.

Young, Iris Marion, *Justice and the Politics of Difference*, Princeton, 1990.

Zukin, Sharon, *Landscapes of Power: From Detroit to Disney World*, Berkeley, 1991.

INDEX